Hellenic Studies 57

PAIDEIA AND CULT

Recent Titles in the Hellenic Studies Series

http://chs.harvard.edu/chs/publications

PAIDEIA AND CULT

CHRISTIAN INITIATION IN THEODORE OF MOPSUESTIA

DANIEL L. SCHWARTZ

CENTER FOR HELLENIC STUDIES
Trustees for Harvard University
Washington, D.C.
Distributed by Harvard University Press
Cambridge, Massachusetts, and London, England
2013

Paideia and Cult
   by Daniel L. Schwartz
Copyright © 2013 Center for Hellenic Studies, Trustees for Harvard University
All Rights Reserved.
Published by Center for Hellenic Studies, Trustees for Harvard University, Washington,
   D.C.
Distributed by Harvard University Press, Cambridge, Massachusetts, and London,
   England
Production: Ivy Livingston
Cover design and illustration: Joni Godlove
Printed by Edwards Brothers, Inc., Ann Arbor, MI

EDITORIAL TEAM

Senior Advisers: W. Robert Connor, Gloria Ferrari Pinney, Albert Henrichs, James
   O'Donnell, Bernd Seidensticker
Editorial Board: Gregory Nagy (Editor-in-Chief), Christopher Blackwell, Casey Dué
   (Executive Editor), Mary Ebbott (Executive Editor), Scott Johnson, Olga Levaniouk,
   Anne Mahoney, Leonard Muellner
Production Manager for Publications: Jill Curry Robbins
Web Producer: Mark Tomasko

On the cover: Paros Baptistry, 4th century. Photo, Jelena Bogdanovic.

LIBRARY OF CONGRESS CATALOGING-IN-PUBLICATION DATA

Schwartz, Daniel Louis, 1973-
   Paideia and cult : Christian initiation in Theodore of Mopsuestia / by Daniel L.
   Schwartz.
      p. cm. — (Hellenic Studies Series ; 57)
   Includes bibliographical references (p.   ) and index.
   ISBN 978-0-674-06703-5 (alk. paper)
 1. Theodore, Bishop of Mopsuestia, ca. 350-428 or 9. 2. Theology, Doctrinal--Early
   works to 1800. 3. Catechetical sermons. I. Title.

BR65.T75746S39 2012
265'.92--dc23

                                                                    2012038440

In memory of Louis Wilson Greenwood (1917–2011)

Contents

Contents

Acknowledgments

IT IS MY GREAT PLEASURE to recognize the numerous debts I have acquired in the production of this book. The scholar who has most influenced this project is clearly my doctoral supervisor, Peter Brown. I greatly appreciate his patience with my first faltering steps into the world of Theodore of Mopsuestia and his constant encouragement throughout every stage of this project. His enthusiasm for all things late antique continues to inspire me and I know that most of the questions I find interesting derive in one way or another from conversations with him. Many of the most enjoyable of these conversations took place along with his wife, Betsy Brown, who never lacks a kind word of encouragement, or a delightful story of far off travel. I owe a debt of gratitude to them both.

Princeton University offered many people and programs whose influence appears in the pages that follow. William C. Jordan, Tia Kolbaba, John Gager, Peter Schäfer, and AnneMarie Luijendijk, as well as Kathleen McVey at Princeton Theological Seminary, have all had a hand in shaping my intellectual interests. Most of them have offered their insights on portions of this book at one stage or another of its production. While Peter Brown urged me to pursue Syriac, Emmanuel Papoutsakis actually gave me my first instruction in the language. Without him I would have likely ended up working on very different sources and certainly would not have produced this book. I am grateful for his patience and dedication as a teacher. The Hellenic Studies Program, under the very capable direction of Dimitri Gondicas, offered a stimulating contribution to my thinking and a friendly place for scholarly interaction throughout my time at Princeton. The Center for the Study of Religion provided a welcome home for several years, my thanks to the director Robert Wuthnow, associate director Jenny Wiley Legath, and program manager Anita Kline. I owe many thanks as well to the participants in the Center's Religion and Culture Workshop for reading my early drafts and providing very helpful comments and critiques. The Group for the Study of Late Antiquity and the Program in the Ancient World also played vital roles in my development at Princeton.

I owe a special debt of gratitude to several people at the University of Oxford where I spent one year as a graduate student and another as an Andrew W. Mellon Postdoctoral Research Fellow. Averil Cameron has consistently offered encouragement and insightful comments on my work, for which I am deeply grateful. David Taylor showed great patience and true charity by meeting with me to read through Theodore's *Catechetical Homilies* in Syriac. Neil McLynn and Arietta Papaconstantinou also provided a hospitable and stimulating environment in which to consider questions of conversion from a great variety of perspectives. I would also like to thank Johannes Hahn. The research position he provided in the Exzellenzcluster in "Religion und Politik" at Westfälische Wilhelms-Universität Münster allowed me to finish the dissertation and his comments on that project provided food for thought as I have pursued the completion of this volume.

Many other friends and colleagues have commented in part or in whole on the book that follows and have provided invaluable intellectual and personal support. I would like to extend a special thanks to Kutlu Akalin, Philip Booth, Sara Brooks, Side Emre, Jan Willem Drijvers, Scott Johnson, Maja Kominko, Derek Krueger, Volker Menze, David Michelson, Yannis Papadogiannakis, Richard Payne, Lisa Ramos, Brian Rouleau, Richard Snoddy, Jack Tannous, Katherine Unterman, and Erin Wood. Jelena Bogdanovic graciously provided the photos for the cover of the book. I am very grateful to her for sharing those photos and for her friendship.

I could not have written this book without the love and support of my family. My parents, Donald Schwartz and Lois Schwartz have tirelessly supported me through many years of pursuing intellectual interests that often seemed obscure to them. The generosity and affection of my sister and brother-in-law, Kristen Robinson and Jon Robinson, never cease to amaze me. Megan Schwartz, the linchpin of my life and its greatest joy, has enthusiastically embraced this project as it has led us to three countries and two states. Her love sustains me each day and I am deeply grateful for her support. I dedicate this book to the memory of my maternal grandfather, Louis Wilson Greenwood. I remember him as a loving husband, father, and grandfather with a playful wit and a true generosity of spirit. He was a veteran of the Second World War and a construction contractor for over forty years. And while his love and support remained unwavering, I know he never quite understood how it could take me so long to produce anything substantial. This is for you Gramps.

Author's Note on Citations and Translations

THE *CATECHETICAL HOMILIES* of Theodore of Mopsuestia stand at the heart of this study. Unfortunately, the resources available for doing work on these sermons present certain logistical problems. Scholars have known for many years that Theodore preserved his catechesis. However, the scholarly community did not have access to them until 1932 and 1933, when Alphonse Mingana discovered and published in his Woodbrooke Studies series an edition and English translation of the first and only known manuscript of the sermons.

A careful study of Mingana's edition of the homilies, however, shows that Mingana often took liberties with the Syriac text when he reproduced it. He emended the text with some regularity, usually without including any notes to that effect, and only very rarely explaining his reasoning. As such, Mingana's text cannot be considered a critical edition. Fortunately, in 1949, Raymond Tonneau and Robert Devreesse published a facsimile of the manuscript with facing-page French translation in their *Les Homélies Catéchétiques. Reproduction phototypique du ms. Mingana Syr. 561 (Selly Oak Colleges' Library, Birmingham)*. I have endeavored to point the reader toward both Mingana's English translation and the published manuscript facsimile.

In this text I will cite Mingana's edition as *WS* (for Woodbrooke Studies), followed by the volume number and page number of Mingana's English translation. This is necessary, as Mingana offers the only complete English translation of these homilies. I have based the English translations of the catechesis on Mingana's, emended as necessary, but the footnotes contain the Syriac text based on the manuscript facsimile. For this reason, alongside the reference to the English of Mingana, I cite the facsimile as *Homélies Catéchétiques*, followed by the sermon number and the manuscript folio number:

> *WS* 5.27; *Homélies Catéchétiques* 2.8v

This practice will allow readers to access easily the available Syriac and English sources discussed in the text.

Abbreviations

ACO	*Acta conciliorum oecumenicorum*
ANF	Ante-Nicene Fathers
BO	Bibliotheca orientalis
CCSL	Corpus Christianorum Series Latina
CSCO	Corpus Scriptorum Christianorum Orientalium
CSEL	Corpus Scriptorum Ecclesiasticorum Latinorum
GCS	Griechischen christlichen Schriftsteller
LCL	Loeb Classical Library
NPNF[1]	Nicene and Post-Nicene Fathers, Series One
NPNF[2]	Nicene and Post-Nicene Fathers, Series Two
PG	*Patrologia graeca*
PL	*Patrologia latina*
PO	Patrologia orientalis
SCh	Sources Chrétiennes
TTH	Translated Texts for Historians
WS	Woodbrooke Studies

Introduction
Catechesis, Christianization, and Conversion

T HEY SPEND THE SATURDAY NIGHT OF HOLY WEEK in the church, keeping vigil in prayer and song. They have gathered with the clergy and their baptismal sponsors in order to be initiated as Christians. Very early on Easter Sunday morning, long before the sun comes up, the rites begin. Before they can be baptized, they must declare their fidelity to Christ and their rejection of demonic influences. They fall to their knees as supplicants, renouncing Satan and claiming the power of Christ to protect them from the devil. A recitation of the creed summarizing Christian teaching and the prayer Jesus taught the disciples follows. Then the priest signs them on the forehead in the name of the Father, the Son, and the Holy Spirit, a mark designed to single them out as belonging to Christ and to warn Satan who might still try to attack them. The sponsors help the catechumens to their feet and prepare them for baptism. They enter the baptismal font naked where the priest immerses them three times, again in the name of the Father, the Son, and the Holy Spirit. They exit the font as new creations, born again through this ritual of baptism. A second signing on the forehead with chrism finalizes and confirms the ritual of initiation. They immediately receive brilliant white linen garments as a symbol of their new birth and purified state. As they leave the baptistery, they do so as fully initiated Christians. Soon they will partake of the ritual meal of the church, the bread and wine of the eucharistic service.

Such initiation rites took place within numerous Christian communities throughout the Mediterranean world during the fourth and fifth centuries. They generally took place at Easter to symbolize the connection between the cleansing rebirth of baptism and the resurrection of Jesus from the dead. These rites were strategically crafted ritual moments designed to make a significant impact. They took place early in the morning after a long night of prayer. They entailed a confrontation with Satan and a claim of affiliation with Christ. The rites engaged the whole body through kneeling and immersion in water. The sources that discuss these rites often emphasize these dramatic elements and highlight a belief in their immediate efficacy. The language of awe and fear pervades discussion of these rites, with priests using their sermons on these topics to make the hair of their audiences literally stand on end.[1]

Despite the emphasis on the dramatic moment, the rites of Christian initiation required more than a single incident of spiritual battle, ritual cleansing, and formal affiliation with a new religion. These rites assume a significant background, with considerable interaction between the various participants. A range of Christian clergy took part in these rituals. A presbyter could perform the rites, but those being baptized expected their bishop would perform the ceremony. Priests and deacons assisted while exorcists facilitated the renunciation of Satan. The assistants involved extended beyond the hierarchical ranks of the clergy to include lay members of the congregation as well. Each person being baptized needed a sponsor who knew their life and character. The sponsor gave assurances to the bishop of the person's sincerity and pursuit of Christian morality. The ability to provide a credible report on such matters required considerable familiarity and assumed substantial interaction between these individuals. All of this interaction took place before a formal procedure, usually at the beginning of Lent, during which the church took down the names of those intending to receive baptism at Easter. Whatever history the sponsor and the person seeking baptism shared, their relationship would soon intensify. Both were expected to attend church several times a week during Lent. Together they would hear the preaching of the bishop who taught them the doctrine of the church and prepared them for the baptismal rites. As we have seen, these rites included the recitation of the creed and the Lord's Prayer. The creed, along with the substance of the baptismal and eucharistic rites, was meant to remain secret from all the uninitiated. In order to maintain this secrecy, the creed had to be committed to memory rather than written down. Baptismal sponsors assisted in this task of memorizing the creed and supplemented the preacher's technical theological teaching.

This process by which late antique people could move from having some interest in Christianity to undergoing full initiation into the church is generally known as catechesis. This term, derived from a Greek word meaning "hearing," places an emphasis on the fact that candidates for baptism were expected to listen to the sermons preached by the clergy. As they did so, they encountered carefully constructed introductions to the basic theology and practice of the church. However, catechesis was not simply a cognitive activity and the process accomplished far more than merely conveying information. Catechesis took place within the context of the church with its internal power structures of religious authority and access to God. Throughout the fourth century, however,

[1] Yarnold 1994:60.

political power in the Roman Empire became increasingly entwined with the church, making it a tremendously important institution on the imperial stage. This situation formed an important component of what it meant to associate oneself with the church as a fully initiated Christian. Though the bishop played an important role in connecting his congregation to the highest levels of power, the institutional and political appeal of conversion to Christianity did not develop in a vacuum. Interaction with the church entailed social integration. A person desiring baptism needed a baptismal sponsor who would stand before the bishop as an advocate for him or her. This baptized lay-person invested a considerable amount of time in the one seeking baptism and facilitated social integration into the community, as well as an understanding of the norms of belief and practice within the church. And finally, this complex process of initiation culminated in ritual acts aimed at sacralizing a person's decision to become a part of a Christian community.

The preachers used instruction and ritual, embedded in community, to create a Christianized culture. In doing so, these preachers produced something reminiscent of classical *paideia* (παιδεία). The term *paideia* means both "education" and "culture." In the classical Greco-Roman context, it refers to a form of highly literate education designed to create a ruling elite well versed in a canon of authoritative texts and capable of using that knowledge to wield influence through the delivery of public speeches. The use of *paideia* in the context of catechesis should not, however, be taken as an indication that Christians proposed catechesis as an alternative to classical Greco-Roman education or culture. Nor does it suggest a democratization of education in Late Antiquity.[2] Many Christian preachers came from among the elite levels of their society and rarely expressed interest in spreading that elite culture among the lower classes. Rather, the use of *paideia* in this context seeks to capture the idea of the formation of a culture through a system of education. Just as classical *paideia* served to differentiate elites from the rest of society, so the distinctly Christian culture promoted through catechesis sought to create a group set apart from the rest of society and embedded within a community that shared unique beliefs and rituals.

This book contends that the complex process of catechesis outlined above was essential to the production of Christians. Late antique preachers certainly thought of initiation rites and the educational activities that preceded them as efficacious and transformative. The dramatic events and language surrounding the initiation rites that sought to ensure the efficacy of catechesis also urge this interpretation. A central interpretive difficulty arises, however, when one

---

[2] Cameron 1991:7–8.

gives due weight to the fact that the preachers do not offer objective descriptions of personal perceptions and internal dispositions. Preachers offer hortatory addresses that seek to urge particular behavior, attitudes, and beliefs rather than disinterested descriptions of what happened as people sought initiation. This evident gap between preacher and audience forces the consideration of conversion, what it meant and to whom. Subsequent discussion will explore the difficulties in speaking about conversion in the context of the ancient world. Suffice it to say at the moment that a properly analytical definition of conversion is difficult to obtain, insofar as the term suggests something radical, transformative, and usually instantaneous. This is precisely what late antique preachers would have us believe Christian initiation was all about. On the contrary, however, careful analysis of catechetical preaching shows catechesis to entail a lengthy process with multiple facets. However transformative catechesis may or may not have been in various cases, the process was a long and slow one. While catechetical sermons took many forms and suggest numerous different emphases, three particularly significant means of producing Christians emerge in these sources. Catechesis entailed immersion into a social context that included lay Christians, baptismal sponsors, and clergy, including the bishop. It also offered opportunities for education, which engaged people cognitively through memorization and training in Christian theology and practice. Finally, catechesis culminated in ritual activity through which people became initiated into a worshipping community.

This book uses catechetical sermons to analyze these social, intellectual, and ritual components of catechesis in order to unpack their individual features and combined impact on converts to Christianity as they pursued initiation into the community, creed, and cult of the church. While many sources discuss these three components of catechesis—social integration, intellectual engagement, and ritual participation—the catechetical curriculum of Theodore of Mopsuestia resides at the center of this study. The sixteen sermons of Theodore's catechesis, delivered while he was a priest in the city of Antioch between 383 and 392, clearly demonstrate the important roles played by community, creed, and cult in the process of Christian initiation.[3] While the emphasis on community remains implicit in Theodore's preaching, his emphasis on belief and ritual engagement emerge clearly from the structure of his catechetical curriculum. Theodore used the first ten sermons of this series to preach on the creed that his students would need to recite before baptism. He went into considerable detail regarding the fine points of Trinitarian theology, but ultimately placed the strongest emphasis on how Christians should think about theology within

---

[3] See chapter one on the date of Theodore's catechetical preaching.

the context of the confessing community. Intellectual rigor and sophisticated argumentation did not necessarily constitute the aim of theological inquiry. His eleventh sermon focuses on the Lord's Prayer that the catechumens would need to recite at baptism but that also formed a staple of regular Christian worship following initiation. Sermons twelve to fourteen explain the components of the baptismal liturgy, as well as its spiritual interpretation. Sermons fifteen and sixteen do the same for the eucharistic liturgy. While the first ten sermons focus on cognitive understanding of theology and sermons eleven through sixteen focus more on ritual, we will see that these sermons employ a pedagogy that consistently integrates these components while also maintaining a focus on community formation and the integration of converts into that community.

In addition to the fact that Theodore treats the social, intellectual, and ritual components of catechesis, his homilies offer an important perspective on the catechetical process. Considerable source material relevant to the study of catechesis comes down to us in sermons, letters, and treatises.[4] Nevertheless, Theodore's *Catechetical Homilies* arguably offer the only catechetical curriculum that has been preserved in the form in which it was designed and delivered. The corpus of collected catechetical sermons by Cyril of Jerusalem, which dates from the early part of his episcopal tenure around the middle of the fourth century, contains his instruction given before baptism. He likely did not produce the post-baptismal instruction that we have until the end of his tenure in the mid-380s, and some have questioned whether he is the author at all.[5] Likewise, John Chrysostom's works contain a substantial number of sermons used to catechize converts. Once again, however, this corpus includes a collection of sermons written and delivered at different times and under different circumstances.[6] This makes the *Catechetical Homilies* of Theodore a uniquely complete catechetical curriculum from Late Antiquity.[7]

The structure, themes, and preservation of Theodore's sermons thus offer compelling reason to give them a place of prominence in the study of catechesis. Relevant comparative material from a range of catechetical sources will appear

---

[4] This should not be taken to suggest that other catechetical material is unimportant or somehow faulty for not presenting a single series of sermons. Indeed we learn much from these catechetical sources. However, a single curriculum delivered in one Lenten season offers a valuable contribution to the study of catechesis. For discussions of additional catechetical sources, see Harmless 1995; Sandwell 2007; Yarnold 2000:22–56; and Satterlee 2000.

[5] On the authorship of the so-called *Mystogogic Catecheses*, see Doval 2001.

[6] Harkins 1963:8–19.

[7] Bruns (1995, esp. 15–19) takes the approach of looking at these sermons in their entirety, as opposed to mining them for individual theological statements made by Theodore. However, his concern remains primarily theological, rather than the pedagogical concerns that occupy us here.

alongside the analysis of Theodore's *Catechetical Homilies*, but we will focus on these sermons as a coherent catechetical curriculum designed to produce the kinds of initiated Christians Theodore, and many late antique clergy, desired. The rhetorical strategies that will emerge offer a critical approach to understanding the attempts of the Christian church to multiply its membership and to position itself in a rapidly changing religious and political landscape as it sought to effect what is often called the Christianization of the Roman Empire.

The Problem of Christianization

The transformation of Rome from an empire thoroughly at ease with its traditional religious worship to a self-identified Christian state has interested observers since the time the process began. Whether seen as abrupt, decisive, and miraculous or slow, halting, and incomplete, observers have consistently considered the religious, political, and even economic changes occasioning the transformation to be problems requiring explanation. The problem of the Christianization of the Roman Empire can be summarized in short: how did a cultural system as vibrant as ancient Rome's make the transition from simply assuming the validity of its widespread pagan worldview to emphatically asserting its affinity with Christianity, which began its existence as a small provincial sect of a monotheistic religion? This question would be an interesting one even if its effects were short-lived. However, the impact of this transformation has had a tremendously long history. The Byzantine Empire's distinctive Orthodox Christian identity would, in part, define it until its final collapse in 1453, over a millennium after the process of Christianization began in earnest. Furthermore, this Christian identity would prove significant for the formation of Eastern European cultures to the present day. The Roman imperial presence in the western Mediterranean would not enjoy a similar length of tenure, but the prominence that Christianity gained in the late Roman west served to cement its place in western European culture well into the modern period. The Middle East also included vibrant Christian populations that flourished throughout the Medieval period and continue to the present. Indeed, we continue to live today with many of the consequences of these events, and thus the persistent interest in the processes that brought them about should come as no surprise.

The profound changes that occasioned the religious transformation of the Roman Empire have inspired many interpretations, a thorough discussion of which would require a volume of its own. Positions on the Christianization of the empire came early and very often from partisan quarters. Contemporaries of the first Christian emperor, Constantine, already took bold imaginative positions on Christianization. Eusebius of Caesarea concluded his ecclesiastical history (begun under pagan emperors as a story of imperial persecution and righteous Christian recalcitrance) with the conversion of Constantine and a discussion of his support for the church.[8] Eusebius sometimes leaves the impression that he would not know what we mean by the phrase, "the problem of Christianization." With the utmost confidence in Christian supremacy, Eusebius presented the Christianization of the Roman Empire as a *fait accompli*. However, Eusebius' presentation of Constantine offered an idealized view of a Christian Roman state that would not be realized for generations, if it were ever fully realized at all. Of course, Eusebius' historical writings ought to be read more as means of achieving Christianization rather than as a proper description of the process. One clear example of this can be seen in Eusebius' discussion of Constantine's sons in the *Life of Constantine*.[9] We must remember that they were present in the audience as Eusebius discussed them. With this in mind, the treatise in praise of Constantine's life reads more like an exhortation to the future emperors to live up to the ideal image of Christian imperial rule put forward by Eusebius.[10] Thus we can see even in Eusebius an implicit acknowledgement of the problem addressed here.

Plenty of other ancient authors would have had no difficulty relating to the concept of the "problem of Christianization." Many maintained their adherence to traditional Greco-Roman religion. Even generations after the conversion of Constantine, elite pagans held positions of considerable influence in Roman society, including high-level positions in the imperial administration.[11] Governors on one side of a growing religious divide took up posts where they inevitably encountered important and powerful local people who held different convictions or religious affiliations.[12] Themistius presents the image of a very capable imperial advisor who remained a pagan but served under most of the Christian emperors of the fourth century, at times even counseling them on religious matters.[13] Likewise, Libanius, who pursued a very prominent career as a teacher of rhetoric in the city of Antioch, remained a pagan. His academic post engaged him in extensive patronage networks with people of various religious

---

[8]   Barnes 1981:128–129.
[9]   *Life of Constantine* 4.40.
[10]   Barnes 1981:267.
[11]   Barnes (1995:135–147) insists on a very high estimate for the number of Christians promoted to elevated posts within the imperial administrations of the fourth century. Even if he is right, however, the number of pagans in high government posts under Christian emperors remained between 25 and 50 percent, a considerable percentage.
[12]   For two discussions of the sort of balancing act required by these realities, see Sandwell 2007 and Van Dam 2002.
[13]   Daly 1971:65–79. On Libanius' political career and literary production, see Heather and Moncur 2001.

commitments: pagan, Jewish, and Christian.[14] Libanius rarely spoke explicitly on the topic of Christianity or religious observance in general, which seems to have been part of his strategy for dealing with the problems Christianization presented to him.[15]

Other exchanges between Christianity and the ancient religions of the empire were less irenic. Those to whom Augustine responded in his *City of God* famously blamed the sack of Rome, and the attendant weakness of the Roman state, on the advent of Christianity as a political presence in the empire. Their denunciation of Christianity focused on the abandonment of the ancestral gods of the Romans.[16] The refusal to honor the gods who had made Rome great was essentially an act of hostility which those gods repaid by allowing Rome to suffer in turn. Unfortunately this was not the only violence inflicted in the process of Christianization. Pagans had not simply given up their ancestral cults when Christianity emerged as an imperial religion with Constantine and later as the imperial religion under Theodosius. Pagan worship was actively suppressed and often in a violent manner.[17] Likewise, Jews along with their synagogues suffered greatly as Christianity separated itself from its spiritual parent and asserted its religious supremacy.[18]

The legacy of violence, however, did not stop there. Christians who held views out of favor with the ecclesiastical policy of the state were also subject to violence at the hands of the state. The Donatist church in North Africa already felt the oppressive weight of imperial Christianity under the reign of Constantine.[19] Various parties during the course of the so-called Arian controversy found themselves out of favor with imperial religious policy and liable to banishment or worse. The situation would grow graver still in the fifth and sixth centuries, and the church would eventually see itself split into at least three distinct communities, with divisions that persist to this day. Too much has occasionally been made of political concerns associated with regional and ethnic tensions within this process.[20] However, even if the origins of these conflicts were entirely a matter of formal theological disagreement (a dubious assumption), one could still not discount the importance of imperial policy for the ways in which the controversy played out.[21]

---

[14] See Cribiore 2007.
[15] See Sandwell 2007.
[16] *City of God* 1.
[17] See Hahn 2004 and Gaddis 2005.
[18] Gaddis 2005; Becker and Reed 2003; Wilken 1983.
[19] Drake 2000:219–221.
[20] A. H. M. Jones 1959:280–297.
[21] For an excellent study of imperial policy in the development of the non-Chalcedonian church, see Menze 2008.

But these well-known subjects are not the central aim of this study. They remain very relevant, however, as they remind us of what we might call the ancient problem of Christianization. They remind us that religious change was often turbulent and that the contemporary responses to it happening on a large scale within the Roman Empire were never simple. Regions, communities (defined religiously and otherwise), and individuals had very different experiences of, and responses to, the complicated process of the Roman empire coming to identify itself as a Christian state. Being reminded of this ancient problem of Christianization should help put into perspective the modern historiographical problem of Christianization. The complexity of the processes is enormous, the causes of events diverse. It may be that the avenues of approach to Christianization and indeed the solutions to this "problem" are inexhaustible.[22] This study aims to take one approach and address the problem of Christianization from the perspective of the catechetical sermons delivered by Theodore of Mopsuestia.

Christianization and Conversion

Before we discuss catechesis, however, we must address the role of conversion in the scholarship on Christianization. For better or worse, contemporary scholarship on the Christianization of the Roman Empire has inherited much from Edward Gibbon, even where it has come to disagree with him.[23] The model of decay and final collapse (not coincidentally commencing with the rise of Christianity), suggested by the title of his magisterial *The Decline and Fall of the Roman Empire*, has been the focus of considerable attention since the latter half of the twentieth century.[24] Even where that model rightly highlights the waning or outright disappearance of some impressive accomplishments of Roman culture, it has come to be seen by many as too pejorative and condescending to capture accurately the rich texture of the later Roman Empire.[25] Nevertheless, Gibbon does represent a considerable improvement over some of the ways people before him had understood the process of Rome's adoption of Christianity. In particular, Gibbon made advances by trying to isolate historical causes for the

---

[22] Harris (2005) expresses a similar sentiment in the introduction to the collection of essays he edited; see also the similar caveat of Brown 1995:x.

[23] S. Schwartz 2005:145–160.

[24] While certainly not alone in this endeavor, most of the work of Peter Brown has, in one way or another, critiqued this model. See Cameron 2002:165–191.

[25] However, it must be noted that some recent scholarship has shown an increasing interest in returning to the model of decline, even if not to a full-blown acceptance of Gibbon's approach. Among a growing number of recent studies, see Liebeschuetz 2001; Ward-Perkins 2005; Wickham 2005; Ando 2008:31–60; and Marcone 2008:4–19.

rise of Christianity that did not simply assume its divinely ordained ascendency and inherent superiority to paganism.[26] This attention to the natural causes of Christianity's growth has predominated since, but radically different ideas about the cause and nature of Christianization still remain.

Arthur Darby Nock brought to the discussion of Christianization a study of religious conversion in antiquity that gave a privileged position to conversion to Christianity.[27] His work was based on the application of psychological theory to ancient conversion undertaken by William James in 1902.[28] James used the conversion of Paul, as recounted in the canonical Acts of the Apostles, to argue for a radical psychological transformation at work in the process of conversion. He defines conversion as "the process, gradual or sudden, by which a self hitherto divided, and consciously wrong inferior and unhappy becomes united and consciously right superior and happy, in consequence of its firmer hold upon religious realities."[29] Nock's dependence on James emerges clearly in the way that he defined conversion: "By conversion we mean the reorientation of the soul of an individual, his deliberate turning from indifference or from an earlier form of piety to another, a turning which implies a consciousness that a great change is involved, that the old was wrong and the new is right."[30] The inward and transformative approach taken by Nock betrays his psychological orientation toward conversion and Christianization. But for Nock, this transformation was also highly cognitive, entailing "the adhesion of the will to a new theology, in a word faith ..."[31] This places Christianity, along with Judaism, into a category distinct from traditional Greco-Roman religion with its emphasis on performing cult rather than on theological ideas. The only comparable comparison Nock found outside of the Judeo-Christian tradition is in ancient philosophical circles.[32]

This notion of conversion has not fared well in recent scholarship.[33] In general, it is seen as far too intellectual and far too psychologically transformative to reflect accurately anything that happened on a mass scale in Late Antiquity. At best, these notions of conversion might apply to a person like Augustine. In reality, his *Confessions* clearly offers a considered and highly polished presentation

---

[26] For this observation and several points that immediately follow, see Drake 2005:1–14.
[27] Nock 1933.
[28] James 1902. For a discussion of James and his influence on Nock, see Crook 2004:23–26 and Taves 2009:4–5.
[29] James 1902:189.
[30] Nock 1933:9.
[31] Nock 1933:14.
[32] Nock 1933, chap. 11.
[33] Among the many critiques, see Lane Fox 1987; Markus 1990; and Crook 2004.

of how he wanted his conversion to be remembered.[34] As such, it is better to think of the *Confessions* as a prescriptive text that attempts to establish a normative position regarding the nature of true conversion. Augustine's actual thoughts and feelings at the moment he took up the epistle to the Romans and read are lost to us and perhaps were also lost to him by the time he sat down to write his account of them.[35] We can see here that, almost by definition, the accounts of conversion that we have are atypical, composed as they were by the small percentage of highly literate elites and subsequently found worthy of being copied at least several times over between Late Antiquity and today.[36]

While some recent work addresses the role of conversion in Christianization,[37] overall the literature has shifted away from thinking about such questions. Recent discussions of Christianization have taken a great variety of approaches and have yielded much fruit, but without giving particular attention to the thorny issue of conversion. One particularly important development is the application of social scientific models to the problem of Christianization.[38] Harnack's tentative estimate that 7–10 percent of the Roman population was Christian by the end of the fourth century has found general approval, even though the types of sources required in order to confirm such a number are almost entirely wanting.[39] Recent attempts to understand in demographic terms what these numbers mean have been a great help in conceptualizing the process of Christianization. Rodney Stark has shown that Harnack's 10 percent could have been reached if Christianity had maintained a rate of growth of about 3.4 percent annually.[40] While this suggests a flourishing community, the growth rate is certainly not out of the question.

Many recent studies surrounding issues of Christianization have turned to a more institutional approach. These have addressed questions about the behavior and self-presentation of important institutions in the Later Roman Empire. The religious orientation of the imperial administration, the aristocracy,

---

[34] Brown 2000:156–157.

[35] Stark 1996:19.

[36] It is rightly held that literacy rates in the ancient world were very low by modern standards. The most frequently cited work on literacy is still Harris 1989. His estimate of literacy rates is very pessimistic and, in my opinion, does not take seriously enough the wide range of functional literacy that remained below that of the highly educated. As a supplement to Harris, see Cribiore 1996.

[37] See the essays in Mills and Grafton 2003. Also, Neil McLynn and Arietta Papaconstantinou convened a Mellon-Sawyer Seminar at the University of Oxford in 2009–2010 called "Conversion in Late Antiquity: Christianity, Islam, and Beyond." The papers from this series of colloquia are scheduled for publication by Ashgate in 2013.

[38] Drake 2005:1–14.

[39] Drake 2005:2.

[40] Stark 1996; see also Hopkins 1998:185–226.

and the army have all received attention.[41] They have asked when these institutions began to look Christian. When did the symbols of their place in society take on a demonstrably Christian image? What political, economic, and spiritual demands drew the individuals who made up these institutions to such an affinity with Christianity? Many of these studies have centered on the west, where imperial power was relatively weaker than in the east, and the resulting cracks in the imperial system allow glimpses on religious matters that might otherwise not have appeared. We know a great deal about these institutions. Epigraphy alone yields tremendously valuable information about religious self-presentation. Literary sources help fill out the picture as well and contribute to substantive understanding of late Roman institutions. Particularly when literary sources are emphasized, these institutional histories often border on intellectual histories. R. A. Markus' *The End of Ancient Christianity* is an excellent example of this genre.[42]

In addition to these institutional approaches to Christianization, scholars have written many other types of historical accounts. Legal histories of Christianization are able to show the ways in which the law was used to promote Christianity and restrict pagan practices, but also some of the ways in which emperors allowed room for the reality that many late Romans remained pagans.[43] A number of scholars have pursued what could be called an architectural history of Christianization.[44] The aim of this research is to investigate the physical space of cities and towns. When did they begin to look Christian? When did churches become prominent features of cities, to what extent and when did they come to replace other forms of civic architecture? This work has shown important ways in which distinctively Christian architecture could play a role in Christianization. Monuments displayed wealth, power, and stability. They could be used as part of a comprehensive plan to proselytize, a phenomenon that Peter Brown has aptly described as the construction of "arguments in stone."[45]

All of these studies propose different avenues of approach to the complex process of Christianization. Many of the studies undertaken since Nock wrote on conversion have looked at Christianization without addressing questions related to the conversion of individuals. Some studies that have included a discussion of conversion are at their weakest precisely on this point. Ramsey MacMullen's *Christianizing the Roman Empire (A.D. 100–400)* begins with a strong

---

[41] Among the many institutional studies of this sort, see Brown 1995:1–26; and Salzman 2002.
[42] Markus 1990.
[43] Trombley 1994, 1:1–97; Hunt 1993; Joannou 1972; and Sandwell 2005.
[44] Nicholson 2009:45–84; Harl 2001: 301–322; Kidner 2001:349–379; Trombley 1994, 1:98–146.
[45] Brown 2003:30. See also, Trout 1996:175–186.

critique of Nock.[46] MacMullen demonstrates that many of the conversions that appear in the sources do not look at all as Nock suggests they should. His introduction suggests a new paradigm for understanding late antique conversion. He draws attention to the Bedouin discussed by Theodoret in his *Historia religiosa*:

> [Even the bedouins] in many thousands, enslaved to the darkness of impiety, were enlightened by the station upon the pillar. ... They arrived in companies, 200 in one, 300 in another, occasionally a thousand. They renounced with their shouts their traditional errors; they broke up their venerated idols in the presence of that great light; and they foreswore the ecstatic rites of Aphrodite, the demon whose service they had long accepted. They enjoyed divine religious initiation and received their law instead spoken by that holy tongue (of Symeon). Bidding farewell to ancestral customs, they renounced also the diet of the wild ass or the camel. And I myself was witness to these things and heard them, as they renounced their ancestral impiety and submitted to evangelic instruction.[47]

Impressed by the charismatic power of Symeon atop his pillar, the Bedouin flock to him. MacMullen, following Theodoret, emphasizes that central to their conversion is the rejection of their pagan idols, which they break to pieces at the foot of Symeon's column. However difficult it may have been for these Bedouin to make such a transformation in their religious thinking and behavior, the conversion described by Theodoret does not immediately call to mind Nock's reasoned and heartfelt reorientation of a life away from one religious system and towards another.

In this way, MacMullen has drawn our attention to an important point: individual conversions can look very different from one another. What one might consider a conversion, another might view as superficial or even a conscious act of duplicity. Clearly what Theodoret praised as the true conversion of thousands of Bedouin, MacMullen dismisses as merely ephemeral. Nock was not entirely wrong in his thinking about conversion. Some conversions, indeed even some of the most well-attested from antiquity, appear just as Nock described them. Others, and Theodoret's account of the Bedouin is just one, simply do not.

We must ask how one should assess these differences. Although critiquing Nock, MacMullen has also followed him in working from an assumption of what Christianity is and in concluding with what a "true" conversion would look like. However, what Nock sees behind virtually every reference to a conversion,

---

[46] MacMullen 1984:4–5.
[47] Theodoret *Religious History* 26.13–14, quoted in MacMullen 1984:2.

MacMullen apparently sees almost nowhere. MacMullen takes the Bedouin swarming around Symeon's column as the proper paradigm for understanding the majority of conversions in antiquity. They maintained their primitive religious culture but instead of looking to their old gods to supply their material needs and to offer help in taking vengeance upon their enemies, they looked to the holy man Symeon and the bishop Theodoret as their new sources of power.[48] Applying this notion of "actual" conversions, as opposed to Nock's "ideal" conversions, MacMullen concludes that the Christianization of the Roman Empire was largely superficial.

What should be clear from this discussion is that addressing the issue of conversion in Late Antiquity presents considerable methodological difficulties. This subject is problematic enough for scholars of contemporary conversion who can conduct interviews and surveys. When the ancient historian tries to address the subject, conclusions are very hard to reach indeed. The sources we would need in order to assess thoroughly the conversions of a representative sampling of late antique converts to Christianity are not available. Institutional histories deal mainly with the elites. Epigraphy usually only tells us when and how people self-identified as Christians. Architectural studies reveal similar information. When literary sources tell us about conversion, they are usually too literary—that is, they present literary re-workings of experiences in which the time of composition is often removed from the events by decades of formative experiences that color the interpretation of the past events.[49] Furthermore, the ability to leave such literary traces of one's Christianity was not available to a large majority of ancient people. This material cannot offer the widespread evidence required to speak meaningfully about conversion on a mass scale. Sources like Theodoret help us here by describing the conversion of Bedouin, who were likely illiterate, but their story only reaches us through his interpretation—that is, across a substantial divide of language, culture, and class.

Such difficulties have even led some scholars to suggest that the term "conversion" is too misleading to be of any real analytical value. David Frankfurter makes this argument in the process of analyzing the variety of ways in which late antique Egyptians approached their local holy men and saints' shrines.[50] He begins by emphasizing the idea that all people are constantly in the process of developing practices they find authentic as they appropriate some ideas and practices while passing over others. He argues that the term "conversion" suggests a reified and stable religious tradition to which a person

---

[48] MacMullen 1984:2–3.
[49] This problem also confronts the contemporary sociologist or anthropologist who wants to study conversion.
[50] Frankfurter 2003:39–85.

adheres when, in fact, no such stable or pristine entity exists. He prefers the term "syncretism," which he uses to emphasize the various contributing factors that have gone into particular religious practices.[51] Frankfurter takes care to emphasize that "syncretism" must not be understood as suggesting the idea that two or more concrete systems have been combined into a new syncretic system. After all, he rejects the notion of concrete systems of religion to begin with. This approach offers the benefit of emphasizing the diversity of late antique religious practice and maintaining the agency of the practitioner who approached religious shrines and persons in ways that held significance for him or her.

Though such an approach has its merits and any study of late antique religion that failed to take Frankfurter's concerns seriously would be poorer for it, the rejection of conversion as an analytic category seems unwarranted. Religious experiences gain significance as people ascribe it to them.[52] For many in Late Antiquity this likely had little to do with scriptural texts or authoritative statements from bishops or church councils, and any account of late antique religious life must be capable of capturing these realities. Nevertheless, the fact that Frankfurter must be so careful to redefine the straightforward meaning of syncretism as a combination of two or more things suggests that the term cannot be more than marginally helpful in overcoming the difficulties involved in discussing religious conversion. It seems preferable to maintain the term conversion, while understanding it in a way that can deal with the blurry categories and the variety of ideas and practices that emerge in the sources. The communal context of Christian practice helps make this point. No community has clear and impenetrable boundaries. Nevertheless, communities establish formal and informal mechanisms of recognizing insiders and outsiders, policing their boundaries, and initiating new stakeholders. In the study that follows, the term "conversion" will be used in the analysis of these complex processes. So long as it is not taken to indicate the reified categories Frankfurter rightly critiques, it offers the best hope of accommodating the variety of late antique Christian practice, while also considering the decision of converts to ascribe religious significance to the church and to join themselves to this particular religious community.

Given these difficulties, it is with good reason that many studies of Christianization have moved away from addressing conversion and its causes. But however well founded these concerns may be, shifting too heavily toward social institutions runs the risk of eclipsing the human agency involved in the process. The institutional, material, and literary evidence necessitates that

---

[51] Frankfurter 2003. On syncretism and the history of its fall from and return to theoretical discussions of theory in the study of religion, see Stewart and Shaw 1994:1–26.

[52] Taves 2009:17–20.

individuals, families, and communities adopted and came to identify themselves with Christianity. Furthermore, the fact that later Roman and Byzantine culture came to identify so strongly with Christianity also demands explanation. While an overly teleological approach to this identification would be problematic, the process had to begin somewhere. One significant setting in which it took place early on was the catechetical classroom, in which considerable attention was given to cultivating Christianity. Even though this does not take us nearly as far as we would like toward hearing the voice of the ever-elusive representative sampling of Christian converts in Late Antiquity, it at least has the benefit of redirecting our attention toward the people who were the objects of Christianization. Seth Schwartz nicely articulates a similar perspective in his contribution to a recent collection of essays on the spread of Christianity. After surveying the diversity of Christian expression in Late Antiquity and the variety of explanations advanced to explain the phenomenon, he states, "In sum, it may be better to imagine that even the mass of Christian converts was, if not as sophisticated as Augustine, more active and conscious than the reaction to Nock has supposed. Notwithstanding the paucity of evidence, speculation about the *subjectivity* of non-elite early Christians may be due for a revival."[53]

Though such a revival surely is in order, it would likely err significantly if it took the approach of returning to the old discussion of individual motivation for conversion, not to mention stressing intellectual or psychological transformation. Besides the problem of sources, one of the main reasons for the difficulty of talking about conversion is the terminology surrounding it. The term "conversion" suggests a binary system in which the labels "converted" and "unconverted" apply to every individual. The most flexibility allowed by these terms is a certain amount of qualification applied to each. Thus one can speak about the Arab nomads before the stylite as "barely" converted because they had undergone certain rites and made certain superficial changes to their behavior or, alternately, as somehow interested in Christianity but remaining unconverted because of a lack of sufficient mental or moral transformation. Which of these two descriptions rightly applies, even in their qualified state, is almost impossible to determine in the vast majority of cases. As a result, when such dichotomous language is forced, it tends to reflect the particular pre-conceived notions of the scholar and it certainly flattens what in reality was a more fluid set of conceptual frameworks operative during the period. This complexity demands that we pause for a moment to consider some of the relevant categories and terminology applied to this situation in Late Antiquity before we return to some of the theoretical concerns associated with catechesis.

---

[53] S. Schwartz 2005 (emphasis his).

Late Antique Catechesis

Late antique Christianity had a host of descriptive categories for people who were a part of it in one way or another. Chapter two will discuss in greater detail a number of the roles for fully initiated Christians. In the present context, however, it is most important to focus attention on those who had not yet received baptism but were nevertheless associated with the church. The broadest category for such persons is catechumen (Gk. *katēchoumenos*, Lat. *auditor*). The most basic meaning for the verb *katēcheō* is "to echo." The more common meaning deriving from this, however, is "to teach or instruct."[54] Thus the catechumens were those instructed or taught by the church. They attended public portions of the Christian service where they could hear regular preaching on Christian scripture or on the lives of saints and martyrs. Many of the people who made up this group would even meet Nock's definition of a convert. The clearest example of this comes from martyrologies. Take the famous account of the martyr Perpetua. She was an unbaptized catechumen but considered herself a Christian who could not recant her commitment in order to avoid martyrdom.[55] It was commonly held that catechumens who chose to accept martyrdom instead of renouncing Christianity were actually baptized in their own blood.[56] Thus initiated, they could expect the full eternal reward of any baptized Christian. We can see here that many catechumens had come to appropriate some version of the Christian message and were even willing to make the ultimate sacrifice for the sake of that belief.

Other catechumens, however, had a very different relationship to Christianity. Let us look briefly at another famous example. Augustine tells us of his conversion in dramatic terms in Book nine of his *Confessions*. The story is well known and need not be recounted here in detail except to emphasize what preceded this account. Augustine speaks at length of the delight he took in his sin and rebellion, his stealing of pears purely for the pleasure of it reflecting the state of his heart with respect to God's law.[57] A more mature Augustine spent time as a Manichaean "hearer," a position within that community that was roughly parallel to the catechumenate of the church. However, throughout all of his early years, Augustine was a catechumen of the church; his mother Monica had seen to that.[58] "Even as a boy," Augustine professes, "I had heard of eternal life promised to us through the humility of the Lord our God, who came down to visit us in our pride, and I was signed with the sign of his cross, and was

---

[54] Lampe 1961:732.
[55] *The Martyrdom of Perpetua and Felicitatis* 3.
[56] Cyprian *On the Glory of Martyrdom* 7; Cyril of Jerusalem *Catechesis* 3.10.
[57] *Confessions* 2.4.9.
[58] Yarnold 1994:3.

seasoned with his salt even from the womb of my mother, who greatly trusted in thee."[59] The rites of signing and salt described here (along with the laying on of hands and exorcism) were signs of entrance to the catechumenate, which developed some time in the course of the fourth century as people increasingly sought a way to associate themselves with the church while putting off baptism for fear of committing sin after the cleansing rite of baptism.[60] That Monica had these rites performed while Augustine was an infant is likely somewhat out of the ordinary. Nevertheless, this account, taken together with the testimony of Perpetua, gives us a clear indication of the tremendously broad range of commitment to Christianity among the catechumens. Some we may want to consider converts already, others we almost certainly should not. Nevertheless, all were hearers of the church's teaching. For that matter, even complete unbelievers apparently attended Christian services, although they did not enter the ranks of the catechumens.[61]

How long a person remained in the state of being a catechumen was a highly individual matter. Many postponed things as long as they could, only accepting baptism toward the very end of life. Others sought baptism earnestly. What one would consider a normal length of time is rather difficult to determine.[62] The early-third-century *Apostolic Tradition* stipulates a three year catechumenate but there is little indication that this was practiced anywhere outside of Rome, the place of this text's origin.[63] The Council of Elvira (ca. AD 305) stipulates two years for catechetical instruction under normal circumstances.[64] Part of the reason for having a waiting period before baptism was to observe the individual's progress in conforming to Christian morality. Committing certain sins could postpone one's baptism for three or even five years and, in the case of particularly grievous sin, one might not be allowed to receive baptism until the very end of one's life.[65] Alternatively, other sources suggest a much shorter period of time, mandating instead a period of forty days, usually during Lent, during which a catechumen received pre-baptismal instruction.[66] In such cases, the baptismal sponsors who assisted during the catechetical process were expected

---

[59] *Confessions* 1.11.17. See also Augustine's *On the Catechizing of the Uninstructed* 27.50.

[60] Yarnold 1992:131.

[61] *Apostolic Constitutions* 8.6.2 required that none of the unbelievers (μήτις τῶν ἀπίστων) be permitted to remain in the church during the eucharistic liturgy. How common it would have been for people without any belief to attend a Christian service is very difficult to determine.

[62] Johnson 1990:90.

[63] *Apostolic Tradition* 17.

[64] Canon 42.

[65] Canons 4 and 73.

[66] This is the requirement of the *Canons of Hippolytus* 12. Furthermore, the catechetical sermons of Cyril of Jerusalem, John Chrysostom, and Theodore of Mopsuestia all appear structured for delivery within this framework.

to give assurance of the moral state of the catechumens.[67] Such mandates only required a minimal amount of time for instruction and have little bearing on the length of time a catechumen would spend in an associated, but not fully initiated, position within the church.

As suggested by the clearly defined period of baptismal instruction, the broad group of catechumens contained within it a smaller group of people preparing to undergo the right of baptism. This rite was intended to cement the relationship between the catechumen and the church. It took one from the position of hearer to being a fully initiated member of the church. These received the title *phōtizomenoi*, "those being illuminated."[68] This illumination referred simultaneously to the instruction of the catechetical homilies and to the spiritual enlightenment of the baptismal ritual itself. However, some who entered this state also remained in it for a time.[69] Being found worthy and attending catechetical homilies during Lent did not oblige the catechumen to receive baptism on the coming Easter Sunday. Lingering concerns about one's ability to live the Christian life could continue to urge caution and the postponement of baptism. Such people were considered worthy of baptism, and the book of those registered for the rite contained their names. Cyril of Jerusalem refers to such baptismal candidates as "the registered ones," *oi apographentes*.[70] They will be referred to here most often as candidates for baptism.

This group of candidates from among the catechumens received the teaching of the catechetical homilies that form the basis of this study. In many cases, they would have had long-term exposure to the church, its preaching, and its charismatic holy men, as well as access to many of the institutional manifestations of Christianity mentioned earlier. All of these things served as a backdrop to the process of approaching baptism. Even when many of these preparatory components were lacking, Christians made an effort to inculcate their ideals among those claiming Christianity. Recall from above that even Theodoret's Bedouin accepted instruction in the Christian faith and baptism. Thus, in the case that MacMullen used as an example of the low bar that could be set in considering someone a Christian, we see the converts being taught and undergoing the rite of baptism. MacMullen is curiously silent on this point. He simply assumes a lack of understanding on the part of the Bedouin. He cites their nomadic lifestyle and

---

[67] *WS* 5.25.

[68] This term appears throughout Cyril of Jerusalem's catechetical homilies. See also *Apostolic Constitutions* 8.8.2, 8.8.6, 8.35.2; as well as John Chrysostom *Homilies on the Epistle to the Romans* 2 and *Homilies on Hebrews* 13. The Latin sources also use the term *competentes*, "the competent ones." This name stresses the fact that the catechumens had to be found worthy of baptism before they could be admitted to the group of those about to receive baptism.

[69] Yarnold 1992:133.

[70] Cyril of Jerusalem *Procatechesis* 13.

ignorance of Greek and probably Syriac too. These certainly presented obstacles to their understanding, but such a pessimistic view of cross-cultural communication is hardly warranted. Less warranted still is the conclusion that the most pessimistic reading of the Bedouin and their conversion should be the model for understanding Christian conversion throughout the empire.[71]

The aim here is not to respond to MacMullen's minimalism with a maximalist interpretation. It would be a mistake to suggest that these Bedouin returned to the desert having mastered the precepts of Christian ethics, vast portions of scripture, the theological treatises current among the elites of Mediterranean cities, or even all the doctrines contained in the relatively basic creeds. However, suggesting that questionable assumptions about the abilities of Bedouin should be seen as paradigmatic of Christian conversion is equally problematic. Most important in the context of the present study is to note that even under such difficult circumstances, in which Christian authorities were attempting to Christianize a non-sedentary population on the fringes of the empire, the church could still make considerable efforts to educate and initiate converts. It would be a mistake to ignore the commitment to such an endeavor and also to ignore the possibility that it might have been a priority for the church because it actually had an impact on the people who chose to join the audience of those hearing the instruction.

In this connection we must also keep in mind the common practice of postponing baptism. People often put off baptism until they neared their deathbed.[72] In response, many preachers urged everyone to seek baptism early on in their Christian lives. The failure of many to do so created problems of boundary maintenance, as unbaptized Christians would occasionally attempt to pass themselves off as baptized.[73] Isabella Sandwell has urged caution, therefore, when considering the relevance of catechesis to the impact of Christianity on Roman society.[74] The present study of catechesis makes no claim to universal adoption of the expectations of catechetical preachers. Neither does it assume that even all catechumens adopted the outlook of the clergy who preached to them. It does, however, argue that catechesis demonstrates the range of tools

---

[71] MacMullen 1984:3: "But what started this discussion was my wish to understand how the empire was converted; and in a conventional sense (the sense to be found in all the ordinary history books), populations exactly like the Bedouins in the degree of their spiritual change are certainly counted as converts—are and *were* counted."

[72] Riley 1974:212–213. I do not doubt that postponement of baptism was common; it is important to see a certain hyperbole in the constant pleading of preachers who claim that no one pursues baptism.

[73] Maxwell 2006:120.

[74] Sandwell 2007.

used by the clergy to create a Christian community of invested converts.[75] It shows how catechesis urged cognitive instruction and ritual participation situated within a robust community. Though the periphery of interested but uninitiated believers may have been sizeable, the core of initiated believers surely contained considerable numbers as well. Furthermore, the efforts of the church to ground catechumens in the community and create Christian identity must be recognized.

Catechesis therefore forms the basis of the present study. It joins the study of institutions, architecture, legislation, and other topics as one very important aspect of the process of Christianization. It is not offered here as the solution to the problem of Christianization, nor is it necessarily intended to supersede other approaches. Nevertheless, catechesis has much to offer in this context, even though surprisingly little has been written on it from this perspective.[76] Many clergy and initiated Christians clearly ascribed considerable religious significance to the process. Even those who studiously avoided catechesis and baptism seem to have done so precisely because they believed it would alter their lives in a way that gave them pause. Furthermore the clergy designed the process of catechesis to do just that, to alter the lives of converts. Catechesis offered far more to the converts than a set of theology lessons. Rather it initiated catechumens into the community of baptized adherents to the Christian church. The process fostered social and spiritual ties between the convert and the church. It ritually enacted the rejection of demonic influence and bound the catechumen to Christ through baptism. Throughout these experiences, the priests also taught the converts about the basic points of Christian doctrine and morality. The process was designed to have an impact, and catechesis gave careful attention to reaching the converts socially, physically, and intellectually. As such, this study addresses each of these catechetical themes.

Two recent studies have spoken to a number of the issues raised here but from somewhat different perspectives. Isabella Sandwell has argued that the sources produced by the Christian clergy are the wrong place to look for gaining an understanding of the process of Christianization. She argues that Christian texts, particularly sermons, were actively engaged in trying to create a Christian society that did not exist and, therefore, cannot tell us about the situation as it was on the ground.[77] She focuses on Chrysostom's sermons as a vigorous

---

[75] Sandwell (2007:195–212) recognizes the potential of catechesis to have an impact on catechumens.

[76] See Trombley 1994. On the face of it, Trombley makes a case for the importance of catechesis. He makes repeated reference throughout his study to what "catechism" and "the catechist" accomplished. However, his bibliography contains no references to catechetical homilies, the best sources available for what catechists actually did.

[77] Sandwell 2007:12–13.

attempt both to present and create a society where Christianity touched every aspect of life. Then, by way of contrast, she turns to Libanius as a valuable source on religious identity that was not engaged in trying to Christianize late Roman society in this way. She argues that in the writings of this prominent pagan we see a world in which religious identity was very fluid, highly relevant in some situations and not at all worth mentioning in many others.[78] In short, she finds Libanius' approach to religious identity in Late Antiquity to be much more representative than that of Chrysostom.

In contrast, Jaclyn Maxwell has written about the sermons of John Chrysostom and their role in Christianizing the population of the city of Antioch.[79] Her work responds to an argument that sees the late antique sermon as limited in its impact due to the inability of the mass audience to comprehend technical rhetoric.[80] Maxwell argues that a broad range of the late antique population, especially in a city like Antioch, would have been comfortable with listening to relatively sophisticated rhetoric.[81] She also shows how preachers and audiences negotiated the content of sermons and other means of Christianizing.[82] Preachers wanted to communicate and made considerable effort to tailor their sermons to the abilities of their audiences.[83]

Sandwell is absolutely correct in drawing attention to the reality of fluid categories of religious identity in Late Antiquity. Chrysostom's particular zeal to conform his congregation to an ideal of Christian behavior that struck them as unnecessary is well known and ably exemplifies the point that his preaching did not always achieve its desired goals.[84] But we should not allow the fact that Chrysostom's homiletical aims were not always realized to lead to the wrong conclusion. Attempts at Christianization did indeed produce Christians. Maxwell is right to stress the give and take between preachers and audiences in this process. Preachers wanted to reach their audiences in meaningful ways, and their sermons show them working diligently to do just that. Perhaps more importantly, audiences wanted to be reached. For a host of reasons people came to the church and sought various kinds of identification with it. Many of them

---

[78] Sandwell 2007:9.
[79] Maxwell 2006.
[80] For a prominent example of this argument, see MacMullen 1989:503–511.
[81] Maxwell 2006:67. Furthermore, just because we have a large corpus of sermons from John Chrysostom does not mean that his sermons were representative of late antique preaching. In fact, their preservation in such large numbers suggests exactly the opposite. For a study on a much more representative set of sermons, see Bailey 2010.
[82] Maxwell 2006:172.
[83] See also Rousseau 1998:391–400.
[84] Take, for example, the difference between Chrysostom and his congregation regarding Christian involvement in Jewish practices he considered unacceptable; see Wilken 1983; also Sandwell 2010.

formalized this relationship by being initiated through catechesis and baptism. Even when the results of the process failed to live up to the ideals of someone like Chrysostom, the efforts to produce Christians could be fruitful. Just because the results did not always satisfy Chrysostom's expectations should not exclude the possibility of their attachment to Christianity being deeply meaningful in terms of their attachment to its community, ritual devotion, and even ideas.

The efforts of Theodore of Mopsuestia to engage baptismal candidates during this period of initiation into the church form the basis for this study. The curriculum he offered was far more than an abstracted or theoretical classroom experience. Rather, it fostered community ties for the purpose of forming the catechumens morally and intellectually. This communal focus extended even to the teaching of the creed. In the sermons that exegete the creed, Theodore taught its theological content line by line, while baptismal sponsors worked with the catechumens to help them memorize it. Furthermore, catechesis drew converts into a highly ritualized set of engagements. Precisely how the catechumens perceived their ritual actions is difficult to determine. Theodore certainly gave considerable attention to defining them, but it would be unreasonable to assume that everyone who heard him followed his instruction to the letter. Nevertheless, Theodore's sermons demonstrate his concern for pedagogy and the comprehension of his students. The analysis of these sermons will argue that catechesis presented a potentially profound pedagogical experience, especially through the confluence of social and ritual components. Even though the reception of these sermons and the rituals they describe could not have been uniformly effective or even perceived entirely as Theodore would have intended, the contention here is that they ought to be taken seriously as pedagogical moments designed to cultivate a habitus.

Pierre Bourdieu's notion of habitus offers a helpful analytical category for approaching the process of catechesis. His understanding of socially and historically embedded ways of being and acting in the world highlights precisely the sort of things Theodore sought to cultivate as he preached these sermons. The roles played by society and hierarchy, ritual and the body, and education as means of inculcating a "second nature" that at once feels comfortable while simultaneously originating outside the objects of such mechanisms hold particular relevance for understanding Theodore's catechesis.[85] This type of habitus formation through catechesis captures nicely what we mean by the construction of a Christian *paideia* in which community structures and ritual activity

---

[85] See, especially, Bourdieu 1977:78–83 and 1990:66–79, for these aspects of his thought. While Bourdieu noted the difficulty of changing one's habitus, he did not leave out the possibility of this happening and, not coincidentally, described it as a second birth in 1990:68.

were brought to bear on people undergoing initiation.[86] These themes will continually reappear as we analyze Theodore's pedagogy and the substance of his catechetical curriculum.

Several scholars have made rather pregnant suggestions about another important aspect in the process of Christianization that we have not yet discussed—that is, the creation of a Christian imagination.[87] Many late Roman people came to imagine their world as a Christian one. Christian angels and demons replaced the ancient *daimones* that inhabited the lower levels of the heavens. Christian holy men and women as well as relics of saints and martyrs became tangible proof that divine power was at work upon the earth. People drew near to God in the liturgy and saw a representative of God in the person of the bishop who administered it. All of this required a shift in the way people imagined their world. It is important, however, that when we speak of this development of a new way of imagining, we avoid overly intellectualized notions of what this means.[88] The formation of a Christian imagination did not necessarily have to engage a convert on an intellectual level, and we should not necessarily have theology in mind here. In fact, we will see very clearly that Theodore orchestrated Christian initiation and the catechetical process to address a broad audience in a host of different ways. Catechesis was a complex process that initiated baptismal candidates into the mysteries of the church. Chapter one discusses the relevant context of Antioch and the intellectual milieu in which Theodore worked as a preacher of catechetical sermons. Chapter two addresses the maintenance of Christian secrecy and the rhetorical effect to which the practice of maintaining it was put. Chapter three places catechesis into the social context in which it was carried out. It addresses the nature of the community visible from outside the church and how the church used the process of initiation to incorporate catechumens. Chapter four addresses Theodore's teaching on the creed with a particular emphasis on his pedagogical approach. Theodore's careful attempts to teach the candidates about the liturgy they were

---

[86] This notion of *paideia* differs from what Becker (2006:112–125) has written about in the context of Theodore's influence on the notion of "divine *paideia*" in the school of Nisibis. Becker deals with Theodore's theological idea that God works through human history to teach humans in historically situated ways. While this understanding of divine *paideia* offers valuable insight into Theodore and his influence in the East Syriac tradition, it is less relevant to what we mean here by *paideia* as a cultural system into which people must be educated through catechesis. See also, Wallace-Hadrill 1982:63; and Reinink 1995:84–85.

[87] Markus 1990:15–16; and Cameron 1991.

[88] Critiques of an overly intellectual focus in the study of Christianization abound. This is the basis of MacMullen's critique of Nock discussed earlier. See also, Sandwell 2007:14–15; and Kile 2005:220–221.

about to experience and about how use the moment of initiation to form a new habitus is the subject of chapter five.

Theodore spoke of catechesis as a process in which the candidates became citizens of heaven.[89] He designed his catechetical curriculum as a multifaceted program of enculturation, a vigorous attempt to naturalize Christian converts. His sermons reveal a thoughtful attempt to craft a holistic approach to catechesis that would engage baptismal candidates with ideas, community, and ritual. Furthermore, we will see that any attempt to maintain firm boundaries between these categories tends to break down, since each was used to reinforce the others. Christian imagination was formed by the cumulative effect of all of these aspects of catechesis, and each had its role to play in making Christian citizens.

---

[89]   *WS* 5.24–26.

1

Theodore's Life, Education, and Ministry

THEODORE OF MOPSUESTIA stands out as an influential figure well situated to observe and contribute to the Christianization of the Roman Empire during the late-fourth and early-fifth centuries. He was born into a well-to-do family in the city of Antioch (Antakya in southern Turkey) around the year AD 350. He was educated, along with his better-known contemporary John Chrysostom, in the school of the famous Antiochene rhetor Libanius.[1] Theodore then pursued an ascetic life along with theological and biblical study outside Antioch under Diodore (d. ca. 390), later bishop of Tarsus. Theodore served as a priest in Antioch from 383 until he was ordained bishop of Mopsuestia in Cilicia (modern Yakapınar in southern Turkey) in 392. Theodore served as bishop of Mopsuestia until his death in 428.

Theodore's training and the offices he held positioned him to engage in some of the most pressing theological debates of his day. He wrote extensively on Christian scripture, both commenting on the texts and articulating a distinctive hermeneutical theory. He also wrote several works defending the theology of the councils of Nicaea (325) and Constantinople (381) against so-called "Arian" opponents and, in doing so, put forward a comprehensive set of ideas on the relationship between humanity and divinity in Christ. Though Theodore was a well-regarded theologian in his day, the positions he took on both of these theological topics, hermeneutics and Christology, would leave him out of step with future generations of Christian thinkers and powerbrokers. At the Council of Constantinople in 553, Theodore was condemned for views deemed heretical at that time.

This development has had a tremendous impact on Theodore's legacy, as it ensured that most of his original Greek writings did not survive into the modern period. Furthermore, much of Theodore's extant Greek stems directly from the collections of questionable statements put together by his theological detractors for the purpose of demonstrating his error and condemning him.

---

[1] Socrates *Church History* 6.3; and Sozomen *Church History* 8.2.

Fortunately, a rather significant number of Syriac translations along with some Latin translations have survived. The *Catechetical Homilies* present a case in point. Theodore delivered his homilies in Greek, most likely sometime in the early 390s while still a presbyter in Antioch.² As a result of Theodore's condemnation during the sixth century, however, the sermons are no longer extant in the original Greek. They remained unknown to the scholarly community until 1932 and 1933, when Alphonse Mingana published the Syriac text of the homilies along with an English translation.³ This manuscript dates to the fourteenth century but contains a translation of the fifth or sixth century.⁴ Many other works by Theodore have not fared as well and remain available only through small fragments.

Consequently, the development of Theodore's career and the circumstances leading to his condemnation have greatly affected his scholarly reception. In addition to his work's poor state of preservation, the controversies in which Theodore engaged have dominated the scholarship on him. To date, this literature has left little room for the consideration of Theodore as a pastorally minded minister. Nevertheless, certain biographical details combine with the nature of many of Theodore's theological positions and the subject of several lost works to show him as a religiously sensitive pastor concerned to communicate the Christian life with great concern for the care of his flock. These concerns relate directly to our treatment of the *Catechetical Homilies,* in so far as Theodore's sermons have generally been treated as a source of evidence for understanding his Christology. While they can serve that purpose, they were not delivered as a piece of systematic theology. Theodore preached these sermons as an act of pastoral ministry in which he sought to engage catechumens and initiate them into the Christian life, and we must attempt to view him in that light. In so far as Theodore did not consider theology unimportant to his pastoral aims, we will

---

² There is some disagreement on the date of Theodore's homilies. Vosté (1925:80) places them during Theodore's episcopate—that is, after 392. McLeod (2009) follows Vosté, but without giving any reason. Tonneau and Devreesse (1949) prefer to place the homilies in Antioch, but again give little argument. Abramowski (1992:481–513) establishes that the discussion of the Holy Spirit best fits the period when Theodore was still a priest in Antioch.

³ I will cite Mingana's edition as *WS* (for *Woodbrooke Studies*), followed by the volume number and page of Mingana's English translation. In footnotes containing the Syriac text of the manuscript facsimile, I will cite the published facsimile as *Homélies Catéchétiques,* followed by the sermon number and the manuscript folio number. See the Author's Note on Citations and Translations for a fuller discussion on citations and abbreviations.

⁴ For a description of *Mingana Syriac 561,* see Mingana 1933–1985, 1:1041–1044. Mid-nineteenth-century missionary accounts contain several vague references to the possibility of additional manuscripts. The most promising mentions "a copy of the history of the Nicene Council by Theodorus of Mopsuestia." The last known location of the manuscript was the American Mission Library in Beirut in 1863. Unfortunately, it can no longer be located; see Laurie 1853:203.

give consideration to an outline of his thought. Nevertheless, in what follows we will take up the events of Theodore's life and career with a particular focus on his concern for pastoral care.

Theodore's Youth and Education

We know little of Theodore's upbringing or family history, except that he likely came from a well-to-do family. Theodore attended the rhetorical school of Libanius in Antioch, one of the most elite educational institutions of the day.[5] Rarely could anyone outside the upper ranks of Roman society afford this sort of training. Under Libanius, Theodore received an education thoroughly grounded in the Greek classics of poetry and prose. This education entailed more than mastery of literary texts, however. Ancient Greco-Roman education oriented students toward the production of rhetorical speeches in political and judicial contexts. Mastery of the tradition's literature thus served as the entryway into public life. When governors conveyed the will of the emperor in provincial capitals, when *curiales* deliberated in the town councils, or when lawyers adjudicated cases, public speech provided the common medium of these interactions. Knowledge of, and facility with, the received canon of literature remained the most effective way to craft compelling speech and thus to advance in late Roman society.[6] This education, designed to produce effective participants in the exercise of power within the late Roman world, bore the name *paideia*, a Greek term encompassing both "education" and "culture." The semantic range of this term nicely highlights the social significance of the course of study. In a large empire made up of people with diverse regional, civic, and ethnic identities, *paideia* served the essential function of offering a common culture for elite Roman subjects from as far afield as Gaul, Syria, or Egypt. Literature provided a mainstay of this shared culture, and elites needed the ability to comprehend and produce complex literary references as they engaged in public life.

At the center of the culture that *paideia* sought to inculcate in Theodore and other young elite males stood a concept of morality focused on a sense of decorum and comportment.[7] The budding members of the curial and senatorial classes needed to possess such skills as second nature. Civic and imperial politics could be brutal affairs, as military might regularly accompanied provincial governors who could find themselves facing an angry mob at any moment.

---

[5] On Libanius' school in Antioch, see Cribiore 2007:30–37.

[6] Already by Libanius' time, however, the study of law as opposed to rhetoric had become an expedient means of advancing one's career, a fact about which Libanius complained bitterly, as he lost good students who went to study law in Berytus (Beirut); cf. *Or.* 62.21.

[7] Brown 1992a:49–61.

Theodore, Chrysostom, and Libanius all experienced this first-hand, probably on many occasions, but certainly during the so-called "Affair of the Statues," in which the city of Antioch erupted in anger over a substantial rise in their tax burden.[8] In the resulting uprising, the crowd pulled down the statues of the emperor Theodosius and his family. This constituted an act of treason and resulted in a very tense situation in which both Libanius and the bishop Flavian urged the emperor to respond leniently. Such situations called for a remarkable level of composure on the part of governors, town councilors, emperors, and bishops. *Paideia* thus shaped the characters as well as the minds of the elites who received this education, in turn helping negotiate relations between rulers and subjects at times of crisis. Control of one's emotions, and even one's physical gestures, was seen as essential in the tense climate of late antique political life. As such, *paideia* sought to shape the minds, characters, and bodies of the young men who would soon enter into positions of social and political prominence. This type of training under the rhetor Libanius constituted the early part of Theodore's education and would have an impact on his intellectual activity throughout his life.

Following his rhetorical training, Theodore would again join Chrysostom in studying Christian scripture and theology under Diodore (d. ca. 390), later bishop of Tarsus.[9] The ancient church historians who discuss this school use the term *askētērion* (ἀσκητήριον), which literally means "a place of asceticism," a monastery. Few details emerge from this period of Theodore's life, but if we can take Chrysostom's experience as an indication, the monks at Diodore's *askētērion* practiced a rigorous form of asceticism. Palladius states that Chrysostom lived for a time as a hermit and pursued an asceticism so severe that he damaged his kidneys permanently, which forced his return to a more normal course of life.[10] It is conceivable that Theodore followed similar practices. However, Diodore's *askētērion* comprised something different from the stereotyped notions of complete poverty and withdrawal from the world that often surround monastic renunciation.[11] Diodore was a productive biblical scholar during these years and Theodore began his literary career in the *askētērion* as well. Theodore almost

---

[8]   Sozomen *Church History* 7.23; Theodoret *Church History* 5.19; Zosimus *New History* 4.41. John Chrysostom delivered his homilies, *On the Statues*, in conjunction with this very episode. They offer an excellent example of public speech urging the general public to adopt the kind of composure emphasized in late antique *paideia*.

[9]   Kelly 1995:19. For the suggestion that Theodore did not complete his rhetorical training, see Carter 1962:97–98.

[10]   Palladius *Dialogue* 5.

[11]   See Athanasius' *Life of Anthony* for the paradigmatic image of complete withdrawal for the Christian monk. For a critical reading of this and similar texts that shows the numerous ways monks engaged with society, see Chitty 1966.

certainly produced his Psalm commentary and his commentary on the minor prophets of the Hebrew Bible during his time at the *askētērion*.[12] This type of study required resources, particularly access to a library of rather expensive books.[13] We must see Diodore's *askētērion* as a school that offered a monastic setting for immersion in Christian scholarship at a high level, rather like a modern Roman Catholic theological seminary, where one would pursue spiritual formation through celibacy, prayer, and fasting, alongside advanced biblical and theological study.

Another well-known event of Theodore's involvement with Diodore's school comes from an incident in which Theodore left and his friend John Chrysostom wrote to him hoping to convince him to return.[14] It seems that Theodore left the *askētērion* in order to pursue marriage, family, and the type of secular career for which studying under Libanius had prepared him. Such a career would have been the norm for someone of his station in life and educational background. Chrysostom understood Theodore's departure as a serious matter demanding attention. "If it were possible," lamented Chrysostom, "to express tears and groans by means of writing I would have filled the letter, which I now send to you, with them."[15] While Chrysostom very likely thought that walking away from the intellectual formation offered at Diodore's school would adversely affect Theodore, he was much more concerned with the state of Theodore's soul. Leaving Diodore's school entailed leaving the monastic life after Theodore had taken vows to pursue it. As such, two concerns appear repeatedly in Chrysostom's personal letter to Theodore. First, Chrysostom cautioned Theodore regarding the pursuit of a secular career. He feared that Theodore's engagement in civic life would entail the pursuit of money and prestige, lead him away from Christ, and ultimately condemn his soul.[16] Chrysostom also argued that abandoning a monastic vow was tantamount to abandoning Christ as one's savior. Theodore had become married to Christ and the monastic community. By leaving it and taking a wife, he rejected this spiritual marriage and sought his security and place in the world. Chrysostom admitted that marriage itself did not harm a Christian, but still insisted that leaving the monastic community for a life of marital comforts and obligations constituted a betrayal of Christ for the monk.[17]

---

[12] Hill 2004:42 and 2001:111–113.

[13] On monks with large libraries, see M. H. Williams 2006:133–166.

[14] Chrysostom's writings include a letter to a Theodore and a treatise to a monk who left the monastic community. It is likely that the letter is to Theodore of Mopsuestia, while the treatise is not; Carter 1962:87–101.

[15] John Chrysostom *Letter to Theodore* 1.

[16] John Chrysostom *Letter to Theodore* 2–3.

[17] *Letter to Theodore* 3.

Theodore's decision may have been personally motivated, stemming from a desire for a wife, family, and civic prominence as opposed to a life of ascetic devotion and biblical study. Most commentators have indeed tended to understand it this way.[18] An alternative explanation presents itself as rather plausible, however. His decision may have been a reluctant one, the result of his succumbing to pressure from his parents to continue the family legacy and use his expensive education to secure the well-being of his family.[19] Several developments suggest this interpretation. We know for certain that Chrysostom's pleas successfully recalled Theodore to Diodore's school and the monastic life.[20] That Theodore chose to return to the *askētērion* even though no serious sanction would have affected him had he chosen otherwise shows his earnest attachment to his religious life. Furthermore, Theodore's activity during this period of his life further suggests the serious nature of his commitment. It seems as though he had already been engaged in a high level of biblical study and commentary while at the *askētērion*. Leontius of Byzantium asserted that Theodore began commenting on biblical texts when merely eighteen years old.[21] Leontius likely exaggerated in making this claim, but Theodore's youth at the time of his Psalm commentary remains certain. We cannot secure precise dating of these events, but it is quite possible that Theodore began writing commentaries before the departure from the *askētērion* that prompted Chrysostom's letter.[22] As such, there remains little reason to suspect the sincerity of Theodore's desire to pursue asceticism and biblical study. It seems most appropriate to see his decision to leave the *askētērion* as motivated by external factors, with pressure from his family being a likely source. These events suggest an image of Theodore as a religiously sensitive young man who took Christian devotion seriously even while family pressures weighed upon him, not as someone bent on escaping a monastic lifestyle for personal gain or marital pleasure. Regardless of exactly

---

[18] Devreesse 1948:3–4; Behr 2011:52. Socrates and Theodoret ignore the incident, while Sozomen (*Church History* 7.23) gives an account that does not discuss motives very deeply.

[19] Festugière (1959:158) suggests a similar interpretation but speculates further that Theodore's decision came about in response to the death of his father.

[20] For a brief discussion of a contested letter claiming to be Theodore's response to Chrysostom, see Dumortier 1966:20–21. The consensus, supported by Dumortier, is that Theodore did not write this letter. Nevertheless, Dumortier includes the Greek text and a French translation of this letter on pp. 220–239.

[21] Leontius of Byzantium *Contra Nestorianos et Eutychianos* 8; Hill 2004:52; Zaharopoulos 1989:30–31.

[22] On the date of Theodore's Psalm commentary, see Vosté 1925:71. Vosté asserts that the Psalm commentary ought to be dated to Theodore's second stay at the *askētērion*. However, his only argument for this is that the commentary shows signs of immaturity but also considerable familiarity with Diodore's exegetical method, a familiarity Vosté does not seem to believe Theodore could have gained on his initial stay. Since the dates and lengths of neither stay are known, there is little reason to adopt this interpretation.

how we read Theodore's motivation, this entire episode casts him in a very human light and urges us to consider him as more than a theological polemicist.

As a final point with respect to Theodore's early life, we must note the combination of classical *paideia* and Christian education that occupied so much of it. The focus of each differed considerably from the other. The classical system of education focused on mastering an elite literature, imbibing a cultural system, and using these resources in pursuit of a public life. The *askētērion* urged withdrawal from public life and attention to a very different literature. However, each sought to train mind and body for proper engagement with particular institutions. It would be misleading to suggest that Theodore set out consciously to replicate either of these pedagogical experiences when taking up the task of teaching Christian catechumens. Nevertheless, by the time he preached his catechetical homilies he had given over two decades of his life to these educational institutions and had clearly gained considerable understanding of how to train minds and bodies, as well as of what it meant to be socialized into two distinctive cultures. These themes will reappear in subsequent chapters as we analyze how Theodore taught theology and ritual participation while grounding it in the life and culture of a community.

Theodore's Ecclesiastical Career in Context

The character of Theodore's youth and education would manifest itself throughout his life. While Theodore did not use his rhetorical training for the secular career his parents likely imagined, he would go on to employ the skills he gained under Libanius to his pastoral ministry and commentaries on the Bible. We know little of the details of Theodore's daily life and what aspects of his ascetic training he continued to exhibit once he entered the ranks of the clergy in 383. The intellectual component of Theodore's training, with its dual focus on theological and Biblical studies, would form his outlook considerably and set the intellectual trajectory for the rest of his career. We will return to a more detailed discussion of these two components of Theodore's thought shortly. First, however, it will be helpful to situate these two intellectual pursuits within the context of Antioch at the end of the fourth century.

Antioch and the Arian controversy

The cultural and strategic prominence Antioch held in Late Antiquity made it one of the four most important cities in the Roman world along with Rome, Constantinople, and Alexandria. Located in ancient northern Syria some twenty miles from the Mediterranean Sea, Antioch was close to Mesopotamia and the northeastern border regions of the Roman Empire. The coastal city of Seleukia Pereia, located near the mouth of the Orontes River, served as the port city of Antioch. As Silk Road trade flourished following the conquests of Alexander and the establishment of Hellenic cities throughout Mesopotamia and the Iranian Plateau, Antioch and its port facilitated, and greatly profited from, this trade.

Antioch exploited this position and wealth to establish itself as a major center of Hellenic culture in the eastern Mediterranean throughout the Roman period. Antioch's several agoras and numerous bath complexes marked it as a paradigmatic Hellenic city within its Syrian context.[22] A tradition of Greek letters and flourishing educational institutions distinguished Antioch as a cultural as well as an economic powerhouse.[23] The Antiochenes who benefited from these civic institutions also had easy access to a world-famous playground for the rich and famous just outside their city. Sometimes called a suburb of Antioch, the resort town of Daphne lay less than ten miles from Antioch and offered the elites of the city a nearby refuge of lush groves, mountain springs, and an extensive array of amenities. The opportunities for wealth and pleasure offered by Antioch and its environs prompted one commentator to describe it as "the fair crown of the Orient."[24]

The obvious appeal of Antioch existed in tension with its relative proximity to a hostile neighbor. The Persians—the Parthians from 238 BC to AD 226 and the Sassanians from AD 226 to 651—presented a persistent threat to the Antiochenes. Indeed, the Sassanians sacked Antioch in AD 256 and again in 260.[25] As long as Antioch offered the Persians a major Roman city accessible from the border regions of Mesopotamia and granting easy access to the Mediterranean Sea, it remained a constant target of Persian ambition. The Romans, in turn, increasingly used it as a staging point for their incursions into Mesopotamia. As such, Antioch presented a well-fortified city with a large military presence and a robust imperial bureaucracy. It also frequently served as an eastern residence for Roman emperors, particularly those preparing to go on campaign against the Persians. This reality produced a situation in which imperial politics were woven into the day-to-day life of Antioch, with all of the benefits and liabilities that entailed.

The clergy of Antioch enjoyed this prominence as much as those of the curial or senatorial classes. As with Theodore and Chrysostom, the clergy often came from prominent families, making their expectations of proximity to political

---

[22] Libanius *Oration* 11.134, 212, 218–248; and Stillwell, et al. 1934–1972, 1:4–48. On the traditional religious monuments and festivals of Antioch, see Soler 2006:13–42.

[23] Cicero *Pro Archia* 3.

[24] Ammanius Marcellinus *Rerum Gestarum* 22.9.14.

[25] Downey 1961:260–262.

power that much greater.[27] The elite rhetorical training Theodore pursued as a young man prepared him for a public career as a local notable serving his city and rubbing shoulders with imperial power brokers. Theodore's involvement with Diodore's *askētērion* set him on a course suited to an ecclesiastical career, but likely did not alter too significantly his expectation of civic prominence. The exact nature and duration of Theodore's monastic study remains unclear, but we know that the bishop Flavian ordained him presbyter in the city of Antioch in 383.

In many cities this would have been a rather straightforward matter. However, Antioch was a tumultuous place for Christians, laity and clergy alike. As an important Roman city garnering so much imperial attention, Antioch had little hope of escaping the most contentious theological disagreements of the day. For much of the fourth century, Antioch was one center of what came to be known as the Arian controversy. The issues at stake in this contentious series of disagreements can be summed up rather succinctly as a question regarding the relationship between God and Jesus, between the Father and the Son. In the early 390s when Theodore preached his catechetical sermons, this controversy continued to divide Christians. As we will see, Antioch continued to have three distinct Christian churches. These divisions provide essential context for understanding Theodore's theological instruction and attempts to create Christian community through catechesis.

Early in the fourth century, the Alexandrian presbyter, Arius, had proposed that the nature of Jesus' divinity was derivative, that the ontological gap between creator and creature fell in such a way as to include Jesus, the Son, among the created. The biblical phrase "only-begotten Son of God"[28] provided one of the strongest proof-texts offered by Arius and those in agreement with his theology. Those who disagreed saw Jesus as a fully divine figure who did not come into being in time but rather existed with the Father before time began. Each position held that Jesus was divine and that Jesus existed as a divine mediator between God and human beings. The difference came down to the fullness or completeness of that divinity and where one should recognize the line between creator and creature.[29]

The dispute came to the attention of the first Christian emperor, Constantine, who called a universal council of the church in order to deal with this contentious matter. Held in the city of Nicaea in the year 325, the council aimed to settle the

---

[27] Rapp 2005:183–194.

[28] John 1.14, 18; 3.16; I John 4.9. The canonical New Testament also contains many additional references to Jesus being the "Son of God."

[29] Our main concern here is the political impact of this theological dispute on the history of Christianity. See chapter four for a fuller discussion of the theology at stake in this dispute.

dispute permanently. The council affirmed that the Son is "God from God, light from light, very God from very God, begotten, not made, one substance with the Father ..."[30] The council chose language designed to exclude Arius' theology. The full divinity of the Son whose source is the divine Father comes across clearly. Less clear is the inclusion of the term *homoousios* (ὁμοούσιος), "one substance." It most likely gained acceptance as an expression of what it meant for the Son to be "God from God." Nevertheless, while the participants in the council departed Nicaea in triumphant agreement, they returned to their respective sees in a haze of confusion, with many people left wondering what exactly it meant for the Father and the Son to be *homoousios*. Many bishops, particularly in the east, feared that declaring Jesus to be one substance with the Father might fracture divine unity, simplicity, and impassibility, thus calling into question Christian monotheism. Rather than unify the Christians of the empire, the Council of Nicaea and its creed produced deep divisions that resulted in further religious and political turmoil for most of the fourth century.[31]

The theology discussed by the numerous bishops and theologians involved in these debates was highly technical, but the specifics need not concern us in this context. The important thing for our purposes here is that these issues were highly divisive, especially since emperors throughout this period sought to follow the lead of Constantine and enforce consensus through exiling troublesome bishops and denouncing ideas out of keeping with what they thought would produce harmony within church and empire. This situation produced division throughout much of the empire, but Antioch became the focus of particularly contentious partisanship. Eustathius served as the bishop of Antioch during the Council of Nicaea at which he took a firm position against the theology of Arius. A council held in Antioch in 327 subsequently deposed him.[32] Athanasius would interpret this as part of a grand "Arian" conspiracy to marginalize and eradicate Nicene "orthodoxy."[33] This is likely a misrepresentation but the perception stuck. Those favoring Nicaea and the term *homoousios* considered him the rightful bishop of Antioch until his death. A series of bishops who did not favor the Nicene formula followed, and Nicenes in the city of Antioch continued to oppose the so-called "Arian" theology, which they felt plagued their city.

Diodore, Theodore's teacher, and Flavian, who, as the bishop of Antioch would later ordain Theodore, first appear in the sources in this context during

---

[30] *Symbolum Nicaenum*: θεὸν ἐκ θεοῦ, φῶς ἐκ φωτός, θεὸν ἀληθινὸν ἐκ θεοῦ ἀληθινοῦ, γεννηθέντα, οὐ ποιηθέντα, ὁμοούσιον τῷ πατρί ...

[31] Williams 1987; Vaggione 2000; Gwynn 2007.

[32] This revised date was proposed by Chadwick 1948:27–35. This date is also accepted by Barnes 1978:59–60 and Gwynn 2007:141. Hanson (1988:208–210) continues to assert the conventional date of 330/1.

[33] Gwynn 2007:27–28.

the 340s. Though not yet ordained, they whipped up popular support against the bishop Leontius (344–358) after he tried to ordain the openly non-Nicene Aetius as a deacon.[34] Though forced to relent, Leontius and his successor Eudoxius (358–360) continued to favor non-Nicene interpretations of the relationship between the Father and the Son. Conciliar machinations continued over the next several decades and imperial power secured the exile and return of several bishops.[35] Flavian, bishop from 381–404, eventually won the support of all the major sees of the empire, but a technical division persisted in Antioch until 415. As a result, when Theodore preached his catechetical homilies, he did so in the context of the dispute, and the community he worked to form did not present the only option available to those seeking initiation. The divided nature of Antiochene Christianity made the persuasive articulation of Christianity an essential pastoral duty. Theological polemics demonstrate the process of boundary formation and maintenance in Late Antiquity. The ability to garner popular support even among people who may not have understood the finer points of the theology played an important role in this process.[36]

Theodore's Theological Controversies

The context of the Arian Controversy is also essential for understanding Theodore's thought and the scholarly treatment it has received. As Theodore was groomed for Christian ministry in such a theological atmosphere, it should not surprise that Theodore's intellectual activity continued to center around theological controversy. Most of Theodore's writings engaged in one of the two great controversies that marked his career. The first controversy surrounded the continued discussion of the relationship between the Father and the Son, with the status of the Holy Spirit also becoming contentious as a full-fledged doctrine of the Trinity took shape.[37] Theodore engaged deeply in these debates and became a major figure in shaping the discussions over almost four decades. These Christological debates never fully took him away from his early interest in biblical exegesis, however, and Theodore continued to write commentaries and an important work on hermeneutical theory in which he attacked the Christian use of allegory in the interpretation of scripture.

Theodore's engagement with these theological controversies gained him a great reputation in some circles and considerable notoriety in others. His theological writings made him a prominent figure among the clergy of Antioch and

---

[34] Theodoret *Church History* 2.19; Behr 2011:49.
[35] For a discussion of the schism and its treatment in recent scholarship, see Spoerl 1993.
[36] Gregory 1979.
[37] Theodore of Mopsuestia *Against the Macedonians*.

led to his elevation to the bishopric of Mopsuestia in 392. Theodore even gained the attention of Theodosius and received considerable praise after preaching before him.[38] The canons of the Council of Chalcedon also mention him favorably, accepting Ibas of Edessa's characterization of him as "a herald of the truth and doctor of the Church."[39] However, Theodore also received negative attention as well, particularly from theologians active in Alexandria.[40] The positions Theodore took on these controversies and the reception they received have contributed significantly to the questions that drive the scholarly treatment of Theodore in general and his catechesis in particular. Denunciation of Theodore's theology would continue until reaching a crescendo in the sixth century, when the emperor Justinian secured his condemnation as a heretic. This combination of praise and condemnation has continued to reverberate in the modern scholarship on Theodore, which focuses on the two main controversies he engaged in. The predominance of these controversies in the scholarship on Theodore has made it difficult to appreciate him as a pastoral theologian. Nevertheless, some of Theodore's concern for pastoral matters emerges even in the context of considering his exegetical and Christological thought.

Exegesis

Theodore wrote extensively on almost the entire Christian scripture.[41] As we saw earlier, Theodore commented on the Psalms and the Minor Prophets when still at Diodore's *askētērion*. While many of Theodore's commentaries are no longer extant, important references to these works appear in the tenth- to eleventh-century *Chronicle of Siirt* and the *Catalog* of ʿAbdišōʿ (d. 1318).[42] Between them we can determine that Theodore wrote commentaries on the Pentateuch, Joshua, Judges, 1 and 2 Samuel, Job, Ecclesiastes, Isaiah, Jeremiah, Ezekiel, and Daniel.[43] ʿAbdišōʿ mentions commentaries on each of the Synoptic Gospels and Acts, while we have extant Theodore's commentary on John. Theodore

---

[38] Facundus of Hermiane *Defense of the Three Chapters* 2.2. In this section, Facundus quotes John of Antioch on Theodore.

[39] *Acts of the Council of Chalcedon* 10.138; ACO 2.1:392.

[40] Behr 2011:88–100; and Wessel 2004:278.

[41] Theodore is sometimes referred to as the "founder" of the so-called "School of Antioch." This "school" is marked by a historical and grammatical approach to scripture and by displeasure with allegorical interpretation. As long as we understand by "school" a general approach to interpretation and keep in check overwrought ideas of a radical disjunction between Antioch and Alexandria on this score, the use of the term is acceptable. We must also note that the set of ideas associated with this school are really attributable to Diodore rather than Theodore. See Hill 2004:17–24; and Viciano 1996:370–405.

[42] ʿAbdišōʿ *Catalog* 30–35; and *Chronicle of Siirt*; see also, Zaharopoulos 1989:33–36.

[43] For more on Theodore's Old Testament writings, see Zaharopoulos 1989:27–43.

commented on the entire Pauline corpus, including Hebrews, which he believed to be written by Paul.[44]

The interpretive method that Theodore employed in these commentaries focused on drawing attention to the historical events recounted in the text and emphasizing the work of God through those actual events.[45] As a consequence, he strongly opposed the use of allegory in the interpretation of the Bible. His critique focused on the origins and effects of allegorical interpretation. He believed that allegory was a method devised by pagans and therefore incapable of fruitful application to Christian scripture.[46] The fragments of his *Treatise against the Allegorists* often mention the errors of the third-century theologian Origen in adopting this "pagan" method. Theodore saw Origen's use of allegory as leading him away from the words of scripture. He repeatedly insisted that God's Spirit communicated to his people through those very words and that allegory drew one away from them.[47] Antiochene theologians preferred historical readings of texts and openly criticized the use of allegory. As a result, many have characterized the disagreement between the Antiochene tradition of hermeneutics and the Alexandrian as a disagreement over historical versus allegorical interpretation. However, the simple conclusion that Origen promoted speculative readings distanced from the true meaning of the text while Antiochenes promoted a critical, historical reading entails numerous problems. In particular, non-literal, figurative readings do appear in the work of Theodore and other Antiochene exegetes. This problem has inspired a sizeable body of literature on the precise nature of Theodore's hermeneutical theory and how he applied it in practice.[48] The best recent work shows that the root of the disagreement was between rhetorical and philosophical readings.[49]

Theodore's rhetorical education involved more than simply reading texts and practicing the delivery of speeches. Rhetorical training entailed intimate knowledge of texts and as such required proficiency in literary criticism. Teachers spent considerable time analyzing both the background and the content of the literature with their students.[50] In the earlier stages of the

---

[44] See the bibliography for a list of editions and translations of Theodore's writings.

[45] McLeod 2009:19.

[46] *Against the Allegorists* frags. 3–4; translation in McLeod 2009:75–79.

[47] McLeod 2009:19.

[48] Bultmann 1984; Devreesse 1948:53–93; Greer 1961; Kihn 1880; Hill 2005; Thome 2004; Dudley Tyng 1931:298–303; and Zaharopoulos 1989. For an assessment of this work and additional scholarship on Antiochene exegesis, see Nassif 1996:343–377.

[49] Young 2003:334–354; and Young 1989:182–199; see also Viciano 1996:370–405.

[50] Quintilian, although writing in Latin, is very much a representative of the Hellenic tradition of rhetorical education. His *Institutio Oratoria* offers some of the best descriptions of rhetorical education, especially in its early stages. Cribiore 1996 is an invaluable resource for school

curriculum, a grammarian (*grammatikos*) worked with his young students to ensure that they knew how to handle texts. In the ancient world, this was no straightforward matter. All texts were copied out by hand, and variations inevitably crept in. Furthermore, scribes customarily wrote without punctuation or breaks between words, with the result that simply reading a text took considerable effort.[51] Thus grammarians taught their students to pay careful attention to deciphering every word of the text. Students also learned about word choice and style, what type of vocabulary and grammatical constructions accomplished various aims within a text. The rigorous study of the lexical and grammatical components of classical texts formed the basic method (*methodikē*) of textual analysis.[52] In addition to the careful attention to *methodikē*, the grammarian also taught students to analyze the text under consideration within its broader context. Students learned to identify the subject matter (*hypothesis*) of the text, then moved to the consideration of context. Questions such as when and to whom the author wrote, as well as what texts take up similar subjects and how they treated those subjects, thus came under consideration. This analysis of broader context was referred to as *historikē*. The English word "history" derives from *historikē*, but it would be a mistake to see the ancient and modern senses as closely related. Teachers and students in the rhetorical schools did not bring a modern critical approach to their pursuit of *historikē*. Rather, literary concerns motivated the rhetor's emphasis on *historikē*. He sought to reconstruct the context that would help him analyze texts.[53]

These categories of textual analysis largely served the purpose of isolating the proper text and determining its subject matter through a consideration of its context. As such, *historikē* did not provide the fundamental disagreement with Origen's hermeneutical method. Origen also gave considerable attention to the particulars of language and context.[54] His massive work of textual scholarship, the *Hexapla*, sufficiently attests to this interest.[55] Furthermore, Theodore and Origen both moved beyond this level of textual analysis. Their theories ultimately diverged however, on the level of how to effect that move. Rhetorical schools had developed elaborate systems of inquiry for the purpose of considering the higher meaning (*theōria*) contained within classical literature. "Theorizing" literature took many forms, but *krisis*, or the use of judgment in analyzing a text, offers the most important theoretical tool for situating

---

exercises and a very helpful discussion of the contexts in which they were produced. On the educational and social role of educators, see Kaster 1988.

[51] Quintilian *Institutio Oratoria* 1.8; Cribiore 2001:189–190.

[52] Quintilian *Institutio Oratoria* 1.9.1; Marrou 1982:275; Young 1989:186.

[53] Marrou 1982:280.

[54] Young 2003:339.

[55] Grafton and Williams 2006.

Theodore's approach to texts. The type of *krisis* relevant to considerations of *theōria* dealt with ethical judgment, and the application of this judgment thus formed the basis for commentary and exposition of scripture. For Theodore and for the Antiochenes more generally, sound exegesis required that *theōria* find its basis in *historikē*.[56] Historical context determined the legitimate avenues for considering the higher meaning of a text.[57] On the contrary, Origen's allegorical method adopted a more philosophical approach to literature.[58] While this approach took *historikē* into consideration, it never limited the intended meaning of the divine author to the historical circumstances of the human author. By permitting legitimate *theōria* to relate the text under consideration to abstract metaphysical forms and eternal truths, Origen ultimately freed himself from the constraints of *historikē*.

Theodore's emphasis on the historical grounding of revelation appears to stem from the defenses of Christianity that Theodore made in response to the critiques of the pagan emperor Julian.[59] The idea that Christianity contained nothing more than silly fables was a staple of Julian's critique.[60] If unchallenged, Julian's attack on Christianity could be rather devastating. Felix Thome has thoroughly studied the fragments of Diodore and Theodore on the subject of Julian's religious policy. While he has not found definitive proof that they formulated their critique of allegory in order to undermine Julian's attack on Christianity, he has shown a strong resonance between the concerns that motivated the rejection of Julian's religious program and Origen's allegory. While this apologetic connection to Theodore's hermeneutical theory is not, narrowly speaking, a pastoral issue, it relates to the ability of Theodore to articulate a compelling vision of Christianity. Without such a vision, attracting and maintaining parishioners within a religiously competitive atmosphere could become difficult.

Christology

Another major area of scholarly inquiry concerns Theodore's view of the relationship between the Father and the Son. Contemporary debates over the person of Christ most often cast the discussion in terms of theological fine points and high-stakes ecclesiastical politics. While an engagement with Christology certainly required considerable intellectual rigor and while political

---

[56] Wallace-Hadrill 1982:35.

[57] Theodore of Mopsuestia *Commentary on the Epistle to the Galatians* 4.24.

[58] On the use of allegory in philosophical interpretation, see Lamberton 1986:1–43; and Dawson 1992:23–72.

[59] Behr 2011:66–82.

[60] Hoffman 2004:75, 79.

maneuvering usually lurked behind pious statements of doctrine, we must not miss the pastoral concerns that emerge in Theodore's Christology.

Ordained by bishop Flavian of Antioch in 383, just two years after the Council of Constantinople, Theodore was an ardent Nicene. He wrote numerous works attempting to defend what he saw as orthodox doctrine against enemies on many sides. One early work, *On the Incarnation*, gained Theodore a good reputation while he was still a priest in Antioch.[61] Here he tackled various positions he believed to be in error. On the one hand, he argued against Arius and Eunomius, who diminished the humanity of the Son by considering him a creature.[62] This aspect of *On the Incarnation* addressed the familiar Nicene question of whether or not the Son should be considered fully divine. On the other hand, he also argued against the theology of Apollinaris, who strongly emphasized the divinity of the Son. Apollinaris had argued that two substances becoming one constituted a logical impossibility. Thus, he thought it illegitimate to speak of two natures in Christ, one human and the other divine.[63] Theodore's sense that these theological systems continued to threaten the church persisted; later in his career, he wrote additional works on similar themes, *Against Eunomius* and *Against Apollinaris*.

Theodore did not see these debates as merely academic. Human salvation depended upon the full humanity of Christ.[64] "However, if he had not received a soul and it was the Deity who conquered [sin]," argued Theodore, "then nothing he did would benefit us. For what advantage would there be for the perfection of our way of living in having the Deity [acting] as the human soul? For then our Lord's struggles would seem to have no advantage for us, but rather to have been [done] for the sake of show."[65] Theodore insisted on the true humanity of Christ as a way to ensure that the salvation accomplished by Christ might apply to human beings. Furthermore, he seems to suggest that despair would befall a Christian struggling to live the Christian life, if the Son had only managed to overcome sin because of his divine soul. Theodore wrote often of the activity of Christ's free human will in this connection.[66] Faced with one theology that diminished Christ's divinity and another that diminished his humanity, Theodore focused on asserting two natures in Christ. He insisted that Christ was fully divine but also fully human. Furthermore, this humanity and divinity existed together in

---

[61]   Theodore of Mopsuestia *On the Incarnation*.

[62]   On this topic, Theodore also wrote *Against Eunomius*, of which only two small fragments remain.

[63]   Behr 2011:9–11.

[64]   McLeod 2009:35.

[65]   *On the Incarnation* 15: "Animam autem si non recepisset, sed deitas est quae euicerat, nullatenus eorum quae facta sunt ad nos respicit lucrum—quae enim ad conversationis perfectionem similtudo deitatis et animae humanae?—et viderentur Domini certamina non ad nos respiciens habere lucrum, sed ostentationis cuisdam gratia fuisse."

[66]   *On the Incarnation* 7; *PG* 66:976–977; McLeod 2005; and Norris 1963.

one person according to Theodore.[67] Theodore understood this emphasis on full humanity and full divinity as an attempt to combat the theological errors that he believed threatened the idea that God had truly become human in a way that could guarantee the availability of salvation. The ability to assure parishioners that they worshipped a savior truly capable of securing their salvation drove much of his Christological theory.

The Reception of Theodore and His Works

This cursory summary of Theodore's Christology greatly simplifies what can only be described as a highly complicated set of theological problems that have received a great deal of attention from historians of Christian dogma. The ways in which Theodore and the larger Antiochene tradition described the precise relationship between the humanity and the divinity of Christ have presented considerable interpretive difficulties. In particular, the language he used to explain the unity of the two natures would prove problematic to many. Theodore preferred the idea that Christ's human nature and divine nature each had its own *hypostasis* (ὑπόστασις) and that these two *hypostases* were united in one *prosōpon* (πρόσωπον).[68] Theodore understood *hypostasis* to refer to a substantial nature, thus emphasizing the concrete completeness of each of Christ's natures. The use of *prosōpon* for the union of Christ's two natures was the source for much of the trouble with Theodore's formula. *Prosōpon* could be used in a theatrical context for the masks worn by actors and thus suggested to Theodore's detractors that the unity of the human and divine natures in Christ was not a real unity.[69] Theodore insisted that the unity of the natures in Christ was a real unity.[70] While it seems unlikely that he intended to communicate unreality by using the term *prosōpon*, many detractors found Theodore's language problematic. It did not help Theodore's case that he regularly sought to distinguish between some actions of Jesus that were proper to his human nature and others that were proper to his divine nature. Theodore's most troublesome manifestation of this practice came in reference to the birth of Christ from Mary. Theodore insisted that "the divine nature is not born from a virgin. Rather, it is the one composed from the substance of the virgin who is born of the virgin. In no way had God the Word been born of Mary!"[71] This idea would cause consider-

---

[67] *On the Incarnation* 7; PG 66:977.
[68] McLeod 2009:48.
[69] Mcleod 2009:49.
[70] *On the Incarnation* 7, 8.
[71] *Against Apollinaris* 3: ἀλλ' οὐχ ἡ θεία φύσις ἐκ παρθένου γεγέννηται, γεγέννηται δὲ ἐκ τῆς παρθένου ὁ ἐκ τῆς οὐσίας τῆς παρθένου συστάς· οὐκ ὁ θεὸς λόγος ἐκ τῆς Μαρίας γεγέννηται.

able trouble for Antiochene theology and ultimately play a significant role in Theodore's downfall.

This troubling statement did not immediately bring about the downfall of Theodore as an orthodox theologian, however. Indeed, when he died in 428 he maintained a solid reputation among many in the church. Nevertheless, when his Antiochene compatriot Nestorius took up the bishopric of Constantinople in that same year, he almost instantly caused an uproar by rejecting the use of the term *Theotokos* (Θεοτόκος), "Mother of God," to describe Mary.[72] The Council of Ephesus in 431 would condemn Nestorius for holding too great a distinction between the two natures of Christ and, in doing so, would explicitly affirm the use of *Theotokos*. Despite these events, Theodore still maintained his good name and standing. This is so even though Cyril of Alexandria, the driving force behind Nestorius' condemnation, would begin attacking the theology of Theodore.[73] Theodore would have a mixed reception during the rest of the fifth and much of the sixth century. As those who did not consider the theology of Nestorius to be problematic came to settle in Sassanian Persian territory just outside the Roman Empire, the theology of Theodore spread widely in the East Syrian tradition, where he came to be known as "The Interpreter."[74] Theodore's theology also found support in some western parts of the Roman world.[75]

Despite the many people interested in Theodore and his theology, he fell out of favor in a rather decisive way in the events surrounding the so-called Affair of the Three Chapters in 544–545 and the Council of Constantinople in 553. In this period, the Emperor Justinian sought to reunite his empire religiously after the fractures caused by the formula of the Council of Chalcedon in 451.[76] The Council of Chalcedon had exonerated the Antiochene theologian Theodoret along with Ibas of Edessa, whose writings included a letter in praise of Theodore. In short, Justinian hoped to sidestep non-Chalcedonian charges that the Council

---

[72] Socrates *Church History* 7.32; Cyril of Alexandria *Letter 2*.

[73] Behr 2011:88–100.

[74] ʿAbdišōʿ *Catalog*; *Chronicle of Siirt*. See also Becker 2006:112–125; and McLeod 2007:18–38.

[75] Becker 2006b. There was considerable disagreement with the condemnation of Theodore among bishops in the west. Particularly problematic was the fact that Theodore's two-nature theology looked enough like Chalcedon that they believed an anathema against Theodore was an anathema against Chalcedon. Furthermore, Theodore had died at peace with the church and in some quarters it was seen as deeply problematic to condemn someone who had died in such a position. However, detailed knowledge of Theodore in the west was by no means widespread, and Justinian's inability to exert his influence over the entire Christian west actually made little difference for the preservation of Theodore's Greek writings. What texts of Theodore could be found in the west were circulating in Latin translation; his commentary on the so-called Minor Pauline Epistles even circulated throughout the Middle Ages under the name of Ambrose of Milan; see Swete 1880, 1:ix–xvi.

[76] On Justinian's religious policy, see Menze 2008 and Price 2009:8–42.

of Chalcedon asserted Nestorian theology by condemning Theodore's writings, declaring him a heretic, and also condemning suspect writings by Theodoret and Ibas' letter praising Theodore.

The results of these sixth-century developments have had a tremendous impact on Theodore and his reception. Most importantly, the majority of Theodore's original Greek compositions have disappeared.[77] Fortunately, a number of Syriac and Latin translations remain extant, along with many fragments collected in florilegia used to secure the condemnation of Theodore in the sixth century. The fragmentary nature of this evidence has led to many interpretive difficulties. Serious questions arose over whether or not the fragments collected for hostile purposes had been manipulated, with some scholars suggesting that they could not be used to assess Theodore's theology.[78] Francis Sullivan has argued convincingly that the fragments do indeed provide valuable sources for Theodore that can be corroborated by unproblematic material.[79] A related issue has driven most of the scholarship on Theodore's Christology as many scholars have taken up the question of whether or not the fifth ecumenical council rightly condemned Theodore.[80] Theodore's insistence on a two-nature Christology can indeed sound compatible with Chalcedon's emphasis on two natures in Christ. However, as we have seen, Theodore's language can also suggest a false unity between those natures. The issues do not resolve themselves easily.

While these remain interesting questions of historical theology, this book makes no pretense of attempting to resolve them. Instead, this study poses very different questions about Theodore and his ministry. The nature of Theodore's condemnation and the uneven preservation of his work have led to a scholarly literature consumed by theological and hermeneutical intricacies.[81] This work can result in an image of Theodore as little more than a polemical figure with a theological agenda. With this mindset, we can miss his early struggle with the tension between Christian vocation and family obligations. We can miss Theodore's earnest attempts to steer the believing community toward right belief. We can miss the pastoral concern behind his emphasis on Christ's

---

[77] The only complete work extant in Greek is Theodore's commentary on the Minor Prophets.

[78] Richard 46:55–75; and Devreesse 1930:362–377.

[79] Sullivan 1956:35–158.

[80] For a synopsis of the earliest scholarship, see Norris 1963:246–262. For discussions of the more recent scholarship, see Clayton 2007:53–74; Behr 2011:28–34; and McLeod 2009:8–16. On the theologically invested nature of much of this literature, see Bruns 1995:5–15.

[81] The *Catechetical Homilies* have also been the focus of this scholarly interest; many of the scholars cited in the note above have used the *Catechetical Homilies* as a source. Furthermore, two recent studies focused on these sermons take considerable motivation from questions of Christology and Theodore's condemnation: Bruns 1995 and Gerber 2000.

free human will and the related ability of ordinary people to live the Christian life. We might be more likely to understand Theodore as a pastoral figure if we had not his lost treatises, *On the Priesthood*, *To a Monk*, and *On the Perfection of Observances*. We have no reason to speculate in any detail on the content of these treatises, but it remains significant that they bear titles suggestive of his concern for pastoral ministry.[82] Furthermore, Theodore's corpus of letters, the so-called *Book of Pearls*, is also no longer extant, an unfortunate fact that hampers efforts to understand Theodore's personality. Chrysostom's *Letter to Theodore*, delivered while Chrysostom was in exile, demonstrates a deep sense of appreciation for Theodore's devoted friendship. Additional assessments of Theodore's personality remain rare.

These lacunae make it difficult to think of Theodore as someone actively engaged in pastoral care. Several bishops, particularly John Chrysostom with his rich corpus of sermons and letters, attract the attention of an active group of scholars who work on pastoral care.[83] Preaching, missionary activity, and philanthropic work emerge as regular pastoral activities in this literature. If we had extant the full corpus of his writings, Theodore would have his place within this body of literature as well. One aim of this book is to consider what we can say about Theodore's contribution to this important field of study. The *Catechetical Homilies* demonstrate considerable attention to pastoral ministry and sensitivity to reaching people with a compelling presentation of the Christian life. They show Theodore using a wide range of tools to craft a Christian *paideia* and communicate it to a new generation as they approached initiation into the Christian community.

[82] ꜥAbdišōꜥ *Catalog* 34–35.
[83] Mayer 2001:58–70; Mayer and Allen 2000:345–397; Greer 2007:567–584; Allen 1999:387–400; and Bailey 2010.

2

Approaching Catechesis

W**E HAVE NOW CONSIDERED** T**HEODORE'S LIFE** and the circumstances surrounding his education, ecclesiastical career, and writings. Subsequent chapters address three key components of Theodore's catechesis, but first we must take a step back from Theodore to consider several important factors surrounding the way clergy framed catechesis and the rites of initiation. Many preachers catechized Christian converts and they did so within a cultural and religious context far wider than simply one preacher in one location. This chapter assesses the context in which full initiation into the church took place, the way clergy presented initiation to outsiders, and some of the variety of emphases the teachers of Christian faith presented to those pursuing initiation.[1]

We often hear of Christianity as a proselytizing religion that emphasized the spread of its message of salvation. While in some ways this is indeed an accurate representation of the missionary focus of Christianity, it can easily lead to false impressions of openness and transparency regarding Christian beliefs and practices. In reality, initiated Christians shrouded in secrecy some of their most important distinctive features. Those interested in Christianity but who had not yet been catechized and baptized would have encountered claims of secrecy on a regular basis. A close look at Christian secrecy, however, calls into question the validity of the claim to a well-maintained practice of secrecy. Nevertheless, the persistence of the claim raises important questions about why Christians went to such lengths to insist they kept secrets.

In claiming secrecy, the church fit itself into a broadly held set of expectations regarding religious truth and practice. Religious secrecy recurs as a common feature of a late antique culture in which many religious traditions guarded, or attempted to guard, the rites, myths, or beliefs that they did not want outsiders to know. These traditions regularly constructed dramatic rites of initiation designed to overawe initiates and produce lifelong devotees to the cult. Both these claims to secrecy and the dramatic educational and cultic

---

[1] An earlier version of this material appears as D. L. Schwartz 2011.

mechanisms used to reveal these secrets served the purpose of maintaining boundaries and lending authority to the officials who presided over the rites. Christian attempts to appropriate secrecy and the dramatic revelation of secrets provide an important backdrop for the consideration of what it meant for a person to approach baptism and catechesis. It also provides critical context for understanding the various rhetorical approaches Theodore and other catechists used in revealing Christian secrets. While preachers crafted different strategies to disclose the beliefs and practices of the church, they all used catechesis as a dramatic liminal period in which to impart what they understood as uniquely Christian truths essential for proper insiders within the community.

The *Disciplina Arcani*

"Let none of the catechumens be present; none of the uninitiated; none of those who are not able to pray with us. Take note of one another! The doors!"[2] This exclamation of the deacon marks a turning point in the fourth-century version of the liturgy of St. James. With this cry, the public portion of the weekly service ended and, from that point on, only those who had been properly initiated into the church through catechism and baptism were allowed to remain. The *Apostolic Constitutions* urged the clergy to follow the proper procedure for insuring the secrecy of the service after the uninitiated left: "Let the subdeacons stand at the door of the men and the deacons at the door of the women, so that no one may depart and the door may not be opened at the time of the offering, even if it is one of the faithful."[3] In short, it was preferable to exclude fully initiated Christians from the secret portions of the service than to run the risk of disclosing the mysteries even to catechumens, some of whom may have regularly attended the public portion of the liturgy for years. What could motivate such a rigorous exclusivity? The question is particularly interesting given the frequency with which Christians and their scriptures spoke in universal and inclusive terms about the availability of Christian salvation. Insofar as fourth-century Christian authors give both the idea of secrecy and the idea of universality some of its fullest expression of the late antique period, they will provide the basis for the present analysis.

---

[2] *The Liturgy of St. James* 16: Μή τις τῶν κατηχοθμένων, μή τις τῶν ἀμυήτων, μή τις τῶν μὴ δυναμένων ἡμῖν συνδεηθῆναι· ἀλλήλους ἐπίγνωτε· τὰς θύρας.

[3] *Apostolic Constitutions* 8.11: Οἱ δὲ ὑποδιάκονοι ἱστάσθωσαν εἰς τὰς τῶν ἀνδρῶν θύρας καὶ αἱ διάκονοι εἰς τὰς τῶν γυναικῶν, ὅπως μή τις ἐξέλθοι μήτε ἀνοιχθείη ἡ θύρα, κἂν πιστός τις ᾖ.

The question of Christian secrecy has long been the object of scholarly attention.[4] Modern liturgists often label the idea that certain aspects of the Christian liturgy ought to be kept secret from those who have not received baptism the *disciplina arcani*, or the discipline of secrecy. The liturgical enactment of the discipline mentioned above provides the clearest expression of this Christian ideal. However, this was not simply a matter of worship in a narrow sense. Christian secrecy applied equally to the ritual performance of the sacraments and to some of the doctrines bound up with them. It is precisely this matrix of Christian secrets that occupied the catechetical instructors charged with initiating converts. As such, the catechetical sermons of Cyril of Jerusalem, John Chrysostom, and Theodore of Mopsuestia, in particular, bear directly on the *disciplina arcani*, in that they were the mechanism used to reveal the secrets of Christian doctrine and worship.

By the time these fourth-century catechists preached their sermons, secrecy had had a long and varied history in the Christian tradition. The theme of secrecy plays a prominent role in many of the earliest Christian texts. The Gospel of Mark presents a prime example. Jesus responds to the inquiries of his disciples who want to know why he teaches in parables with the famous saying, "To you has been given the secret of the kingdom of God, but for those outside, everything comes in parables; in order 'that they may indeed look, but not perceive, and may indeed listen, but not understand; so that they may not turn again and be forgiven.'"[5] Gospels, canonical and non-canonical alike, depict Jesus as regularly teaching through parables that were difficult to comprehend,

---

[4] For a summary of this literature, see Perrin 2008; and Stroumsa 1996. Stroumsa nicely treats the way in which scholars have focused on the ritual aspect of this secrecy and downplayed the doctrinal. In the first four centuries, a variety of so-called Gnostic groups claimed secret knowledge as an essential component of the way they understood salvation. Many mainstream Christians denounced this idea as an elitist restriction on the universal offer of salvation explicitly articulated in several esteemed Christian texts. Stroumsa traces the repetition of this idea into the modern period, arguing that scholars have often simply accepted the idea that secrecy of worship was an acceptable Christian position, while secrecy of doctrine should be seen as a pagan or heretical error. One of the main objectives of his book is to emphasize the secrecy of doctrine in the works of Christians within orthodox traditions. In doing so, Stroumsa maintains a division between cult and doctrine, always stressing, against the prevailing interpretive traditions, that mainstream Christian secrecy in Late Antiquity pertained to doctrine as much as to worship. Several times in his work, however, Stroumsa suggests that these two might not be very easy to separate from one another. This chapter develops Stroumsa's suggestion through a discussion of liturgical secrecy and demonstrates how maintaining a close connection between doctrine and practice is important for understanding how late fourth-century catechesis functioned as a type of revelation of Christian mystery.

[5] Mark 4.11–12, citing Isaiah 6.9–10: καὶ ἔλεγεν αὐτοῖς, Ὑμῖν τὸ μυστήριον δέδοται τῆς βασιλείας τοῦ θεοῦ· ἐκείνοις δὲ τοῖς ἔξω ἐν παραβολαῖς τὰ πάντα γίνεται, ἵνα βλέποντες βλέπωσιν καὶ μὴ ἴδωσιν, καὶ ἀκούοντες ἀκούωσιν καὶ μὴ συνιῶσιν, μήποτε ἐπιστρέψωσιν καὶ ἀφεθῇ αὐτοῖς.

and scholars have repeatedly wrestled with the significance of this gospel theme.[6]

Early Christians developed this and other themes from Christian scriptures in articulating a rather extensive maintenance of Christian secrecy.[7] The *Didache*, already by the turn of the second century, cited the Gospel of Matthew as the impetus for preserving the secrecy of the eucharistic meal.[8] "Do not give what is holy to dogs; and do not throw your pearls before swine, or they will trample them under foot and turn and maul you."[9] Here, the most cherished components of the Christian cult are the pearls and the swine are, of course, unbelievers. The author of the *Didache* expresses the concern that unbelievers will not only mistreat the holy things of the Christian liturgy but might also use the knowledge of these things against believers in some unspecified way. Likewise, Athanasius used Matthew 7.6 to critique his so-called Arian opponents, writing, "And they are not ashamed to parade the sacred mysteries before Catechumens, and worse than that, even before heathens ... We ought not then to parade the holy mysteries before the uninitiated, lest the heathen in their ignorance deride them, and the Catechumens being over-curious be offended."[10] Others focused more on the harm that might come to one who learns about the eucharistic meal without proper initiation.[11] They appealed to Paul's instruction in 1 Corinthians 11.29. In teaching about the Lord's Supper, Paul warned, "For all who eat and drink without discerning the body, eat and drink judgment against themselves." The implication drawn from this passage was that the clergy had an obligation to keep the elements of the sacred meal away from unbelievers, because if they were to eat without "discerning" the body, they would run the risk of divine judgment.

John Chrysostom struggled to explain the meaning of 1 Corinthians 15.29 to his congregation without divulging the creedal formula used in the baptismal rite:

---

[6] Cf. Wrede 1901; Kermode 1979; and Oepke on κρύπτω, *TDNT* 3:957–1000.

[7] For a more comprehensive collection of second- to fourth-century texts assuming or advocating the maintenance of Christian secrecy, see Yarnold 1994:54–66.

[8] *Didache* 9.5.

[9] Matthew 7.6: Μὴ δῶτε τὸ ἅγιον τοῖς κυσίν, μηδὲ βάλητε τοὺς μαργαρίτας ὑμῶν ἔμπροσθεν τῶν χοίρων, μήποτε καταπατήσουσιν αὐτοὺς ἐν τοῖς ποσὶν αὐτῶν καὶ στραφέντες ῥήξωσιν ὑμᾶς.

[10] Athanasius *Defense against the Arians* 11.2: καὶ οὐκ αἰσχύνονται ταῦτα ἐπὶ κατηχουμένων, καὶ τό γε χείριστον, ἐπὶ Ἑλλήνων τραγῳδοῦντες τὰ μυστήρια, δέον, ὡς γέγραπται, «μυστήριον βασιλέως καλὸν κρύπτειν», καὶ ὡς ὁ κύριος παρήγγειλε «μὴ δῶτε τὰ ἅγια τοῖς κυσὶ μηδὲ βάλητε τοὺς μαργαρίτας ἔμπροσθεν τῶν χοίρων». οὐ χρὴ γὰρ τὰ μυστήρια ἀμυήτοις τραγῳδεῖν, ἵνα μὴ Ἕλληνες μὲν ἀγνοοῦντες γελῶσι, κατηχούμενοι δὲ περίεργοι γενόμενοι σκανδαλίζωνται.

[11] Origen *Commentary on Matthew* 10.25 and 11.14. Cyprian *Letters* 9.2 and 74.21 express similar concern although not without developing the idea.

But first I wish to remind you who are initiated of the response which on that evening they who introduce you to the mysteries bid you make; and then I will also explain the saying of Paul … And I desire indeed expressly to utter it, but I dare not on account of the uninitiated; for these add a difficulty to our exposition, compelling us either not to speak clearly or to declare unto them the ineffable mysteries. Nevertheless, as I may be able, I will speak as through a veil.[12]

Even the golden-mouthed preacher preferred this sort of inelegance to the premature disclosure of the church's mysteries. Cyril of Jerusalem urged caution with respect to matters of Christian theology. He warned the catechumens that it was unsafe to discuss the Father, Son, and Holy Spirit with unbelievers because such ideas ran the risk of causing them harm: "The sun blinds people suffering from poor sight, and those with weak eyes are distressed and blinded by its light; not that the sun of its nature is blinding, but because the human eye cannot look upon it. Similarly, unbelievers, whose sickness is of the heart, cannot look upon the splendor of the Godhead."[13] He even insisted that the baptismal candidates refrain from mentioning any of his instructions to the other catechumens.[14] Theodore preached at length about the power of the sacraments of baptism and the eucharist. He explained how these sacraments joined a person to God and the Christian community. If a person had not been properly catechized, he or she would fail to understand the deeper meaning of the sacred meal and miss its significance to his or her detriment.[15] Thus converts received warnings regarding the mortal danger associated with discussing secret matters with a person not properly prepared by catechesis.

Liturgical forms developed over time and by the fourth century came to include secret components beyond the celebration of the eucharist. The public portion of the worship service contained a series of prayers, scripture readings, and the homily. Only after the dismissal of the uninitiated did the kiss of peace

---

[12] John Chrysostom *Homilies on I Corinthians* 40.2: Πρῶτον δὲ ἀναμνῆσαι βούλομαι τοὺς μεμνημένους ὑμᾶς ῥήσεως, ἣν κατὰ τὴν ἑσπέραν ἐκείνην οἱ μυσταγωγοῦντες ὑμᾶς λέγειν κελεύουσι, καὶ τότε ἐρῶ καὶ τὸ τοῦ Παύλου· οὕτω γὰρ ὑμῖν καὶ τοῦτο ἔσται σαφέστερον. Μετὰ γὰρ τὰ ἄλλα πάντα τοῦτο προστίθεμεν, ὃ νῦν ὁ Παῦλος λέγει. Καὶ βούλομαι μὲν σαφῶς αὐτὸ εἰπεῖν, οὐ τολμῶ δὲ διὰ τοὺς ἀμυήτους· οὗτοι γὰρ δυσκολωτέραν ἡμῖν ποιοῦσι τὴν ἐξήγησιν, ἀναγκάζοντες ἢ μὴ λέγειν σαφῶς, ἢ εἰς αὐτοὺς ἐκφέρειν τὰ ἀπόρρητα. Πλὴν ἀλλ' ὡς ἂν οἷός τε ὦ, συνεσκιασμένως ἐρῶ.
[13] Cyril of Jerusalem *Catechesis* 6.29: Τυφλοῖ καὶ ὁ ἥλιος τοὺς ἀμβλυωποῦντας·καὶ οἱ ὀφθαλμιῶντες τυφλοῦνται, βλαπτόμενοι ὑπὸ τοῦ φωτός· οὐχ ὅτι τυφλωτικός [ἐστιν] ὁ ἥλιος, ἀλλ' ὅτι ἡ ὑπόστασις τῶν ὀμμάτων οὐ βλέπει. Οὕτω καὶ οἱ ἄπιστοι, νοσοῦντες τὰς καρδίας, οὐ δύνανται ἐνιδεῖν τῆς θεότητος ταῖς ἀκτῖσιν.
[14] Cyril of Jerusalem *Procatechesis* 12.
[15] Theodore of Mopsuestia WS 6.21–26. Augustine makes a similar point in his *Homilies on the Gospel of John* 96.3–5; see also *Apostolic Constitutions* 7.25.

and the Lord's Supper take place. The kiss of peace fell into this portion of the liturgy because it provided a liturgical enactment of unity and fellowship within the Christian community. One could not extend this gesture towards the uninitiated, since proper affiliation with the church formed the basis of the Christian fellowship expressed through the kiss.[16] Traditional practice and exegesis of the scriptural passages mentioned above served to keep the eucharist in the restricted part of the service as well. A Trinitarian formula associated with early baptismal professions of faith likely provided the impetus for later creedal formulations, as well as for the secrecy associated with baptism and creed.[17] The details of this development remain somewhat obscure, but by the fourth century, clergy and theologians assumed that the doctrine encompassed all of these liturgical components.[18]

Catechesis and baptism form part of what clearly constitutes a set of initiation rituals or rites of passage.[19] The insistence on secrecy played an important role in creating distance between those on each side of these rites. Those converting to Christianity in this period were expected to undergo a time of moral testing and doctrinal instruction as a part of the process of being initiated into the church. This probationary period usually lasted a year, with the bulk of the instruction taking place during Lent and baptism being administered early on Easter Sunday morning.[20] During this Lenten instruction, the catechumens learned the creed, basic Christian theology and, in some cases, the meaning of the sacraments they were about to take part in for the first time.

---

[16] Michael Penn (2005) discusses the ways in which the ritual kiss created and reinforced community. Secondary functions of the ritual kiss, such as the demonstration of forgiveness given to a repentant sinner, served to add further meaning to the primary function of defining community. On ritual kissing in early Christianity, see also Phillips 1996.

[17] Cf. Matthew 28.19; *Didache*, 8–10; the *Apostolic Tradition* 3–4; and the Old Roman Creed. The details of this development are rather difficult to tease out. For a general study of the relevant sources and what they have to say on the topic, see Noakes 1992; Cobb 1992:228; and Bradshaw 2006:101–102.

[18] See, in particular, the catecheses of Cyril of Jerusalem, John Chrysostom, and Theodore of Mopsuestia. Sermons of Ambrose and Augustine show these preachers falling silent about the details of the mysteries when they happened to come across the topic during a homily. For a more comprehensive collection of third- through fifth-century sources that speak to the matter of the *disciplina arcani*, see Yarnold 1994:55–59.

[19] On rites of passage, see Van Gennep 1960 and Turner 1995.

[20] Hall 1973. This presents the prescribed pattern, but deviations from this norm are attested in the sources. Allow a few examples to suffice. Cyprian advocates infant baptism in his Letter 64. Numerous fourth-century bishops comment on the baptism of infants. Their differing opinions of the practice confirm the fact that it was common enough to be a point of contention. Another baptismal option was the practice of baptism at a saint's shrine or a pilgrimage site associated with a holy man. Theodoret (*History of the Monks of Syria* 26.13) referred to this practice in discussing the throngs of Arab nomads who received baptism in the presence of Symeon the Stylite. In such cases, catechetical instruction receives minimal attention in the sources.

How Secret were the Mysteries?

Despite the fact that at least from the beginning of the second century Christians were being encouraged to maintain some sort of liturgical secrecy, the actual practice of the *disciplina arcani* is surprisingly difficult to determine. Liturgical scholarship has traditionally assumed that secrecy was diligently maintained.[21] Some have called this position into question by cataloging references in public sermons to the liturgical elements that were supposed to remain secret, concluding that "there can have been few secrets left for a fourth-century catechumen as he commenced his instruction."[22]

This later position is bolstered when one looks at late Roman elites who were well positioned to have exposure to Christianity yet maintained the traditional cult. Several important examples illustrate the knowledge of the Christian mysteries among the uninitiated. In the early second century, Pliny derived a rudimentary sense of Christian worship, including the ideal of secrecy through interviewing Christians, or at least former Christians.[23] Justin Martyr seems to have felt little reluctance in disclosing components of Christian worship in his defense of the faith to the emperor Antoninus Pius.[24] Origen's refutation of the attack on Christianity by Celsus shows that at least this one critic knew the scriptures fairly well and was at least familiar with the practice of Christian baptism.[25]

In the fourth century, as advocacy for the maintenance of the *disciplina arcani* reached a crescendo, even more evidence of lax enforcement appears. The anti-Christian treatise by the emperor Julian, *Against the Galileans*, offers a strong case for the disclosure of Christian mysteries. Julian quoted several times from the first chapter of the Gospel of John and then concluded, "But if the only begotten son is one thing and God the Word something else, as I have heard it said by some of the members of your sect, then it seems that not even John was foolish enough to declare that [Jesus was God]."[26] While Julian did not reveal the wording of the creed, he did mention some of the central sticking points in the fourth-century controversies over the incarnation of Christ.

[21] Dix 1954:16–18; Yarnold 1994:55–66; Yarnold 1992:141–142.

[22] See, in particular, Day 2001:270.

[23] Pliny *Letters* 1.10.96–97.

[24] Justin Martyr *First Apology* 61, 65–67.

[25] Origen *Against Celsus* 40, 44, 46.

[26] *Against the Galileans* 225: εἰ δὲ ἄλλος ἐστὶν ὁ μονογενὴς υἱός, ἕτερος δὲ ὁ θεὸς λόγος, ὡς ἐγώ τινων ἀκήκοα τῆς ὑμετέρας αἱρέσεως, ἔοικεν οὐδὲ ὁ Ἰωάννης αὐτὸ τολμᾶν ἔτι. Cf. also, Libanius *Orations* 18.178.

Julian also disclosed information about the secret rites of the church. He ridiculed the doctrine of baptism, first quoting Paul and then arguing for its utter foolishness:

> "Do not be deceived, for neither idolaters nor adulterers nor homo-sexuals, nor sexual libertines nor thieves nor the greedy nor drunk-ards nor extortionists shall inherit the kingdom of God. And of this you are not in ignorance, brothers, because you were these things; but you washed yourselves and you were sanctified in the name of Jesus" [*1 Corinthians* 6.9–11]. Do you not see that he admits the men he addresses *were* these things, and then he says they were "washed" and they were "sanctified," as though water itself had acquired the power to cleanse and purify not the body only, but even the soul! But baptism does not take the sores away from the leper, or the scabs and boils, the wens and disfigurations, or gout or dysentery or dropsy, or a whitlow—in fact, [water] takes away no disorder of the body, however great or small: so shall it then do away with adultery, theft, and all of the sins of the soul?[27]

Julian again appeals to scripture in his critique of Christian practice. He simply mocks the idea that baptism removes sin. If its cleansing ability cannot even remove diseases that afflict only the surface of the skin, how could it possibly reach down into a person's soul and cleanse the heinous sins that so stain it?

The eucharist also came under Julian's attack. He touched on this Christian practice while critiquing Christians for their failure to maintain the ancient performance of sacrifices, whether pagan or Jewish.[28] The Christians had so rejected the Jewish cult that they even refused to observe the Jewish feasts:

> And the Galileans say, "But we cannot keep the rule concerning the feast of unleavened bread, the Passover. For [we believe] Christ was sacrificed

---

[27] *Against the Galileans* 109: «μὴ πλανᾶσθε· οὔτε εἰδωλολάτραι, οὔτε μοιχοὶ, οὔτε μαλακοὶ, οὔτε ἀρσενοκοῖται, οὔτε κλέπται, οὔτε πλεονέκται, οὐ μέθυσοι, οὐ λοίδοροι, οὐχ ἅρπαγες βασιλείαν θεοῦ κληρονομήσουσι. καὶ ταῦτα οὐκ ἀγνοεῖτε, ἀδελφοί, ὅτι καὶ ὑμεῖς τοιοῦτοι ἦτε· ἀλλ᾽ ἀπελούσασθε, ἀλλ᾽ ἡγιάσθητε ἐν τῷ ὀνόματι Ἰησοῦ Χριστοῦ.» ὁρᾷς, ὅτι καὶ τούτους γενέσθαι φησὶ τοιούτους, ἀγιασθῆναι δὲ καὶ ἀπολούσασθαι, ῥύπτειν ἱκανοῦ καὶ διακαθαίρειν ὕδατος εὐπορήσαντος, ὃ μέχρι ψυχῆς εἰσδύσεται· καὶ τοῦ μὲν λεπροῦ τὴν λέπραν οὐκ ἀφαιρεῖται τὸ βάπτισμα, οὐδὲ λειχῆνας οὐδὲ ἀλφοὺς οὔτε ἀκροχορδῶνας οὐδὲ ποδάγραν οὐδὲ δυσεντερίαν, οὐχ ὕδερον, οὐ παρωνυχίαν, οὐ μικρὸν, οὐ μέγα τῶν τοῦ σώματος ἁμαρτημάτων, μοιχείας δὲ καὶ ἅρπαγὰς καὶ πάσας ἁπλῶς τῆς ψυχῆς παρανομίας ἐξελεῖ;

[28] Resumption of sacrifices was one of Julian's main aims. He actively promoted pagan sacrificial cults that he felt had been neglected and attempted to restore the Temple in Jerusalem. See Sozomen *Church History* 5.22; Socrates *Church History* 3.20; Theodoret *Church History* 3.15; and Bowersock 1978:88–89.

for our sake once and for all." Indeed, and did he then command you himself not to eat unleavened bread? With the gods as my witnesses I count myself among those who avoid the festivals of the Jews. But I venerate without hesitation the God of Abraham, Isaac, and Jacob, [for they were] members of a sacred race, the Chaldeans, learned in the arts of divination, who became acquainted with the rite of circumcision during the time of their wandering among the Egyptians."[29]

Julian suggests that he keeps the ancient cultic traditions of the Jews better than do the Christians. How he does this is not entirely clear. Perhaps he refers to his attempts to rebuild the temple of the Jews in Jerusalem. He may also be suggesting that both he and the Jews follow their ancestral cult, whereas the Christians worship in a way that is unprecedented. He clarifies this point later, in the context of discussing Jewish sacrifices in the temple in Jerusalem: "You have invented a whole new way of sacrificing that does not need Jerusalem."[30] Julian's critique focuses on the charge of Christian innovation. However, in doing so, he mentions that Christians have a sacrifice of their own, one that does not need the temple of Jerusalem.

Gregory of Nazianzus indicates that Julian had been baptized and was not simply a catechumen; indeed, he had even served as a reader in the church.[31] Furthermore, Constantius II, Julian's cousin and predecessor as emperor of the western half of the empire, saw to it that he received a Christian education under Eusebius, the bishop of Nicomedia.[32] His knowledge of the Christian scriptures, evidenced even in the few quotations discussed above, confirms this training. Thus it is no surprise that Julian possessed ample material for the critique he leveled against Christianity, including the details of Christian liturgy.

---

[29] *Against the Galileans* 230: «τηρεῖν ἄζυμα καὶ ποιεῖν τὸ πάσχα οὐ δυνάμεθα» φασίν· «ὑπὲρ ἡμῶν γὰρ ἅπαξ ἐτύθη Χριστός.» καλῶς· εἶτα ἐκώλυσεν ἐσθίειν ἄζυμα; καίτοι, μὰ τοὺς θεούς, εἷς εἰμι τῶν ἐκτρεπομένων συνεορτάζειν Ἰουδαίοις, ἀεὶ <δὲ> προσκυνῶν τὸν θεὸν Ἀβραὰμ καὶ Ἰσαὰκ καὶ Ἰακὼβ, οἳ ὄντες αὐτοὶ Χαλδαῖοι, γένους ἱεροῦ καὶ θεουργικοῦ, τὴν μὲν περιτομὴν ἔμαθον Αἰγυπτίοις ἐπιξενωθέντες.

[30] *Against the Galileans* 219: ὑμεῖς δὲ οἱ τὴν καινὴν θυσίαν εὑρόντες, οὐδὲν δεόμενοι τῆς Ἰερουσαλήμ.

[31] Gregory of Nazianzus *Orations* 4.52. "For no sooner had he inherited the empire than he publicly professed his impiety, as if ashamed of ever having been a Christian, and on this account bearing a grudge against the Christians in whose name he had participated: and the very first of his audacities, according to those who boast of his secret doings, into which details am I forced to enter! with unhallowed blood he rids himself of his baptism, setting up the initiation of abomination against the initiation according to our rite, 'a swine wallowing in the mire,' according to the proverb; and he unconsecrates his hands by cleansing them from the bloodless sacrifice by means whereof we are made partakers with Christ, both in His sufferings and in His divinity."

[32] Gregory of Nazianus *Orations* 4.23. For a fuller discussion of Julian's education, see Bowersock 1978 23–30.

Not only did Julian know these things, he publicized them in his attack against the Christians. Since the majority of the literary manuscripts we have from this period were at one point copied by a churchman or monk, it is no great surprise that this attack on the church does not have a strong manuscript tradition. In fact, what we know about the content of this text comes mostly from refutations of it.[33] Thus it is difficult to determine just how widely this text might have circulated. That Libanius' funeral oration for Julian mentions the work suggests that it was something that his contemporaries would have at least known about.[34]

Nevertheless, one would likely err in concluding that Julian's diatribe against the Christians was widely disseminated or broadly known, even among the relatively small literate portion of the population. Julian was not a particularly well-liked emperor, and one can imagine his written work failing to captivate his subjects. The significance of this text for us is that it supplies an example of the mysteries being disclosed to an uninitiated audience. One can imagine this happening on a much smaller scale with some frequency. Julian was not the only apostate after all.[35] A person might leave the church and as a result lose the desire to keep the mysteries a secret. Others may simply not have been as concerned as the clergy who stressed secrecy.[36] One only needs to read a few sermons by a preacher like John Chrysostom before learning that his congregation frequently failed to live up to the high ethical standards he set for them.

Furthermore, the council of Nicaea and the creed promulgated after 325 had become a hugely contentious matter affecting the whole empire. Numerous clergy were exiled and recalled repeatedly throughout the fourth century. The creed itself, particularly the precise terminology of the text, stood at the very heart of the matter. As we will see in chapter three, the recitation of the creed held an important position in the process of initiation and the teaching of the creed received considerable attention. Clergy often warned catechumens not to

---

[33] Julian *Against the Galileans* 76–77.

[34] Libanius *Orations* 18.178: "As winter lengthened the nights, besides many other fine compositions he attacked the books in which that fellow from Palestine is claimed to be a god and a son of god." There is a brief discussion of this in Julian *Against the Galileans* 75.

[35] See Julian *Letter to a Priest* for the case of a former Christian bishop recruited by Julian to serve as a local pagan priest.

[36] Ambrose lists four faults that result in the revelation of the mysteries: flattery, avarice, boastfulness, and incautious speech, *Expositions on the Psalms* 118.2.26: "Periculum itaque est non solum falsa dicere, sed etiam uera, si quis ea insinuet quibus non oportet. Quod uitium quadripertitum est, uel adulationis uel auaritiae uel iactantiae uel loquacitatis incautae, quia, dum adulari uult aliquis, ei cui loquitur effundit mysterium; nonnulli etiam studio lucri mercedem proditionis secuntur, ut tegenda silentio uendant loquendo; alii, ut plura nosse uideantur et scientiam suam iactitent, aperiunt quod celare deberent; plerique, dum sine praeiudicio locuntur, uerbum emittunt, quod reuocare non possunt."

reveal it to outsiders, even to other catechumens who had not yet been accepted to receive baptism. However, a matter of such importance for imperial politics would not have escaped the attention of administrators for long. Interested parties could hardly have failed to know at least the basic issues at stake, the idea that the controversy dealt with the person of Christ and how Christians were to understand him in relationship to God.

One prominent example of this can be found in Themistius, a fourth-century pagan philosopher and rhetor who acted as an advisor to most of the eastern emperors who held the throne during his adult life.[37] His orations contain several references to Hebrew and Christian scriptures.[38] These references, focusing primarily on political life and statecraft, usually remain rather vague. Nevertheless, they bear witness to Themistius as the sort of interested individual who did not convert but who had considerable professional motivation to maintain an awareness of Christianity.

Particularly relevant for the discussion of Christian secrecy, Themistius also showed an understanding of some of the issues at stake in the theological controversy over the incarnation. His *Oration* 1 was addressed to Constantius and delivered in Ancyra in the year 350. The oration took up the topic of *philanthrōpia*, the love of humankind. In the relevant passage, Themistius sought to explain how it could be considered good for either God or an emperor to condescend in showing love towards the mass of humanity. In this context, Themistius stated:

> But, as I said, while we consider these names to be unworthy of God as too trifling or inferior for Him, we are not ashamed to call Him a lover of mankind. And this is why. Man's intelligence naturally considers everything inferior to Him which is able to find in any of the things which derive from Him. Thus intelligence ascribes to the source of all things being beyond being, and Power beyond power, and goodness beyond goodness, hesitating, however, and moreover being cautious in the association of the terms.[39]

[37] Vanderspoel 1995. On the role of rhetoric under Christian emperors, see Kennedy 1983.

[38] For a discussion of these references, see Downey 1957:262–263 and 1962a.

[39] Themistius *Orations* 1.8b: ἀλλ’ ὅπερ ἔφην, ταῦτα μὲν ἀπαξιοῦμεν τοῦ θεοῦ τὰ ὀνόματα ὡς φαυλότερα καὶ ἐλάττω, φιλάνθρωπον δὲ αὐτὸν καλοῦντες οὐκ αἰσχυνόμεθα. αἴτιον δέ·πέφυκεν ἀνθρώπου διάνοια πᾶν ἔλαττον ἐκείνου νομίζειν, ὃ καὶ ἔν τινι τῶν ἀπ’ ἐκείνου δυνατὸν ἐξευρεῖν. οὕτως οὖν οὐσίαν τε ὑπερούσιον καὶ ὑπερδύναμον δύναμιν καὶ ὑπεράγαθον ἀγαθότητα προστίθησιν ἡ διάνοια τῇ πάντων πηγῇ, ὀκνοῦσα ὅμως καὶ ταῦτα καὶ εὐλαβουμένη τὴν κοινωνίαν τῶν ὀνομάτων. See, also, n34 above and the brief quotation of Libanius *Oration* 18.178. Even Libanius’ casual comment about Julian’s attack on the Christians indicates at least a vague understanding of the two affirmations that led to the disagreements regarding the person of Christ—namely, that he was understood as “god and the son of god.” Thus even Libanius, who is

The idea that anything other than God derives from him and is, as a matter of necessity, lesser than God, coincides nicely with Constantius' theological commitments.[40] Furthermore, commentators agree that this passage very likely refers directly to the contemporary controversy over the Christian understanding of the relationship between God and Christ.[41] Themistius clearly had some understanding of the contentious theological issues that focused on the supposedly secret doctrines of the creed. This awareness is further evidenced by comments made in speeches to Jovian[42] in 365 and to Valens[43] in around 375. In each case, Themistius urged the emperor to adopt a policy of religious toleration in dealing with the various Christian factions within the empire.[44] Themistius clearly had substantial, even if not comprehensive, understanding of important points of Christian difference.

All of this strongly suggests that people, particularly those who would have cared to discover it, would likely have had access to much of the basic information about the secret matters of the church: a statement of faith regarding the divinity of Christ, a ritual bath meant to purify a person from sin, and a ritual meal or symbolic sacrifice. Nevertheless, calls for secrecy and the liturgical practice of secrecy were a regular occurrence in this period. In considering the motivation for maintaining this fiction, we must think about this Christian practice within the broader context of late antique religion.

Inspiring Awe in Late Antique Religion

Of course, Christianity does not offer the only religious context in which secrecy played a significant role.[45] The so-called mystery religions based their cults on the maintenance of boundaries between insiders and outsiders who had not been initiated into the myths and rites of the community.[46] In general, the

---

known for avoiding excessive references to Christianity, knew something about the theology of the new religion.

[40] Barnes 1993:168–175.

[41] Downey 1962a:484. See, also, Heather and Moncur 2001:85–86n115, as well as 57–68. All agree that Themistius references the Christian theological debates of the fourth century. However, where Downey concludes that Themistius is being sarcastic and effectively mocking the debate, Heather and Moncur see it as the sincere application of Themistius' philosophical assumptions to the debate. I incline towards the latter interpretation. However, either reading substantiates the point advanced here.

[42] *Orations* 5.69c.

[43] This is the lost *Oration to Valens*. Socrates *Church History* 4.32 provides a summary of the speech. For the argument demonstrating that the Latin oration is a Renaissance forgery, see Foerster 1990.

[44] For a fuller discussion of Themistius' desired religious policy, see Daly 1971.

[45] Yarnold 1994:59–66.

[46] On mystery cults in general, see Burkert 1987 and Bowden 2010.

mysterious nature of these religions means that we are forced to piece together knowledge of their practices. Although the secrets of these enigmatic cults were rather well maintained, a common feature is a concern for personal transformation through participatory ritual.[47]

Apuleius' *Metamorphoses* takes its name from the transformations experienced by its fictional protagonist Lucius. While dabbling in magic, he was turned into an ass. Eventually moved by the devotion of Lucius, the goddess Isis frees him from this fate and transforms him back into a human. This act of divine intervention precedes the further metamorphoses Lucius would experience as an initiate into the cult of Isis. Describing his initiation into the cult of Isis, Lucius expresses the desire to disclose the initiation rites but resists for fear that he will incur the displeasure of the goddess:

> Perhaps, my zealous reader, you are eager to learn what was said and done next. I would tell if it were permitted to tell; you would learn if it were permitted to hear. But both ears and tongue would incur equal guilt, the latter form its unholy talkativeness, the former from their unbridled curiosity. Since your suspense, however, is perhaps a matter of religious longing, I will not continue to torture you and keep you in anguish. Therefore listen, but believe: these things are true.[48]

He proceeds to describe an emotional encounter with the divine in rather vague terms, just enough to pique the interest of his readers, but not enough to give a clear sense of what the rites entailed. Here we see secrecy used to entice the audience of the novel by offering the promise of a profound experience.

Interestingly, this discussion follows a description of Lucius' transformation from an ass back into a human in which Apuleius describes in some detail rites in honor of Isis that would have been part of a secret cult ritual:

> There were women gleaming with white vestments, rejoicing in their varied insignia, garlanded with flowers of spring; they strewed the flowers in their arms along the path where the sacred company would pass. Others had shining mirrors reversed behind their backs, to show homage to the goddess as she passed; or carried ivory combs, and

---

[47] Beard, North, and Price 1998, 1:287.

[48] Apuleius *Metamorphoses* 11.23: "Quaeras forsitan satis anxie, studiose lector, quid deinde dictum, quid factum. Dicerem si dicere liceret, cognosceres si liceret audire. Sed parem noxam contraherent et aures et lingua, ista impiae loquacitatis, illae temerariae curiositatis. Nec te tamen desiderio forsitan religioso suspensum angore diutino cruciabo. Igitur audi, sed crede, quae vera sunt."

moving their arms and curving their fingers pretended to shape and comb the royal tresses.[49]

This text depicts the ritual enactment of a theophany in which the devotees of the goddess minister to her needs. The description of the rite then rises to a crescendo with the entrance of the members of the cult:

> Then the crowds of those initiated into the divine mysteries came pouring in, men and women of every age. They shone with the pure radiance of their linen robes; the women's hair was anointed and wrapped in a transparent covering, while the men's heads were completely shaven and their skulls gleamed brightly—earthly stars of the great religion. All together made a shrill ringing sound with their sistrums of bronze and silver, and even gold. Next came the foremost high priests of the cult, tightly garbed in white linen cinctured at the breast and reaching to their feet. They carried before them the distinctive attributes of the most powerful gods.[50]

He proceeds to describe these items: an ornate lamp in the shape of a boat, an altar, a golden palm branch, a deformed left hand, a golden fan, and an amphora. The significance of these objects remains unclear in most cases, but the scene obviously amounts to one of absolute sensory overload. The jostling surge of the crowd, the smell of perfume, the deafening rattle of the sistrums, all contribute to an intense atmosphere. Later, when Lucius refuses to disclose the details of his initiation into the cult, he encourages the reader to imagine even more elaborate rites.

This fictional account of a mystery cult in action clearly resonates with other practices of Greco-Roman mystery cults whose adherents participated in secret rituals not disclosed to outsiders. Among these are the Mithraic rites, carried out in dark man-made caves where worshippers encountered an elaborate set of cosmological symbols and the dramatic image of the god Mithras

---

[49] Apuleius *Metamorphoses* 11.9: "Mulieres candido splendentes amicimine, vario laetantes gestamine, verno florentes coronamine, quae de gremio per viam qua sacer incedebat comitatus, solum sternebant flosculis; aliae quae nitentibus speculis pone tergum reversis venienti deae obuium commonstrarent obsequium, et quae pectines eburnos ferentes gestu brachiorum flexque digitorum ornatum atque obpexum crinium regalium fingerent."

[50] Apuleius *Metamorphoses* 11.10: "Tunc influent turbae sacris divinis initiatae, viri feminaeque omnis dignitatis et omnis aetatis, linteae vestis candore puro luminosi, illae limpido tegmine crines madidos obuolutae, hi capillum derasi funditus verticem praenitentes—magnae religionis terrena sidera—aeries et argenteis, immo vero aureis etiam sistris argutum tinnitum constrepentes; et antistites sacrorum procures illi, qui candido linteamine cinctum pectoralem adusque vestigia strictim iniecti potentissimorum deum proferebant insignes exuvias."

slaying a bull.[51] The rites that took place in these Mithraea led devotees through the grades of "raven," "male bride," "soldier," "lion," "Persian," "sun-runner," and "father," with each successive elevation effecting a new personal transformation.[52] While the Mithraic rites arose toward the end of the first century AD, the cult of Demeter dated back to the eighth century BC. The Eleusinian mysteries were a fertility cult celebrated annually in the city of Eleusis, just west of Athens. A pair of powerful priestly families in Athens administered the cult, but anyone who was not ritually impure and could afford the fees could be initiated into the cult.[53] This would allow participation in the annual cult, which sought to ensure the return of fertility following the infertility of winter. The rites associated with initiation to the cult seem to have included the ritual search for the goddess Persephone. This act entailed a personal quest for the goddess with the results often described as dramatically transformative: "Blessed are earth-bound mortals who have seen these rites, but the uninitiated, who has no share in them, never has the same lot when dead in misty darkness."[54] Blessed happiness, particularly in the afterlife, appears consistently in the claims of the initiated: "Beautiful indeed is the Mystery given us by the blessed gods: death is for mortals no longer an evil, but a blessing."[55] Finally, there is the dramatic participatory rite of the *taurobolium* associated with the worship of Magna Mater.[56] In this rite, the celebrant was concealed in a pit in the ground covered with perforated boards onto which a bull was led: "When the beast for sacrifice has been brought into position here, they pierce his breast with a hunting spear consecrated to the gods; the vast wound pours forth a stream of steaming blood, and over the bridge of planks below a reeking river gushes out and seethes all around."[57] The celebrant emerged from the pit, as from a grave, a transformed person, one born again into the world as a new man. The Christian Prudentius offers our only description of this rite. His derisive tone and even the details of the rite he describes call his account into question. Regardless of the specific

---

[51] Beck 2006:102–104. For photographs of the cave of Mithras at S. Maria Capua Vetere, see Beard, North, and Price 1998, 2:89–90.

[52] Beard, North, and Price 1998, 1:285.

[53] Mylonas 1961:229–237.

[54] *Hymn to Demeter* 480–482: ὄλβιος ὃς τάδ' ὄπωπεν ἐπιχθονίων ἀνθρώπων· ὃς δ' ἀτελὴς ἱερῶν, ὅς τ' ἄμμορος, οὔ ποθ' ὁμοίων αἶσαν ἔχει φθίμενός περ ὑπὸ ζόφῳ εὐρώεντι.

[55] Inscription found at Eleusis, translation in Angus 1925:140: ἦι καλὸν ἐκ μακάρων μυστήριον, οὐ μόνον εἶναι τὸν θάντοῖς οὐ κακὸν ἀλλ' ἀγαθόν.

[56] Rutter 1968. For a detailed discussion of the *taurobolium* with a particular interest in its evolution prior to this description by Prudentius, see Duthoy 1969.

[57] Prudentius *Peristephanon* 10.1026–1030: "Hic ut statuta est inmolanda belua, pecatus sacrato dividunt venabulo; eructat amplum vulnus undam sanguinis ferventis, inque texta pontis subditi fundit vaporum flumen et late aestuat."

form of the rite, the *taurobolium* is well attested in inscriptions, and fourth-century participants in the rites understood it as a ritual of rebirth.[58]

Christian sources also offer glimpses of the way catechesis could captivate a group of catechumens being initiated. The pilgrim Egeria noted in her travel log that those just baptized in Jerusalem in the middle of the fourth century received their instruction in the mysteries with a great deal of enthusiasm: "The bishop relates what has been done, and interprets it, and, as he does so, the applause is so loud that it can be heard outside the church."[59] This instruction, called mystagogy, entails an explanation of baptism and the eucharist to those who have just experienced these rites. Even if Egeria's description contains some exaggeration, it strongly suggests a significant response, and likely a rather emotional response. Such a clamor surely requires a crowd, and the communal nature of catechesis must not pass unnoticed in this context. Chapter three deals more fully with the community, but suffice it to say here that catechumens underwent initiation in groups and with the assistance of a previously initiated layperson who helped lend credibility to these rites. In disclosing the rituals of baptism and the eucharist, Theodore and Chrysostom both showed a strong inclination toward the dramatic and the participatory. They repeatedly employed the term "awe-inspiring" (Greek *phriktos* or *phrikōdēs*; Syriac *dḥl*), which captures this emphasis nicely.[60] Theodore preached:

> As often, therefore, as the service of this awe-inspiring sacrifice is performed, which is clearly the likeness of heavenly things and of which, after it has been perfected, we become worthy to partake through food and drink, as a true participation in our future benefits—we must picture in our mind that we are dimly in heaven, and through faith, draw in our imagination the image of heavenly things, while thinking that Christ who is in heaven and who died for us, rose and ascended into heaven and is now being immolated.[61]

---

[58] Rutter 1968; he also discusses a separate civic function of the rite. See also Beard, North, and Price 1998, 2:162; McLynn 1996:325–328.

[59] *Travels* 47.2: "Disputante autem episcopo singula et narrante, tantae voces sunt collaudantium, ut porro foras ecclesia audiantur voces eorum."

[60] φρικτός, φρικώδης both denote something that causes a person to shiver. Lampe 1961:1490; and Yarnold 1994:60. Various forms of the root ܕܚܠ recur throughout Theodore's catechesis where they refer to the awe associated with proper worship, Payne Smith 1879, 1:862.

[61] WS 6.83; *Homélies Catéchétiques* 15.125r: ܟܠ ܐܡܬܝ ܡܟܝܠ ܕܡܫܬܡܫܐ ܗܕܐ ܬܫܡܫܬܐ ܕܕܚܝܠܐ ܕܒܚܬܐ ܡܝܬܪܬܐ: ܕܓܠܝܠܐܝܬ ܕܘܡܝܐ ܠܐܝܠܝܢ ܕܫܡܝܐ ܐܝܬܝܗܘܢ ܟܕ ܫܠܡܐ. ܗܐ ܘܡܢ ܕܠܐ ܐܟܬܡܐ ܬܘܒ ܡܠܘܐܐ ܗܘܝܢ ܡܫܘܚܢ: ܡܬܩܢܝܢ ܠܫܡܫܬܗ ܟܠ ܕܐܬ ܒܡܘܥܕܐ ܕܥܝܕܐ ܒܠܚܬܐ ܕܚܙܝܐ ܕܚܟܡܬܢ. ܐܘܝܢ ܠܢ ܕܒܝܘܬ ܕܗܕܪܒܝܢ ܠܢ ܕܘܟܬܐ ܕܟܠܗܘܢ. ܕܠܘܝ ܗܘ ܕܝܬܒ ܒܝܡܝܢ. ܘܟܕ ܣܠܩܐܐ ܣܘܥܪ ܕܝܬܗܢ ܬܫܡܫܬܐ

Theodore teaches here that the ritual of the eucharist virtually places the person partaking of it in heaven. The rites inspire awe, and Theodore urges his audience to imagine themselves in heaven with Christ through the act of partaking.

At this point, discussions of Christian worship and the mystery religions often turn towards comparison and the sticky questions of influence, genealogy, and syncretism.[62] The important thing to note, however, is that secrecy and the language of personal transformation exists across late antique religious groups. The expectation of an interaction that was both personal and efficacious provides the background for individual religious experience. Furthermore, the use of highly emotive language and rites to punctuate divine encounters has analogues across a broad range of religious traditions. We witness in this context a variety of phenomena emerging from a cultural milieu with an apparent consensus regarding religious secrecy. State and civic cults aside, guarding central religious secrets and employing ritual for disclosing those secrets pervaded late antique religion. Even when the mysteries did not remain entirely secret, an insistence upon secrecy allowed Christians and practitioners of many other cults to assert a claim to a unique status. It helped maintain a distinction between insiders and outsiders. Furthermore, it strengthened the position of the clergy who functioned as the keepers of the secrets and the only official mechanism through which one could receive the key to the divine mysteries. This habit could even serve a proselytizing function with religious communities attempting to increase their appeal by insisting that they have something worth hiding from outsiders. Secrecy was important enough that people pressed the claim to it even when that claim entailed a certain falsehood. As such, the disclosure of those secrets became equally important, and considerable effort went into creating a profound experience of the divine in the rites and even in the process of teaching the rites. It remains to note that these expectations extended to literary sensibilities, which demanded ornate language,[63] as well as public displays of state power presented in similar terms.[64]

This consideration of some of the features of late antique religious initiation more broadly helps us understand the context in which catechumens approached the Christian community for the purpose of being initiated. A certain level of secrecy surrounded Christian belief and worship, and catechumens approached

---

ܢܕܚܡܗ ܕܝܒܝ̈ܟ. ܚܕ ܡ̈ܗܕܟܢܝ ܕܡܢܝܣܢܐ ܗ̇ܘ ܕܢܐܡܗܘ ܚܬܡ̈ܢܐ: ܗ̇ܘ ܕܣܝܠܩܒ ܡܢܗ ܡܒܓ ܘܟ̈ܚܡܢܐ
ܡܠܡܥ. ܗ̇ܘ ܓܠ ܡܬܐ ܚܕ ܠܩ̈ܩܗܡܐ ܘܠܒ ܡܗܢܚܚ.

[62] See Smith 1990; though slightly dated, this work provides a thorough and helpful overview of many of the methodological problems that have recurred in the study of early Christianity since the Reformation.

[63] Roberts 1989.

[64] MacCormack 1981.

initiation with the expectation of experiencing something profound. The catechists we know of used a wide variety of rhetorical strategies as they approached the task of meeting these expectations. The remainder of this chapter focuses on some of the variety of rhetorical strategies used in catechesis.

Rhetorical Strategies of Catechesis

As clergy negotiated the process of maintaining the boundaries of the community and initiating new Christians, they used the anticipation of the dramatic rites and the tradition of catechetical instruction to produce the maximal impact on the catechumens. These preachers insisted that converts needed more than to have their names placed on the rolls of the church. They needed education and orientation towards Christian worship. In the chapters that follow, we will analyze the catechetical curriculum of Theodore in depth, but here we consider various different approaches catechists took to their sermons.

On the one hand, catechetical sermons cover a relatively consistent range of topics, with doctrine, ritual, and ethics predominating. Cyril, bishop of Jerusalem during the middle of the fourth century, took a rather straightforward systematic approach to his catechetical preaching. The first sermon in the collection by Cyril, called the *Procatechesis*, addresses introductory matters of faith. Cyril stresses the importance of pursuing baptism and the great understanding that will come as a result of catechetical teaching.[65] Sincerity and earnest pursuit of baptism dominate the sermons.[66] Cyril follows this with eighteen sermons comprising the *Catechesis*. The first three discuss baptism and faith. Cyril stresses the cleansing impact of exorcism and baptism.[67] He elaborates on God's grace and the forgiveness of sin but also insists that catechumens make progress in avoiding sin.[68] The next fifteen sermons teach the creed then held in the city of Jerusalem. Cyril preaches on God and his attributes, the Son, and the Holy Spirit. His final sermon treats the church and the resurrection of the saints.

As we will see, this arrangement of lessons follows pretty closely Theodore's approach in so far as Theodore preaches through the creed in a similar fashion. The biggest difference between Theodore and Cyril is that Cyril waited until after baptism and the eucharist to explain the details of these rites, while Theodore explained them beforehand. Cyril argues in the first of these mystagogical catecheses that he has waited to explain the mysteries because "seeing is

---

[65] Cyril *Procatechesis* 6.
[66] Cyril *Procatechesis* 16.
[67] Cyril *Catechesis* 1.2, 5; 3.3.
[68] Cyril *Catechesis* 2.1; 3.8.

believing."[69] He thought allowing the candidates to experience baptism without any real idea of what it meant offered the best way to exploit the impact of ritual secrecy. Hearing the interpretation of what had already happened to them then apparently prompted the response recorded by Egeria. Theodore seems to have thought just the opposite, that understanding the meaning of the rites before experiencing them would heighten the dramatic impact. In each case, the catechist sought to create an atmosphere in which his teaching would have the greatest impact.

While John Chrysostom also frequently instructed his catechumens in the doctrine of the creed during their catechetical training, he took a much less systematic approach to the presentation of this material. It seems that his primary strategy to approaching catechesis entailed enfolding the catechumens into a definitively Christian moral world. Chrysostom addressed in detail how Christians should perceive things such as jewelry, spectacles, oracles, drunkenness, leisure, and worldly goods, to name but a few topics of moral concern. In his tenth *Baptismal Instruction*, Chrysostom was about to instruct the catechumens in the mysteries of the Christian church when he broke off mid-thought to return to the theme that had dominated the previous sermon, the swearing of oaths: "Therefore, I wished to initiate you in all these matters today. But what is happening to me? My concern over your oaths—a concern that makes my soul waste away—does not let me go."[70] His audience apparently found his concern tiresome;[71] nevertheless, he proceeded to warn them against the error of making oaths. A number of Chrysostom's moral precepts would have been shared by his contemporaries outside the church, particularly Stoic philosophers. Whatever similarities may have existed between Stoic and Christian ethics, however, Chrysostom emphasized the uniquely Christian nature of proper behavior. The moral conduct of the believer ought to flow from Christian theology and a desire to relate rightly to the God of the creed. Thus he sought to present a thoroughly Christianized moral code without reference to any wider philosophical influences.

Such proper conduct required nothing shy of open combat with the devil, and a bold confrontation with the *daimones* that inhabited the world.[72] God provided baptism as a cleansing from sin and anointing with oil as a sign and seal to protect the Christian from diabolical temptations. Chrysostom preached

---

[69] Cyril *Mystagogy* 1.1.

[70] John Chrysostom *Baptismal Instructions* 10.3.

[71] John Chrysostom *Baptismal Instructions* 10.3. As if responding to a groan from the crowd, he replied, "And I know that many of you condemn the excess in my language, because you heard me say that my concern makes my soul waste away."

[72] John Chrysostom *Baptismal Instructions* 9.29. See, also, Kalleres 2002.

extensively on the exorcisms that were a part of the catechetical program because he was convinced that the full benefit and appropriation of exorcism and baptism required catechesis. An uninitiated Christian baptized on his deathbed, who then went on to recover, would lack necessary training. In his first homily on the *Acts of the Apostles*, in the midst of a lengthy discourse on avoiding post-baptismal sin, Chrysostom argued concerning such a person, that "if he recovers from his illness, [he] is as vexed as if some great harm had been done to him. For since he has not been prepared for a virtuous life, he has no heart for the conflicts which are to follow, and shrinks at the thought of them."[73] Chrysostom insisted that sound catechesis prepared candidates to pursue a proper Christian life. Furthermore, by cultivating this sense of danger surrounding baptism, Chrysostom elevated the importance of both the rite itself and the preparation for the rite, each of which the catechumen needed to experience in conjunction with the other and only within the proper context of the church.

We see catechetical preachers using secrecy and emotional language to emphasize the boundary between insiders and outsiders. In doing so, these preachers sought to give their audiences a theological vision of Christianity and their future place within it. Not all of the imaginative tools passed on to catechumens through the catechetical process pertained to the *disciplina arcani*, and secrecy was not the only important strategy for integrating new initiates. Offering ways of thinking about the world and the place of the Christian within it also provided important means of integration. Two brief examples from catechetical contexts will help to elucidate this point.

The first comes from Augustine's *On the Catechizing of the Uninstructed*. The text is actually a letter of Augustine to a young deacon in Carthage named Deogratias. He has been given the charge of teaching catechumens and expresses to Augustine considerable concern regarding his abilities. Although his reputation as a good teacher has already reached Augustine, he fears that he bores his students. Augustine offers a warm response full of encouragement and recommendations for how to approach the process of teaching those uninstructed in Christian doctrine. These were not baptismal candidates, but rather catechumens who wanted instruction in the faith as a way to help them make the decision to seek acceptance into the rank of the *competentes*, those immediately preparing for baptism.[74] Augustine offers two different ways to address the

---

[73]   John Chrysostom *Acts of the Apostles* 1: Καὶ ἐκεῖνος δὲ πάλιν τότε ὀδυνᾶται πλέον, κἂν ἀνενέγκῃ ἀπὸ τῆς ἀρρωστίας, χαλεπώτερον ἀλγεῖ ὡς ἐπηρεασθείς. Ἐπειδὴ γὰρ οὐ παρεσκεύαστο πρὸς ἀρετὴν, ὀκνεῖ λοιπὸν, καὶ ἀναδύεται πρὸς τοὺς ἀγῶνας τοὺς μετὰ ταῦτα.

[74]   Augustine *On the Catechizing of the Uninstructed* 26.50. See the Introduction for a fuller discussion of the terms used for those approaching baptism.

catechumens based on their level of education and their knowledge of pagan as well as Christian literature. Though the two approaches are distinct, they develop out of the same basic approach. Augustine urges Deogratias to begin the education of his catechetical students with biblical history. In each case, the scheme of creation, fall, God's covenantal faithfulness, and the advent of Christ gives structure to the lessons he advocates. In this way, the catechumens will encounter all of human history as oriented toward God and, in particular, toward the coming of Christ for the purpose of redemption.[75] For Augustine, the biblical history necessary for teaching catechumens comprises an account of God's redemptive work from the beginning of time. This story encompassed all of human history. If rightly taught and understood, Augustine believed it would make clear the right choice and urge the catechumen to seek baptism, to secure their position in God's redemptive work. The aim was to present a powerful mental image of a thoroughly Christian past, present, and future.

Though slightly more modest in the expanse of its vision, a similar attempt to articulate a palpably Christian world can be found in Cyril of Jerusalem's catechetical sermons. A theme that ties in with a major emphasis of Cyril's episcopate emerges in these sermons. Jerusalem was ecclesiastically subordinate to its coastal rival Caesarea, and Cyril actively promoted the elevation of Jerusalem as the preeminent see of Palestine. To this end, he focused attention on the biblical history of Jerusalem, the fact that James the brother of Jesus became the first Christian bishop in Jerusalem and, most especially, the presence of the true cross in this city.[76] Cyril also promoted Jerusalem's central role in the eschatological future of the church, as the place where Christ would come again.[77] Cyril imagined a Jerusalem that held a place of central importance in the Christian story, even to the point of being the center of the world.[78] His promotion of this image featured prominently in his catechetical homilies as well:[79] "Yet one should never grow weary of hearing about our crowned Lord, especially on this holy Golgotha. For others merely hear, but we see and touch."[80] Cyril singles out the catechumens of Jerusalem as having pride of place. Their relationship to Golgotha and the cross of their messiah should act as a special reminder of the truth of their faith. Golgotha itself offered an apologetic for Christ's death

---

[75] Augustine *On the Catechizing of the Uninstructed* 3.6.

[76] Drijvers 2004:153–176.

[77] *Letter to the Emperor Constantius* 6; Drijvers 2004:161–162.

[78] Cyril *Catechesis* 13.28. For more on this topic, see Alexander 1994:104–119.

[79] Baldovin (1987:15) counts sixty-seven references to the holy sites of Jerusalem in Cyril's catechetical sermons.

[80] Cyril *Catechesis* 13.22: καίτοιγε οὐκ ἔστι ποτὲ καμεῖν ἀκούοντας τὰ περὶ τοῦ δεσπότου στεφανουμένου, καὶ μάλιστα ἐν τῷ παναγίῳ τούτῳ Γολγοθᾷ. ἄλλοι μὲν γὰρ ἀκούουσι μόνον, ἡμεῖς δὲ καὶ βλέπομεν καὶ ψηλαφῶμεν.

and resurrection against anyone who might doubt: "For if I should now deny it, Golgotha here, close to which we are now gathered, refutes me; the wood of the Cross, now distributed piecemeal from this place over all the world, refutes me."[81] Cyril made every attempt to use the presence of the cross in Jerusalem and the spiritual topography of the city for the education of the baptismal candidates. Jan Willem Drijvers is right to point out the political motives of Cyril's attempts to promote Jerusalem.[82] But that should not diminish our attention to the means he used to accomplish this goal. By stressing the holiness of sites around Jerusalem and their value as mnemonic devices, Cyril presented an image of his catechumen's immediate surroundings that forcefully declared the validity of Christianity. The success of his approach can be discerned in the esteem given to Jerusalem at the Council of Constantinople in 381, where it was declared "the mother of all churches."[83]

Each of these collections of sermons accomplished far more than simply furnishing baptismal candidates with information regarding Christological particularities, moral precepts, or the content of the liturgical mysteries. Rather, these preachers carefully crafted comprehensive curricula for initiation into the Christian church. These sets of sermons aimed at a holistic approach to catechesis and initiation. Any attempt to maintain a distinction between doctrine, cult, and ethics breaks down in this context. The preachers structured their catecheses to affect the entirety of the candidates. They aimed to instruct the thoughts, words, and actions of those seeking initiation into the church. They insisted that catechumens needed more than information about the mysteries, even more than the experience of the mysteries. They maintained that candidates needed the preacher to reveal to them, through catechesis, the nature of the Christian life in a controlled and systematic way. Maintaining the rhetorical efficacy of secrecy allowed the clergy to heighten the gravity and profundity of initiation, to punctuate the experience and the material taught, and to do all of this within the structured community of the church.

These sermons offer various rhetorical strategies for dealing with the transition from an outsider's knowledge of the Christian mysteries to an insider's. In each case, however, the catechist used bold and emotional language to stress the idea that the baptismal candidate was moving into a radically different stage of Christian experience. He or she was leaving behind the other catechumens

---

[81] Cyril *Catechesis* 13.4; translation slightly modified from McCauley and Stephenson 1969 2:6. κἂν γὰρ ἀρνήσωμαι νῦν, ἐλέγχει με οὗτος ὁ Γολγοθᾶς, οὗ πλησίον νῦν πάντες πάρεσμεν. ἐλέγχει με τοῦ σταυροῦ τὸ ξύλον τὸ κατὰ μικρὸν ἐντεῦθεν πάσῃ τῇ οἰκουμένῃ λοιπὸν διαδοθέν.

[82] Drijvers 2004:157–159.

[83] Drijvers 2004:176. Of course, Cyril's catechetical material was simply one portion of this project. For a full account of Cyril's efforts to elevate the position of Jerusalem, consult Chapter six in Drijvers 2004.

and fully joining the Christian community. Though the rigid boundary between members of the church and unbaptized catechumens was liturgically enacted at every eucharistic service with the removal of the uninitiated, the boundary was sometimes very publically shown to be porous. Consider the example of Ambrose's acclamation as bishop when he was yet unbaptized.[84] Though he had to undergo the rites before he could assume his episcopal position, he had clearly come to hold a position of prominence within an important Christian family in Milan, which allowed his dramatic elevation. Similarly, Constantine and Constantius engaged with the formation of Christian doctrine at the highest levels, yet without receiving baptism. The *Apostolic Constitutions* also speaks to a problem of boundary maintenance when it discusses the need for travelling Christians to carry letters from their home church, lest someone unbaptized claim the contrary and receive communion illicitly.[85]

Nevertheless, whatever an individual might have heard from a disgruntled former Christian or a loose-tongued practitioner of the faith, he or she had not been incorporated into the church by the proper clerical authorities. In this way, it did not matter if the person coming for catechesis knew much or only a little about the mysteries of the Christian church. The clergy made every effort to present catechetical instruction, and the community to which it introduced a person, as a proper initiation and incorporation into a life centered on Christ in heaven and the church. Preachers did not primarily reveal to the catechumens the cognitive content of Christianity, but rather the approaching position of the catechumen in an idealized image of a body of Christians directing their lives towards Christ in the course of corporate worship. Creedal theology, ethics, renunciation of the devil, redemptive history, and sacred geography could each be used in different circumstances to engage catechumens and promote this Christianized image of the world. Catechesis permitted many approaches and, at this point, we turn to the consideration of Theodore's catechesis and the context in which it took place, the Christian community.

---

[84] Rufinus *Church History* 11.11.
[85] *Apostolic Constitutions* 2.58.1–3; Sandwell 2007:199; Maxwell 2006:120–121.

3

The Community of Citizens

IN THE LAST CHAPTER, we discussed some of the ways that the church maintained cultic boundaries and rhetorically emphasized its exclusivity. We now turn to a consideration of just what the catechumens were doing as they pursued baptism. Many have sought to answer this question with the cognitive and psychological models discussed in the Introduction. Such approaches, however, tend to downplay if not entirely ignore the fact that the process of Christian initiation had a very heavy communal focus.[1] The people who sought these rites did so in large part because of their desire to become members of a Christian community that was becoming more and more visible as a significant part of the world of Late Antiquity. This community established a robust hierarchy and insisted on the ability of that hierarchy to mediate the connection between people and God. Shrouding Christian doctrine and practice in a cloud of secrecy before ritually revealing it under controlled circumstances offers a clear manifestation of that hierarchy. This chapter addresses additional facets of Christian hierarchy and the role that it played in reinforcing the authority of the clergy. However, one cannot rightly understand the Christian community merely by looking at the top levels of its structure. Catechesis served the important function of creating new members of the community, of integrating them into the church. This chapter also discusses the makeup of the community and looks at the way in which hierarchy served to integrate a broad range of people into a coherent community.

A city made up of citizens is Theodore's preferred metaphor for describing the community of the church in his *Catechetical Homilies*. In attempting to express the profound nature of the catechumens' decision to pursue baptism, Theodore returned regularly to the idea that they were about to undergo initiation into a heavenly kingdom. He appealed to Galatians 4.26 and Hebrews 12.22–23 as the source of this concept.[2] In each passage, the authors refer to the existence of a

---

[1] On the importance of social relations and patronage networks in early Christian conversion, see Crook 2004; Kile 2005; and Stark 1996.

[2] WS 6.23–24. See, also, Theodore *Commentary on the Epistle to the Galatians* 4.26.

heavenly Jerusalem. This city, established by the risen Christ and populated by angels, stands as the future hope of the Christian, and Theodore urged the diligent pursuit of citizenship in this city. Though Theodore genuinely stresses the heavenly nature of this city, he also carefully noted the relationship between the heaven city and the earthly community. Turning again to scripture for his justification, Theodore cited Matthew 16.18–19, in which Jesus gives Peter the keys to the kingdom of heaven and the authority to bind and loose things both on earth and in heaven: "He showed in this [passage] that he granted to the church the power that any one who becomes related to it should also be related to heavenly things, and any one who becomes a stranger to it should also be clearly a stranger to heavenly things."[3] Theodore thus related the earthly Christian community to the heavenly kingdom of God, with clergy taking up Peter's position as heads of the church with authority over its earthly and heavenly manifestations. Furthermore, Theodore insisted in this context that the pursuit of heaven required the pursuit of the earthly community as well. Though catechumens were well on their way in seeking integration into the church, Theodore still stressed to them the importance of attaining full citizenship.

In order to understand catechesis, we must first understand the nature of the Christian community and what it meant to pursue citizenship in that city. While this may seem to be a rather straightforward issue, one ought to be a bit careful when it comes to making assumptions about the matter. Historians of Late Antiquity have followed their sources in emphasizing certain types of Christian religious figures. The bishop looms very large indeed in such literature.[4] We have considerable bodies of literature from individual bishops in numerous genres: letters, sermons, and theological treatises, among others. These are the sorts of characters about whom one can write a proper biography. They often acted on a grand stage within both ecclesiastical and state politics and left a considerable literary legacy. Similarly, holy men and women receive a great deal of attention. They have not tended to leave us texts, but their enigmatic lifestyles piqued the curiosity of many a late Roman biographer and, as a result, the literary record provides ample source material to inspire a lively scholarly literature.[5] Occasionally individual lay Christians also make an appearance. The most prominent representatives in this category are pilgrims, but wealthy lay donors are also worthy of note.[6]

These extraordinary examples, however, make up only a fraction of those actively engaged in late antique Christianity. Surrounding each bishop were

---

[3] WS 6.23.
[4] See Rapp 2005.
[5] See Brown 1998; as well as Hayward and Howard-Johnston 1999.
[6] See Frank 2000; and R. D. Finn 2006.

many presbyters and deacons, particularly in the larger cities of the empire. The varied activities of the church demanded a considerable number of workers. Alongside the cultic function of the church stood educational, charitable, and judicial activities. Throughout all of these activities, the social structures of the church played significant roles. The various official positions held and the ways in which power was exercised and delegated through these positions highlight important aspects of the day-to-day life of the church. Each of these components of the church's activities deserves extensive study. However, the scope of this project does not allow such comprehensive treatment of these matters. Rather, this chapter will bear these multiple conditions and activities in mind as it focuses on material central to the church in Antioch towards the end of the fourth century with the aim of providing the immediate context for Theodore's catechetical sermons.

The Higher Clergy

Our discussion begins with the most prominent figures in the late antique church, the higher clergy. They appear regularly in our sources, but these sources demonstrate an inconsistency in the terminology used to describe the clergy. As it turns out, the terms used of the clergy prove illustrative of the ways in which they presented themselves and how the laity interacted with them in negotiating their engagement with the heavenly city. The sources contain one set of terms that comes out of New Testament scriptures and another set largely absent from those texts. The latter emphasizes the language of priesthood, with all of the attendant ideas of a professional ritual class that performs rites on behalf of the laity. The consideration of the variety of terminology will thus help us as we consider the place of the clergy, laity, and catechumens within the community.

The late fourth-century sources particular to Antioch used a varied terminology when discussing the ranks of the higher clergy.[7] In his commentaries on the so-called Pastoral Epistles, Theodore used only the language contained in those epistles to discuss the clergy: Greek *episkopos* (ἐπίσκοπος), *presbyteros* (πρεσβύτερος), and *diakonos* (διάκονος).[8] While he recognized that the Pauline hierarchy reflected in this terminology only distinguished two offices, overseers/elders and deacons, he interpreted these epistles according to the three-office system current in his day in which overseers held a position higher than

[7] For the historical development of the Christian clergy in the early Christian period, see Schöllgen 1998; and Faivre 1977.

[8] As Theodore's commentaries on these epistles are preserved in Latin, our translation uses the equivalent: *episcopus*, *presbyter*, and *diaconus*.

elders.[9] The compiler of the *Apostolic Constitutions* also used the language of the Pastoral Epistles throughout his treatment of clerical activity as well.[10] However, in addition to that language, he made extensive use of priestly language.[11] In connection with a range of duties, he applied to clerics the Greek term for priest, *hiereus* (ἱερεύς). The *Theodosian Code*, compiled in Latin, followed a similar set of conventions when discussing Christian clergy. Though the term cleric (*clericus*) appears most frequently as a general term for all of the Christian clergy when indicating no specific position in the church, more specific terminology also appears there. The laws sometimes clearly distinguish *episcopi* and *presbyteri*, but several laws refer to both bishops and presbyters as priests, *sacerdotes*.[12] Thus a certain ambiguity of terminology appears in the sources on this point.[13]

Theodore's *Catechetical Homilies* adopt the more priestly approach to clerical terminology. In his explanation of baptism and the eucharist, Theodore apparently used only two terms to refer to the higher clergy. The Syriac translator of this text used *mšamšānā* (ܡܫܡܫܢܐ) to translate Greek *diakonos*. This is the normal word for deacon, appearing consistently in the Peshitta New Testament. It is a participle of the root *šameš* (ܫܡܫ), meaning "to serve," and thus has the same breadth of meaning as Greek *diakonos*, which bears the technical meaning "deacon" but also simply means "servant." The translator used the Syriac *kāhnā* (ܟܗܢܐ) to translate the only other term that Theodore employed in this text. *Kāhnā*, a cognate of the Hebrew *cohen*, is the standard term used in the Peshitta and elsewhere to translate Greek *hiereus* and, as such, it must be the Greek term behind the Syriac *kāhnā* in this text.[14] We should conclude from this that in his

---

[9] *Commentary on the First Epistle to Timothy* 3.8.

[10] The *Apostolic Constitutions* is a book of church order purportedly penned by the apostles themselves. In actuality, it is a text compiled from earlier sources such as the *Didascalia* and the *Didache*. Since the late nineteenth century, many dates and locations have been suggested for this compilation. In the introduction to his recent critical edition, however, Metzger (1985:61–62) argues convincingly that it belongs roughly to the 370s and was compiled in or near Antioch. Thus it holds direct relevance for the consideration of church hierarchy in late fourth-century Antioch.

[11] See also *Canons of the Council of Sardica* 20.

[12] *Theodosian Code* 16.1.3 and 16.2.31.

[13] Rapp 2005:26.

[14] ܟܗܢܐ occasionally means "presbyter," as in the phrase ܟܗܢܐ ܐܘܟܝܬ ܩܫܝܫܐ, "presbyter, that is, priest"; see Payne Smith 1879, 1:1683. However, the central role of the bishop in the Eucharistic service makes it highly unlikely that Theodore is suggesting that only the presbyter administers this sacrament. Likewise, the denominative verb ܟܗܢ can mean "to be a priest," "to celebrate Holy Communion," or even "to serve as a deacon," Payne Smith 1879 1:1683–1684. While the celebration of communion would be most associated with the bishop, this should not be used as a basis for seeing this word as anything other than a translation of ἱερεύς. Since the holder/holders of this office are set off from the deaconate, that meaning cannot apply here either. In

instructions to baptismal candidates, Theodore characterized the higher clergy as consisting of "priests" and "deacons."[15]

A clue to this choice of terminology in the catechesis comes from Theodore's rare use of priestly language in his commentary on the Pauline Epistles. Theodore chose to deviate from his biblical source text and employ priestly language in the context of discussing the administration of the sacraments: "For the presbyters and the deacons alone fulfill the mystery of mysteries; some of them indeed fulfilling the sacerdotal work, others truly administering the sacrifice."[16] The sacerdotal work of the priests is the eucharist, which Theodore refers to here as the sacrifice. But this activity is not merely connected to the "sacrifice" of the eucharist. Theodore, even though he devoted more attention to his discussion of baptism than to his treatment of the eucharist, almost never used anything other than the term *hiereus* when speaking of bishops and presbyters in his *Catechetical Homilies*. For him, the sacred mysteries of the church were simply the province of priests.

Similar language also recurs throughout the *Apostolic Constitutions*. This text refuses to allow women to baptize because it would be "contrary to nature [for them] to be allowed to perform the office of a priest."[17] Likewise, in rejecting the baptism of heretics, the compiler of the *Apostolic Constitutions* argued, "But those who receive polluted baptism from the ungodly will become partners in their opinions. For they are not priests."[18] Therefore, bishops and presbyters were considered priests in part because baptism was reserved for them.[19] Priestly language also bore a connection to ordination. Those who were not themselves properly ordained were not to usurp this authority, and even then presbyters might only ordain certain lower clerical offices, the higher offices being limited to the bishops.[20] The *Apostolic Constitutions* contain detailed regula-

---

only one passage (WS 5.93), when making direct reference to the participants at the Council of Nicaea, did he employ the Syriac term ܐܦܣܩܘܦܐ, a transliteration of Greek ἐπίσκοπος.

[15] I will consistently use "priests" when the sources I am dealing with use the ambiguous *hiereus*, *sacerdos*, or *kōhnō*. When they have *episkopos* or *episkopus* in mind, I will employ the more precise "bishop." Likewise, I will use "presbyter" for *presbyteros*, *presbyter*.

[16] Theodore *Commentary on the First Epistle to Timothy* 3.14–15: "Nam mysterii ministerium presbyteri implent et diaconi soli; alii quidem eorum sacerdotale opus implentes, alii ver sacris ministrantes."

[17] *Apostolic Constitutions* 3.9: Εἰ δὲ ἐν τοῖς προλαβοῦσιν διδάσκειν αὐταῖς οὐκ ἐπιτρέπομεν, πῶς ἱερατεῦσαι ταύταις παρὰ φύσιν τις συγχωρήσει; τοῦτο γὰρ τῆς τῶν Ἑλλήνων ἀθεότητος τὸ ἀγνόημα θηλείαις θεαῖς ἱερείας χειροτονεῖν, ἀλλ᾽ οὐ τῆς τοῦ Χριστοῦ διατάξεως.

[18] *Apostolic Constitutions* 6.15: Οἱ δὲ παρὰ τῶν ἀσεβῶν δεχόμενοι μόλυσμα κοινωνοὶ τῆς γνώμης αὐτῶν γενήσονται. Οὐ γάρ εἰσιν ἐκεῖνοι ἱερεῖς.

[19] *Aposotolic Constitutions* 3.10.

[20] *Apostolic Constitutions* 8.46. On the offices on which a *chorepiscopos* could ordain someone, see *Canons of the Council of Antioch* 10.

tions regarding who may lay hands upon whom for the purpose of ordination.[21] Here again, one encounters a priestly role set aside specifically for bishops and presbyters.

This priestly language denoted mediation and functioned to set apart a hierarchy designed to ensure the proper establishment of order in the church. In order to reinforce and enhance their position in the church, bishops and presbyters applied the old covenant economy to their new context and appealed to the maintenance of proper apostolic authority for justification of this development. According to the compiler of the *Apostolic Constitutions*, the apostles declared, "we distributed the functions of the high-priesthood to the bishops, those of the priesthood to the presbyters, and the ministration under them both to the deacons; so that the divine worship might be performed in purity."[22] Thus the compiler advanced the argument that hierarchy of rank reflected hierarchy of service. The bishop held the top position of the high priest. The presbyters worked under him to support his labors, and the deacons served them both as they ministered to the congregation: "But the weighty matters let the bishop judge; but let the deacon be the bishop's ear, and eye, and mouth, and heart, and soul, that the bishop may not be distracted with many cares, but with such only as are more considerable."[23] In keeping with this, the male laity were often instructed to direct their concerns to the bishop through the deacons, and the female through the deaconesses.[24] The use of priestly terminology aimed at enhancing honor and prestige. As such, it gave the bishop one more tool he could use to consolidate his authority.[25] But this concern for order and authority manifested itself in numerous other ways as well. The following discussion will treat several of the central activities in which the higher clergy engaged. It will highlight the positions various members of the clergy held in the church and begin to outline further the nature of their authority.

Clergy as educators

Education was a clerical task of central importance. Bishop and presbyters alike put considerable effort into the regular preparation and preaching of sermons

---

[21] *Apostolic Constitutions* 3.1; 8.2–3.

[22] *Apostolic Constitutions* 8.46.10: Εἰ μὲν γὰρ μὴ θεσμός τις ἦν καὶ τάξεων διαφορά, ἤρκει ἂν δι' ἑνὸς ὀνόματος τὰ ὅλα τελεῖσθαι· ἀλλ' ὑπὸ τοῦ Κυρίου διδαχθέντες ἀκολουθίαν πραγμάτων, τοῖς μὲν ἐπισκόποις τὰ τῆς ἀρχιερωσύνης ἐνείμαμεν, τοῖς δὲ πρεσβυτέροις τὰ τῆς ἱερωσύνης, τοῖς δὲ διακόνοις τὰ τῆς πρὸς ἀμφοτέρους διακονίας, ἵν' ᾖ καθαρῶς τὰ τῆς θρησκείας ἐπιτελούμενα.

[23] *Apostolic Constitutions* 1.44: Πλὴν ἔστω ὁ διάκονος τοῦ ἐπισκόπου ἀκοὴ καὶ ὀφθαλμὸς καὶ στόμα, καρδία τε καὶ ψυχή, ἵνα μὴ ᾖ τὰ πολλὰ μεριμνῶν ὁ ἐπίσκοπος, ἀλλὰ μόνα τὰ κυριώτερα.

[24] *Apostolic Constitutions* 2.28.

[25] More mundane restrictions existed as well. For example, Canon 20 of the Council of Laodicea insists that a deacon may only sit in the presence of a presbyter or bishop if he is invited to do so.

to their congregations. We have many sermons that John Chrysostom delivered before his elevation to the rank of bishop. Likewise, the fact that Theodore delivered his *Catechetical Homilies* in Antioch means that he had not yet been made bishop of Mopsuestia. Theodore interpreted the command in Titus 1.5 that Titus establish presbyters in the cities as being for the purpose of insuring the presence of those "in the order of the clerics who teach what pertains to common usefulness."[26] Furthermore, 1 Timothy 3.1 contains the requirement that the bishop ought to be "able to teach." Here Theodore distinguished two types of teaching that the bishop needed to master. He had to be able to teach both the dogma of piety and sound doctrine.[27] As the *Apostolic Constitutions* put it, the bishop was a new Moses, both a teacher and a giver of laws to the community.[28]

This ministry of the bishops and presbyters provided one of the foundations for their status of high honor in the church. Indeed presbyters were worthy of double honor because of their ministry in the word and doctrine. Theodore interpreted this teaching from 1 Timothy 5.17 with the following: "And so the blessed apostle evidently places the work of doctrine before all other works."[29] The compiler of the *Apostolic Constitutions* explained the honor in which the bishop was held with reference to the presence of God in the preached word: "For where the doctrine concerning God is, there God is present."[30]

The dual nature of this teaching, exposition of piety and doctrine, as well as the presence of God in the preached word, meant that the preacher had to be pious himself. By the time Theodore was addressing his baptismal candidates, this aspect of the ideal bishop was a staple of the way people wanted to think about bishops.[31] The position had come to entail considerable power, and there was always the threat of the ambitious bishop or presbyter who had his own position and influence in mind when he acted as bishop.[32] People were uncomfortable with the idea that the teaching authority of their priests might be misused. The bishop and the clergy who served under him had to cultivate a demonstrable sanctity if they were to exercise their ecclesiastical prerogatives effectively. Theodore even saw an educational motivation for this life of virtue. He explained that the reason for the cleric to pursue purity was "so that

---

[26] Theodore *Commentary on the Epistle to Titus* 1.5: "... in ordinem clericorum suum officium implerent, per quos explicari poterant illa quae ad communem pertinent utilitatem."

[27] Theodore *Commentary on the Epistle to Titus* 3.2. For a helpful survey of the interpretation of this passage in early Christian literature, see Rapp 2005:32–41.

[28] *Apostolic Constitutions* 2.32.

[29] Theodore *Commentary on the First Epistle to Timothy* 5.17: "Sic enim et beati apostoli videntur doctrinae opus omnibus operibus anteposuisse."

[30] *Apostolic Constitutions* 7.9: Ὅπου γὰρ ἡ περὶ Θεοῦ διδασκαλία, ἐκεῖ Θεὸς πάρεστιν.

[31] Rapp 2005:57–66.

[32] John Chrysostom *On the Priesthood* 4.1.

you might offer yourself as an example to the faithful before whom you direct your life, instructing how it is necessary to conduct oneself, so that on account of these actions of yours, you might present the testimony of your life to each of them."[33] His commentary on Titus 2.7–8 further explained that this type of public life would be a source of credibility for the preacher. A life of sanctity would have a pedagogical function, both teaching by example and reinforcing the credibility of the preacher.

Christian discipline

This credibility had ramifications for ministry apart from the pulpit as well. An example can be found in discussions of the clergy as judges. The compiler of the *Apostolic Constitutions* gave considerable attention to the judicial function of the clergy. The bishop was to use his honored position to act as an impartial judge in all matters pertaining to the life of the church. He should settle disputes between members of his congregation, punish sinners, and restore the repentant. The perception of purity and morality stood at the heart of the bishop's ability to perform these duties from a position of authority.

Our authors located the purpose of this judicial power of the bishop in the maintenance of discipline in the church. However, in portraying the bishop as judge, they preferred the image of the good shepherd. They held that a strong notion of proper pastoral care should guide the bishop in his exercise of judicial authority. A shepherd wielded his staff for the protection of his flock, through teaching and the denunciation of heretics, but also for the purpose of herding his flock through confession, penance, excommunication, and restoration.[34] Theodore further examined one aspect of this through another metaphor that he offered in the catechesis: the priest as physician.

> Since you are aware of these things, and also of the fact that because God greatly cares for us he gave us penitence and showed us the medicine of repentance, and established some men, who are priests, as physicians of sins, so that if we receive in this world through them, healing and forgiveness of sins, we shall be delivered from the judgment to come—it behooves us to draw nigh unto the priests with great confidence and to reveal our sins to them, and they, with all diligence,

---

[33] Theodore *Commentary on the First Epistle to Timothy* 4.12: "... ita ut et ipse formam te praebeas fidelibus pro quibus vitam Regis tuam, instruens quemadmodum conveniat conversari, ita ut ex ipsis actibus tuis testimonium vitae tuae hisdem praebaes."

[34] *Apostolic Constitutions* 2.41.5–7.

pain and love, and according to the rules laid down above, will give healing to sinners.[35]

One such rule that Theodore laid down in the course of commenting on 2 Timothy 2.25–26 was that an offender should be given two opportunities to repent and then be cut off. This shepherd was to be a strong protector who carried out his duties with as much authority as compassion.

Of course, the ideal of Christian discipline being carried out by the bishop as a function of his position as head of the local church must be supplemented by another very present reality. The emperor Constantine had granted to Christian clergy the power to hear cases that would have otherwise been directed toward secular courts.[36] At least some bishops attempted to see this as a natural extension of their church discipline and to use the opportunity to address the hearts and minds of congregations that often struggled with the finer points of Christian ethics.[37] But this task could be tedious and often engaged priests in matters with which they did not wish to concern themselves. Therefore, while this imperial grant of power potentially gave the clergy considerable influence in local matters, it could also be very disruptive of other aspects of their ministry, particularly their study of scripture. The service they performed as judges seems to have been in rather high demand. This duty effectively called upon the bishop to act as an arbitrator whose decision had the force of law.[38] This judicial activity also required a good reputation for impartiality and honest dealing. As a result of this judicial role, the bishop or his clerical representatives held a place of prominence both within the church and outside of it.

The care of the poor

Another important aspect of church administration and pastoral care was the reception and distribution of offerings.[39] The compiler of the *Apostolic*

---

[35] WS 6.123; *Homélies Catéchétiques* 16.151v: ܡܛܠ ܗܟܝܠ ܕܡܣܟܢܐ ܢܘܚܡܗܘܢ. ܘܢܚܙܐ ܠܝܢ ܟܝ ܕܡܟܝܠ

[36] *Theodosian Code* 1.27.1–2; *Sirmondian Constitutions* 1. We hear most about bishops in this context, but the laws refer to *clerici* and *sacerdotes*. As such, it is not entirely clear if this was exclusively episcopal; see Rapp 2005:238.

[37] Lamoreaux 1995:144.

[38] Rapp 2005:242–244.

[39] On alms collected by the bishop in the name of the poor and expectations regarding care of poor, see Brown 2001:24–44.

Constitutions appealed to Old Testament notions of offerings to the temple and priests in discussing Christian gifts to the church: "Wherefore you ought to love the bishop as your father, and fear him as your king, and honor him as your lord, bringing to him your fruits and the works of your hands, for a blessing upon you, giving to him your first-fruits, and your tithes, and your oblations, and your gifts, as to the priest of God."[40] Shortly after this he included an explanation of how Christians could keep the implicit command of Matthew 5.20: "Now herein will your righteousness exceed [that of the scribes and Pharisees], if you take greater care of the priests, the orphans, and the widows."[41] Thus the model at work was one in which the congregation brought to the bishop their offerings, which the bishop then used for the care of the needy within the community.

Episcopal finances, however, could be a tricky matter in Late Antiquity. The distinction between the private wealth of the bishop and the finances he managed in his official role as bishop was not always entirely clear.[42] Many bishops and other clergy as well came from wealthy and influential families.[43] The tax exemptions for clergy were clearly an incentive to seek ecclesiastical office and, as a result, the financial motivations of those seeking ordination were a matter of some scrutiny. Bishops sometimes built elaborate martyr shrines, church buildings, or episcopal residences, to which they might even ostentatiously associate their own name. One such case is evident from a church just outside the city of Antioch. An inscription dated to the 420s captures the efforts of the Antiochene clergy to connect themselves to the beautification of a piece of sacred architecture through the addition of mosaic floors: "Under the most holy and venerable bishop Theodotus and the presbyter and administrator Athanasius, this mosaic of the faithful came into being and this work also came about on account of the deacon and assistant Akkiba."[44] Such building projects had been a part of ancient notions of the wealthy spending their personal finances on the improvement of their city, and these activities were generally

---

[40] *Apostolic Constitutions* 2.34: Διὸ τὸν ἐπίσκοπον στέργειν ὀφείλετε ὡς πατέρα, φοβεῖσθαι ὡς βασιλέα, τιμᾶν τε ὡς κύριον, τοὺς καρποὺς ὑμῶν καὶ τὰ ἔργα τῶν χειρῶν ὑμῶν εἰς εὐλογίαν ὑμῶν προσφέροντες αὐτῷ, τὰς ἀπαρχὰς ὑμῶν καὶ τὰς δεκάτας ὑμῶν καὶ τὰ ἀφαιρέματα ὑμῶν καὶ τὰ δῶρα ὑμῶν διδόντες αὐτῷ ὡς ἱερεῖ Θεοῦ.

[41] *Apostolic Constitutions* 2.35: Οὕτως οὖν πλεονάσει ἡ δικαιοσύνη ὑμῶν, ἐν τῷ πλέον ὑμᾶς πρόνοιαν ποιεῖσθαι τῶν ἱερέων καὶ τῶν ὀρφανῶν καὶ τῶν χηρῶν.

[42] *Canons of the Council of Antioch* 24.

[43] Rapp 2000.

[44] Ἐπὶ τοῦ ἁγιοτάτου καὶ ὁσιοτάτου ἐπισκόπου θεοδότου, καὶ Ἀθανασίου πρεσβυτέρου καὶ οἰκονόμου, ἡ ψηθεὶς τοῦ πειστικοῦ γέγονεν καὶ τὸ ἔργον τοῦτο ἐπεὶ Ακκιβα διακόνου καὶ παραμοναρίου (Lassus 1938:33, my translation). This church also contains four additional inscriptions attributing mosaics to the bishop Flavian and his presbyters, see Lassus 1938:13, 15, 18, 39.

interpreted as such and considered welcome.[45] Nevertheless, members of a bishop's congregations could feel that this expenditure ran contrary to the spirit of financial contributions to the church, which the clergy usually spoke of as money given for the care of the poor. Those critical of bishops (for financial or other reasons) often found that they could effectively slander a bishop by pointing out his expenditures and claiming that he neglected the needy within their congregation.[46] As a result, the bishop had a clear interest in consistently presenting himself as actively engaged in the care of the poor and disengaged from the affairs of the world. Rhetoric and reality surely met somewhere in the middle, with bishops often managing far more wealth than they spent on the care of those dependent upon the church for support. Nevertheless, high profile expenses on hospitals, famine relief, and the redemption of captives, as well as regular support of widows, orphans and the virgins of the church, argued strongly for the philanthropic use of church finances. John Chrysostom claimed that the church in Antioch supported three thousand widows and virgins in addition to many who suffered ill health or poverty.[47] Bishops used these practices to cultivate their role as advocates for a wide range of late Roman people. In doing this, they helped elevate the status of the bishop and his clergy in the life of the city.[48]

The Minor Clergy

This account of clerical activities reveals a very active ecclesiastical organization firmly working to assert itself in late antique society. However, the clergy in late fourth-century Antioch contained far more than the bishops, presbyters, and deacons of the higher clergy.[49] Theodore noted that the lesser orders do not appear in 1 Timothy and was concerned to explain their absence: "These [subdeacons and readers] had been added to the grades of the functions which were held in the churches, as a matter of necessity; on account of the usefulness of [their] service, because, on account of the multitude of those believing, necessity demanded that afterwards they ought to be fulfilled through others."[50] Thus Theodore imagines a situation such as that recounted in Acts 6. When the apos-

---

45 Brown 2001:32.
46 Athanasius *Apology against Arius* 18.2; Brown 2001:32.
47 *Homilies on Matthew* 66.3.
48 Brown 2001:81–84.
49 On the minor clergy of Asia Minor, see Hübner 2005.
50 Theodore *Commentary on the First Epistle to Timothy* 3:14–15: "Illis etenim gradibus functionum qui in ecclesiis necessarium habentur, isti postea magis sunt adiecti propter utilitatem ministerii, quod propter multitudinem credentium per alteros postea impleri debere necessitas flagitauit." See also *Apostolic Constitutions* 8.22.

tles were distracted from their teaching ministry because of a need to serve food, they appointed and ordained deacons who could fulfill these duties. Theodore saw a very pragmatic explanation for the proliferation of clergy. As the church grew, so did the needs of the church. Three offices were no longer enough to meet the liturgical demands of larger congregations. The higher clergy created lower ordained orders to aid in the divine service.

Theodore's sub-deacons and readers do not, however, exhaust the ecclesiastical offices of the late antique church. The *Apostolic Constitutions* also mention the offices of singer (*ōdos*), porter (*pulōros*), minister (*hypēretēs*),[51] confessor (*homologētēs*),[52] exorcist (*eporkistēs*),[53] virgin (*parthenos*),[54] widow (*chēros*),[55] and orphan (*orphanos*).[56] From among these, the readers, singers, porters, and ministers, are specifically called clerics, *klerikoi*.[57] The *Theodosian Code* likewise refers to the offices of exorcist[58] and sexton (*kopiata*)[59] as clerics. The specific concern in the *Code* is the extension of tax benefits to clergy. Legally, in the eyes of the state, all of the people who held these positions had established roles in the church, which required them to be free from onerous tax liabilities. Thus there was considerable consensus about these groups and the important role they played in the management of church affairs. Even though the remaining positions of widows, orphans, and virgins are never singled out in ecclesiastical or legal sources as actually being clergy, they are very strongly associated with the clergy. Particularly in the *Apostolic Constitutions* they repeatedly appear interspersed in hierarchical lists with those offices that are defined as clerical.[60]

The tasks assigned to the majority of these ranks are quite clear from the names they bear. Thus readers and singers performed their duties in conjunction with the divine liturgy. The same was true of porters, although they may have been active throughout the week as the church remained open for prayer twice daily.[61] Confessors and exorcists would have served at various times and

---

[51] *Apostolic Constitutions* 3.11.

[52] *Apostolic Constitutions* 8.23.

[53] *Apostolic Constitutions* 8.26.

[54] *Apostolic Constitutions* 8.24.

[55] *Apostolic Constitutions* 8.25.

[56] *Apostolic Constitutions* 2.26.8.

[57] *Apostolic Constitutions* 3.11.

[58] *Theodosian Code* 16.2.24.

[59] *Theodosian Code* 16.2.15 and 13.1.1. Pharr translates *kopiata* as "grave-digger." Souter 1964 also gives "sexton," which is preferred by Elliott 1978:330–331. I use sexton here because it seems unlikely that many churches needed someone for the sole purpose of digging graves. A sexton's duties entail general property management, which could easily include grave-digging but would not be limited to it.

[60] *Apostolic Constitutions* 2.26 and 8.23–26.

[61] *Apostolic Constitutions* 2.59.

without specific relation to the weekly liturgy. However, exorcists did play a crucial role in the baptismal liturgy. The process of catechesis generally entailed numerous exorcisms, and the catechetical homilies of both Theodore and John Chrysostom discuss at some length the exorcisms preceding baptism.[62] At first glance, the inclusion of virgins, widows, and orphans seems largely oriented towards the system of social welfare within the church which existed primarily to maintain these marginalized groups. In a system of divine reciprocity, the church cared for them, and they prayed for the church, its clergy, and its ministries. But the widows, orphans, and virgins also played an interesting role in the divine service, to which we will return shortly.

Hierarchy and Delegation

We can see in both the ecclesiastical and legal literature that the clergy of the late fourth century had clearly moved well beyond the two or three office system of *episkopoi*, *presbyteroi*, and *diakonoi*. A combination of sacerdotal privilege and an emphasis on maintenance of proper order among the people of God had led to the adoption of priestly language by the presbyters and the bishop. Those at the top ruled over the church in a position of supreme authority and acted as God's representative on earth. The bishop ruled over the church, settling disputes among believers and warning his congregation to seek justice within the church lest they air the grievances of Christians before the pagans and bring the church into disrepute. The bishop trained his congregation in doctrine and piety through example and sermon. He taught about the person and work of Christ and, in turn, urged that this teaching should inform every ethical decision his congregation might make. Likewise, the bishop held the place of prominence in Christian worship, particularly the administration of the sacraments, those mysteries that acted as a sign and seal upon the people of God.

When it came to teaching and the administration of the sacraments, however, the priests clearly had their role as well. Through this activity they alleviated the daily burdens of the bishop and maintained the life of the church whenever the bishop was forced to travel. The matter of travel is an important one and deserves further consideration. We saw above that Theodore explained the proliferation of clergy with an appeal to the growth of the church during the fourth century. Perhaps just as important in this context was the fourth-century growth of the mobility of the clergy. When the Council of Nicaea was called together in 325, no event quite like it had ever taken place in the prior

---

[62] Theodore, especially Sermons 2 and 3 in *WS* 6; Chrysostom, especially *Baptismal Instruction* 2.12–14; and Kalleres 2002.

history of the church. Gathering Christian bishops from so great a geographical range essentially required imperial patronage and access to the *cursus publicus*, the imperial postal system used to transport information, tax revenues, and state officials around the empire. The grant of this privilege to bishops traveling for church councils opened a whole new era in episcopal mobility. Ammianus Marcellinus noted sarcastically that the only thing Constantius achieved through encouraging the episcopal use of the *cursus publicus* was the crippling of the postal system.[63] This is surely an overstatement, but there is no doubt that bishops travelled extensively in this period. From a wide variety of sources we know of nearly 120 church councils that took place during the fourth century. Some of the larger councils saw upwards of 400 bishops in attendance, not to mention the priests and deacons who would have attended as aids.[64]

These numbers are quite high and suggest considerable travel, but it is still difficult to know just how often bishops would have been away from their sees. Fortunately, Othmar Perler has done a thorough study of the travels of Augustine, which can help give some details for at least one late antique bishop.[65] During his thirty-four year episcopacy between 396 and 430, Augustine made at least one trip away from Hippo almost every year. Furthermore, the years he failed to travel are concentrated toward the end of his episcopacy when he was already somewhat advanced in age. Most of the trips he took were for rather local matters, but he was very often in Carthage, a trip of some 150 miles, which could keep him away from Hippo for a considerable amount of time. The occasions for such travel extended far beyond attendance at church councils. Augustine travelled to engage in doctrinal disputes with Donatists and Pelagians, to give assistance to other local congregations, to help dedicate a martyr shrine or basilica, and to take part in the ordination of other bishops. These trips could be as short as several weeks, but on at least four occasions he was away from Hippo for almost five months, and the trip he took in 419–420 lasted the better part of a year.[66] This glimpse into the travels of Augustine demonstrates that the absence of a bishop from his see in the course of his normal duties could be a frequent occurrence. Church councils occasionally recognized the absent

---

[63] *Histories* 21.16.18.

[64] MacMullen (2006:2–3) has provided a helpful table of the great majority of the councils mentioned in the sources between AD 253 and 553. He also mentions that if the canonical rules for holding local and regional synods had been followed, there would have been more than 15,000 councils during that period. The likelihood of that many councils having actually occurred is very low, however, and it seems sufficient for our purposes simply to point out the number of councils that we do know took place during the fourth century.

[65] Perler 1969:436–477.

[66] For a discussion of similar travels by John Chrysostom, see Kelly 1995:162–180.

bishop as a problem and attempted to regulate the movement of bishops.[67] Add to this the suggestion of rather large groups of bishops who spent considerable time in Constantinople attempting to ingratiate themselves at court, and the impression of absent bishops becomes stronger still.[68]

This alone should help make sense of the numerous clerical positions discussed in our sources. With the bishop often away from his see, the church would have required an active and rather extensive group of presbyters and deacons to carry on the many ministries of preaching, administering the sacraments, and caring for the poor. This activity must have occurred, but it very often took place behind the scenes. Our sources usually stress instead the activity of the bishop, as if his role as overseer meant that he was the only actor involved. However, Wendy Mayer has recently argued that just the sort of activity we are suggesting can be seen in the case of John Chrysostom.[69] She looks at the correspondence Chrysostom maintained while away from Antioch as bishop of Constantinople, particularly while in exile from his see. It indicates strong, enduring relationships with elite citizens of Antioch, particularly with wealthy and influential women in the church. In addition to these relationships, we see that Chrysostom expressed deep concern for missionary work among pagans in Phoenicia and hoped to insulate this ministry from the hostile forces that secured his exile from Constantinople. Mayer argues that the strength of these connections to Antiochene people and activities are related to Chrysostom's active engagement in pastoral care while he was still a presbyter in Antioch. His preaching ministry there is well known, but Mayer is able to connect this to a much broader ministry and paints a picture of Chrysostom acting in some ways as the *de facto* bishop of Antioch as the bishop Flavian aged in the years just before Chrysostom was called to Constantinople.

All of this suggests a healthy practice of delegation, which we should expect for purely logistical reasons, even if it can be difficult to locate precisely in our sources.[70] When we are able to tease out the reality of managing a large corporate body like a metropolitan church in Late Antiquity, we can begin to comprehend the multitude of tasks and actors involved. The bishop was indisputably at the head of this corporate activity but he required a considerable amount of assistance to carry out his numerous duties. Many sources seek vigorously to reinforce this hierarchical notion of church structure. Consider this section from Book Two of the *Apostolic Constitutions* in which the compiler expands upon the elevated status of the bishop:

[67] *Canons of the Council of Sardica* 7, 12, 21.
[68] Rapp 2005:265–266.
[69] Mayer 2001.
[70] Greer 2007:573.

But he who is above all these is the high priest, the bishop. He is the minister of the word, the keeper of knowledge, the mediator between God and you in your service toward Him. He is the teacher of piety; and, next after God, he is your father, who has begotten you again to the adoption of sons by water and the Spirit. He is your ruler and governor; he is your king and potentate; he is, next after God, your earthly God, who has a right to be honored by you.[71]

This passage clearly gives priority to the bishop and his supreme position in the ecclesiastical hierarchy. As high priest he was elevated to a position just below God. The compiler imagines him "next after God" in a continuum running from the Father right down through the church. This continuum progresses through the ranks of many of the clergy: presbyters, deacons, sub-deacons, and deaconesses. Immediately preceding this section, he discussed the roles and duties of the readers, singers, and porters. More surprising, however, is the inclusion of widows, orphans, and virgins: "Let the widows and orphans be esteemed as representing the altar of burnt-offering; and let the virgins be honored as representing the altar of incense, and the incense itself."[72] Just as priests, in particular the bishop, had been connected to the sacrificial cult of the old covenant, here virgins, widows, and orphans at the lower end of the hierarchy were connected as well. Without them, the bishop would not have been able to collect offerings. Indeed it was because of his care for these groups that the bishop legitimately requested and received the donations of the congregation. Inasmuch as the people gave offerings, they were caring "for the least of these"[73] who, through the giving and the receiving, became a sweet fragrance unto the Lord.[74] Thus even those who held ecclesiastical positions at the lower end of the church hierarchy had their essential role to play in the church's service, both its service to God and to the needy of the congregation.

These figures also had their parts to play in the process of catechesis. Bishops and presbyters preached and taught baptismal candidates and were engaged, along with deacons, in the rituals of initiation.[75] However, we would do well to consider baptismal sponsors in this context as well, even though the

---

[71] *Apostolic Constitutions* 2.26.4: Ὁ δὲ τούτων πάντων ἀνώτερος ὁ ἀρχιερεύς ἐστιν, ὁ ἐπίσκοπος. Οὗτος λόγου διάκονος, γνώσεως φύλαξ, μεσίτης Θεοῦ καὶ ὑμῶν ἐν ταῖς πρὸς αὐτὸν λατρείαις· οὗτος διδάσκαλος εὐσεβείας, οὗτος μετὰ Θεὸν πατὴρ ὑμῶν, δι' ὕδατος καὶ πνεύματος ἀναγεννήσας ὑμᾶς εἰς υἱοθεσίαν· οὗτος ἄρχων καὶ ἡγούμενος ὑμῶν, οὗτος ὑμῶν βασιλεὺς καὶ δυνάστης, οὗτος ὑμῶν ἐπίγειος θεὸς μετὰ Θεὸν, ὃς ὀφείλει τῆς παρ' ὑμῶν τιμῆς ἀπολαύειν.

[72] *Apostolic Constitutions* 2.26.8: Αἵ τε χῆραι καὶ οἱ ὀρφανοὶ εἰς τύπον τοῦ θυσιαστηρίου λελογίσθωσαν ὑμῖν· αἵ τε παρθένοι εἰς τύπον τοῦ θυμιατηρίου τετιμήσθωσαν καὶ τοῦ θυμιάματος.

[73] Matthew 25.40.

[74] Leviticus 2.2 and 6.15.

[75] See chapter four for a discussion of these rituals.

sources never suggest that they were clergy. The sponsor could be any baptized person from among the laity and the sources do not mention any ordination to this position.[76] However, the sponsors definitely provided another essential link in the hierarchical chain. Baptismal sponsors accompanied the person desirous of baptism and both submitted their names to the church's registrar together:

> A duly appointed person [the registrar] inscribes your name in the Church book, together with that of your sponsor, who answers for you and becomes your guide in the city [of God] and the leader of your citizenship therein. This is done in order that you may know that you are, long before the time and while on earth, enrolled in heaven, and that your sponsor who is in it is possessed of great diligence to teach you, who are a stranger and a newcomer to that great city, all the things that pertain to it and to its citizenship, so that you should be conversant with its life without any trouble and anxiety.[77]

This practice symbolized the fact that in registering along with the convert, the sponsor was acting as his or her surety. John Chrysostom used precisely this language in his catechetical homilies when he described the baptismal sponsor as an *anadechomenos*.[78] In origin, this is a legal term used to denote a third party in a legal action or contract who acts as a guarantor. The situation described is analogous to the co-signing of a loan in modern practice.[79] Chrysostom described this relationship in rather intimate terms as he explained to the candidates what he expected of their sponsors: "They ought to show their paternal love by encouraging, counseling, and correcting those for whom they go surety."[80] Here we can see the ideal sponsor actively engaged in the scrutiny of the catechumen's life and providing assistance in the requisite doctrinal training. Several times in his discussion of baptism in his first sermon, Theodore stresses the importance of the co-registration and the gravity of the sponsor undertaking

---

[76] Some have suggested that ordained deacons, in their capacity as deacons, acted as baptismal sponsors, but the sources do not bear this reading. See Lynch 1986:114. On baptismal sponsors, see also Dujarier 1967.

[77] Theodore WS 6.26; *Homélies Catéchétiques* 12.87v–88r: ܠܚܕܡܐ ܠܕܕ ܚܕܡܐ ܡܝܒ ܠܕܕ ܒܠܕ ܗܘ ܩܘ

[78] *Baptismal Instructions* 2.15–16.

[79] Lynch 1986:106.

[80] *Baptismal Instructions* 2.15: ἐπιδείκνυσθαι ὀφείλουσι, παραινοῦντες καὶ συμβουλεύοντες, διορθοῦντες, πατρικὴν φιλοστοργίαν ἐπιδεικνύμενοι.

such a role. He also addresses the sponsors directly, suggesting that their task includes accompanying the catechumens to church for the sermons that instruct them and helping them to memorize the creed. It is difficult to know just how zealous the sponsors actually were. The fact that both Chrysostom and Theodore address them during their catechetical sermons indicates that they were committed enough to join catechumens daily to aid them in their pre-baptismal instruction.

Another contemporary source on baptismal sponsors is the pilgrim Egeria. She strengthens our understanding of the role of the sponsor by indicating that the absence of a sponsor made it difficult for a person even to be accepted for baptism.[81] In other words, the church relied on these lay members to attest to the acceptance of Christian ethical norms as a sign of a serious intent to live the Christian life. Without this, the bishop and presbyters hesitated to accept someone into the group of the baptismal candidates. The gravity of the scene described by Egeria fits well with Chrysostom's use of legal language. When the bishop scrutinized the catechumens and heard testimony from their sponsors, he literally held court:

> The bishop's chair is placed in the middle of the Great Church, the Martyrium, the presbyters sit in chairs on either side of him, and all the clergy stand. Then one by one those seeking baptism are brought up, men coming with their father and women with their mother. As they come in one by one, the bishop asks their neighbors questions about them: "Is this person leading a good life? Does he respect his parents? Is he a drunkard or a boaster?" He asks about all the serious human vices. And if his inquiries show him that someone has not committed any of these misdeeds, he himself puts his name down.[82]

This scene of catechumens seeking to be numbered among the baptismal candidates of the church bears all the potential dread of appearing before a secular magistrate in a matter of law. The architectural setting of the Great Church displayed the prominence of the institution and the regal presentation

---

[81] Egeria *Travels* 45.4.

[82] Egeria *Travels* 45.1–4. "Ponitur episcopo cathedra media ecclesia maiore, id est ad Martyrium, sedent hinc et inde presbyteri in cathedris et stant clerici omnes. Et sic adducuntur unus et unus conpetens; si uiri sunt cum patribus suis ueniunt, si autem feminae, cum matribus suis. 3. Et sic singulariter interrogat episcopus uicinos eius, qui intrauit, dicens: 'Si bonae uitae est hic, si parentibus deferet, si ebriacus non est aut uanus?' Et singular uitia, quae sunt tamen grauiora in homine, requiret. 4. Et si probauerit sine reprehensione esse de his omnibus, quibus requisiuit presentibus testibus, annotat ipse manu sua nomen illius." "Mother" and "father" in this passage refer to baptismal sponsors and not biological parents. For a discussion of this matter, see Lynch 1986:98.

of the bishop and his clergy thoroughly reinforced their status within the ecclesiastical hierarchy. The day-to-day interaction between candidate and sponsor was likely rather mundane, but those who became catechumens must have been pleased to have such guarantors to see them through this trial. Egeria's use of the language of fictive kinship further enhances the sense of intimacy and comfort within the context of this rather high-pressure scrutiny.

Even in simply presenting themselves as candidates for baptism, the catechumens came face to face with the imposing hierarchy of the Christian clergy. Such a hierarchical understanding of the church might appear inconsistent with Christian scripture that urged the radical equality of Galatians 3.28, where Paul argued that "there is neither Jew nor Greek, there is neither slave nor free, there is neither male nor female; for you are all one in Christ Jesus."[83] Likewise, the reference to the church as "a royal priesthood" in 1 Peter 2.9 might also seem out of keeping with this view of the church.[84] But the compiler of the *Apostolic Constitutions* found a solution to tensions between the potentially egalitarian message of Christianity and the tiered ecclesiology of the church through seeing the earthly hierarchy of the church as a reflection of the divine hierarchy:

> For let the bishop preside over you as one honored with the authority of God, which he is to exercise over the clergy, and by which he is to govern all the people. But let the deacon minister to him, as Christ does to the Father; and let him serve him without blame in all things, as Christ does nothing of Himself, but does always those things that please His Father.[85]

The submission of the deacons and, by extension, the congregation to the bishop was analogous to the submission of the Son to the Father.[86] In this way,

---

[83] οὐκ ἔνι Ἰουδαῖος οὐδὲ Ἕλλην, οὐκ ἔνι δοῦλος οὐδὲ ἐλεύθερος, οὐκ ἔνι ἄρσεν καὶ θῆλυ· πάντες γὰρ ὑμεῖς εἷς ἐστε ἐν Χριστῷ Ἰησοῦ.

[84] Ὑμεῖς δὲ γένος ἐκλεκτόν, βασίλειον ἱεράτευμα, ἔθνος ἅγιον, λαὸς εἰς περιποίησιν, ὅπως τὰς ἀρετὰς ἐξαγγείλητε τοῦ ἐκ σκότους ὑμᾶς καλέσαντος εἰς τὸ θαυμαστὸν αὐτοῦ φῶς·

[85] *Apostolic Constitutions* 2.26.4–5: Ὁ μὲν οὖν ἐπίσκοπος προκαθεζέσθω ὑμῶν ὡς Θεοῦ ἀξίᾳ τετιμημένος, ᾗ κρατεῖ τοῦ κλήρου καὶ τοῦ λαοῦ παντὸς ἄρχει. 5. Ὁ δὲ διάκονος τούτῳ παριστάσθω ὡς ὁ Χριστὸς τῷ Πατρί, καὶ λειτουργείτω αὐτῷ ἐν πᾶσιν ἀμέμπτως, ὡς ὁ Χριστός, ἀφ' ἑαυτοῦ ποιῶν οὐδέν, τὰ ἀρεστὰ ποιεῖ τῷ Πατρὶ πάντοτε.

[86] This view of the relationship between the Father and the Son may be part of the non-Nicene milieu of this text. However, this is not entirely clear. All parties involved in the theological conflicts of the fourth century recognized the importance of Christ's statements in John 14.28 that "the Father is greater than I" and in John 6.38 that "I have come down from heaven, not to do my own will, but the will of him who sent me." They simply had different ways of understanding them. The notion of hierarchy that I describe in what follows is amenable to a variety of the positions articulated in the fourth century and need not be seen as necessarily Nicene or non-Nicene. All parties saw the Father as divine and uniquely separated from creation yet

the ontological equality of Christians urged by the gospel could coexist with the economic hierarchy within the clergy and throughout the church. Though the bishop was "next after God," the image suggested by this passage is one of a continuum that runs from God himself, through the clergy, and on to the laity and catechumens. Thus, this hierarchy, which might appear to distance and divide, was actually constructed to bind the church together, integrating each member into the whole through the delegation of episcopal authority and the distribution of appropriate roles. Our sources suggest an abundance of activity as the clergy served the congregation through liturgy, teaching, disciplining, and collecting charitable donations. If the servants were this numerous, how great must the numbers of those served have been? This point is open to question. The important thing to consider in this particular context is one of proportion rather than size of population. The very large number of clerical and semi-clerical offices suggests that a significant portion of Christians in Antioch held some sort of definable position or office in the church. The proliferation of clerical positions in Theodore and the *Apostolic Constitutions* suggests a similar concern.

R. A. Markus has argued that the influx of new converts challenged the identity of Christians with the result that they urged "a contraction in the scope ... allowed to the 'secular'" and "a tendency to absorb what had previously been 'secular' into the realm of the 'sacred,' turning secular into 'Christian' or dismissing it as 'pagan' and 'idolatrous.'"[87] Markus concerns himself with a certain kind of negative self-definition and delineation in which post-Constantinian Christians involved themselves. The sources discussed in this chapter show a slightly different understanding of this tendency. They are no less concerned with delineation, but at the same time they show a strong inclination toward a positive statement of Christian identity that fully and officially attached a great many people to the Christian church. The result was a vigorous hierarchy with a strong sense of authority that actively sought, through that very hierarchy, to incorporate Christians into the body of the church. The catechumens who sought baptism wanted this attachment and the benefits, both sacred and secular, it had to offer. Through pursuing an image of sanctity, caring for the poor, and cultivating their priestly prerogative, bishops worked to articulate the idea of their church as the means of approaching God. The access

---

thoroughly involved with it through his Son Jesus. The main difference centered on where they chose to draw that line, between Father and Son (the non-Nicene position) or between Son and creation (the Nicene). The hierarchy described here technically works on either account. For an excellent discussion of Nicene and non-Nicene theology in the late fourth century, see Vaggione 2000.

[87] Markus 1990:53.

that he and his clergy provided was desirable and it drew people to the bishop's community. That people sought access to the holy outside of the strict hierarchy of the church and the person of the bishop only confirms the desirability of divine access he offered. Alongside this, however, we must take note of the fact that bishops increasingly had the ear of the emperor and were able to provide benefits from him. Because of their liturgical role and their persuasive claims to sanctity, bishops were able to exercise their freedom of speech (*parrhēsia*, παρρησία) before the emperor for the benefit of their community.[88]

This was a community that catechumens found compelling and to which they wanted to join themselves. As they approached baptism, the candidates became enmeshed in the social world of this community. Assigned baptismal sponsors who acted as their advocates and guides, they began an elaborate process of being acculturated to a new community and a new way of relating to a prominent institution within the life of the late antique city. Certain pieces of epigraphic evidence even suggest that something similar took place in Antioch's rural hinterland, where we catch a glimpse of a careful process of negotiation between clergy and laity. For example, it seems that baptisteries were built only when it was thought that active ministry and the presence of clergy could be sustained in a region. In other words, an established community was seen as a prerequisite for proselytism in the Antiochene countryside. When this activity did go ahead, we can see that the Christians of these regions then went on to appropriate Christian phrases and symbols in very personal ways.[89] All of these texts and material remains show a deep concern for the process by which the church made new Christians and delineated them from those outside the church. Above all, the evidence shows the considerable effort necessary to incorporate people into the ecclesiastical structures of the community in meaningful ways.

One must keep in mind the nature and structure of this community when considering catechesis in late fourth-century Antioch. Initiation into the Christian church entailed initiation into a social network that manifested itself in multiple ways. The Christian community understood ostensibly mundane matters, such as the maintenance of systems of social welfare and justice, as part of a spiritual hierarchy connected to God through the ranks of the clergy and particularly the person of the bishop. Thus the intimate relationship between the baptismal sponsor and the catechumen began the process of rightly relating that person to the community in all of its intricacies as a conduit to God, as well as to other forms of earthly power. The opportunity to obtain citizenship in this

---

[88] Rapp 2005:264–265.
[89] Trombley 2004.

city, to return to Theodore's language, with all of its rights and responsibilities surely played a significant role in convincing people to become Christians. The incremental participation of catechumen, candidate, and full initiate, along with sincere attempts by the church at incorporation along the way, enabled people to feel themselves persuaded by Christianity. I borrow this phrase, "feel persuaded," from the title of a useful essay by Chad Kile, which presents a compelling case for the serious consideration of social networks in attempts to understand Christianization.[90] While this observation certainly points in the right direction, Kile too strongly critiques earlier models for having any significant cognitive component in their approach to Christianization.[91] The acculturation aimed at through the catechetical process placed significant emphasis on instruction and culminated in the conversion rites of baptism and the eucharist. These activities presented regular opportunities for the community to communicate its values to those about to join it and must not be overlooked. At this point, we will turn to the presentation of theology and consider Theodore's approach to the teaching of the creed.

[90] Kile 2005.
[91] Kile 2005 critiques Stark (p. 224) and Nock (p. 222).

4

Teaching the Creed

WE HAVE SEEN THE RICH VARIETY of official positions in the church and considered the construction of a hierarchy as a way to create stakeholders within the Christian community. The higher clergy, especially the bishops, put considerable effort into maintaining their position in matters both secular and religious. However, they exercised that power in part by collecting substantial numbers of lower clergy and non-clerical actors who received official positions within the church. This inclination toward incorporation and the creation of stakeholders extended as well to proselytism and the initiation of new Christians. Through what must have been a range of mechanisms, people encountered Christian ideas, communities, and sources of religious power, such as holy men and healing shrines. These experiences led to the formation of communal ties and relationships. Full initiation into the church, however, went beyond mere participation in community. We have already seen that a key component of the relationship between converts and baptismal sponsors centered on the adoption of Christian moral norms. This acceptance of ethical ideals began the process of forming Christian habits and ways of understanding one's place in church and society. Now we turn to the most overtly didactic aspects of the process of incorporating new Christians. Following the registration of sponsor and cate-chumen with the proper authorities of the church, catechesis proper began. As we consider the teaching component of Christian initiation, we must keep the communal backdrop in mind. Sponsors and catechumens came to the church regularly, at least every other day, for the purpose of listening to the teaching of a priest or bishop. Preachers addressed both directly in their sermons and expected the sponsors to assist the catechumens as they learned the creed and struggled with the theology contained in it.

Theodore's formal preaching of the catechetical homilies began with his teaching on the creed. He devoted ten sermons to his commentary on the creed, which he worked his way through in a straightforward fashion. Homily 1 begins with an introduction to catechesis and the types of things that his catechumens would be exposed to in this teaching. Towards the conclusion of this first sermon,

Theodore moves on to discuss God the Father. He continues his teaching on the Father in Homilies 2 and 3. Fully half of the sermons on the creed, numbers 4 through 8, focus on the Son. Homily 9 focuses on the Holy Spirit, while the final sermon on the creed continues Theodore's presentation of the doctrine of the Spirit and also discusses his theology of the church. These sermons display a method of interpretation and commentary very reminiscent of Theodore's commentaries on the Bible. Theodore's commentaries demonstrate a close reading of his source with the intent of isolating the divine message as expressed in the historical narratives contained in the text.[1] Similarly, Theodore's catechesis moves methodically through the text of the creed. He focuses on a clear presentation of his interpretation of the creed with only minimal embellishments to stress logical connections or provide illustrative examples. As with his commentaries, his catechesis takes particular interest in emphasizing the biblical history behind the teaching of the creed as an argument for its validity.

Given the logical progression of the creed from Father to Son to Holy Spirit to the church, it might appear that Theodore's straightforward presentation sought merely to orient the catechumens to the distinctive theological features of Nicene Christianity.[2] In one sense, this is precisely what his sermons aimed to do. However, a careful reading of these sermons, one that takes into consideration the pedagogical concerns of the sermons and the place of catechesis within the community, reveals a pedagogical method more concerned with incorporating catechumens into the believing community than with the creation of people thoroughly versed in the intricacies of a philosophically demanding theological system. Theodore clearly held education as a critical task but he also consistently situated his theological lessons within the context of communal participation and the liturgical expression of theology in the recitation of the creed. While the procedure for enrolling catechumens aimed to produce converts in pursuit of the moral norms of the community, the teaching of the creed sought to encourage converts to adopt the outlook of the community. We turn at this point to consider Theodore's teaching on the creed and his pedagogical approach to this education.

The Theology of the *Catechetical Homilies*

Theodore's teaching on the creed begins where the creed does, with a discussion of God the Father. His text reads, "I believe in one God, Father Almighty," and Theodore used this text as a starting point for emphasizing the unity of

[1] On Theodore's hermeneutical method, see chapter one.
[2] On the theology of Theodore's preaching on the creed, see Gerber 2000.

God.[3] The concern addressed by this teaching was twofold. Theodore wanted to remove what he saw as the errors of polytheism and Arianism. Indeed, Theodore saw these two errors as related in a significant way. Polytheism was a simple enough error to address. While the Hebrew Bible inherited by Christians had stressed the oneness of God, the Greco-Roman tradition generally considered the divine to be manifest in a variety of divine persons. Even pagan monotheists whose philosophical conception of divinity stressed a supreme divine unity still accepted notions of worshipping the divine that acknowledged diversity of manifestation.[4] We hear so much about Christian monotheism that it is important to note the persistent need Christians had to reaffirm a connection to Jewish monotheism. The Christian world of Late Antiquity was full of angels and demons, not to mention holy men and the deceased, but ever-present, saints of the church.[5] A preacher at the end of the fourth century could not take it for granted that his audience held acceptable views on such matters. When uninitiated catechumens comprised the audience, the situation would have been more acute still.

The most immediate threat to the unity of God that Theodore sought to combat, however, was the error of the so-called Arians. Recall that these sermons were delivered around 392, shortly after Nicene theology emerged victorious at the Council of Constantinople but while Antioch remained a city divided between theological camps. This ecumenical meeting came together in the year 381 in hopes of bringing to an end a bitter theological controversy that had persisted throughout most of the fourth century. As we discussed in chapter one, the issues debated pertained to the divinity of the Son. What was the nature of Christ's divinity? What was the nature of his submission to the will of the Father? Was his divinity somehow derivative in a way that placed him in a category subordinate to the Father? Eventually the ecumenical decision at Constantinople, a slightly modified version of the Nicene formula, would hold sway throughout the majority of Christian communities, but this took some time and, as Theodore preached these sermons, the rifts caused by the theological battles of the fourth century persisted.

While the nature of the Son was the most pressing issue debated, it was impossible to do this without relating the Son to the nature of divinity. The Nicenes were convinced that the non-Nicene position, which they successfully

---

[3] *WS* 5.24.

[4] Frede 1999:55.

[5] On attempts by Augustine and Shenoute to Christianize the late antique concept of spiritual beings, see Brown 1992a:94–95. For an interesting discussion of the ways in which Christians were susceptible to many of the attacks they made against pagans for worshipping lesser divine beings, see Frede 1999:60–68. Regarding saints and holy men, see Frank 2000; Rapp 1999:63–82.

branded as "Arian," contained deep theological errors.[6] They often talked in terms of the non-Nicenes diminishing Christ, of the way that they separated him from God by declaring him to be a lesser divinity. The Nicenes simply refused to believe that any created being could possess a divinity worthy of God's Son. As non-Nicene notions of Sonship entailed a coming into being, it was impossible for Nicenes to accept their repeated claims that they did indeed believe Christ to be divine. The main differences focused on the nature of divinity.[7] When the Nicenes did take at face value the claim that non-Nicenes accepted Christ's divinity, they usually took the occasion to deride them for dividing God.[8] If Father and Son were as ontologically distinct as the non-Nicenes claimed, and they were both divine, then from the Nicene perspective this required a concept of God that was incompatible with Christian monotheism. Theodore adopted this tradition as he stressed the unity of God against the opponents he labels as Arian and Eunomian.[9] Large numbers of the inhabitants of Antioch in the early 390s would have at some point been a part of a community opposed to the Nicene theology espoused at the Council of Constantinople. Theodore sought to ensure that the candidates for baptism knew the proper definition of the faith.

Following the structure of the creed, Theodore turned to the doctrine of the Son for a full five sermons. He stressed throughout these sermons that Christ had two clearly distinct natures (Syriac *kyānā*; Greek *physis*), one divine and one human, dwelling in a single person (Syriac *parṣupā*; Greek *prosōpon*).[10] The fact that this language would get Theodore into trouble later as Christological language developed is not particularly relevant for our purposes here. Rather, we must note Theodore's attempt to articulate for the baptismal candidates an understanding of full humanity and full divinity existing in one Christ. In doing this, Theodore offered Christological themes developed over the preceding decades to counter non-Nicene theology. For example, he insisted that the Fatherhood and Sonship discussed in the New Testament denote eternal relationships and not the normal procreation of humans.[11] Theodore also sought to thwart what he saw as attacks upon the person of Christ by the theology of Apollinaris, who argued that Christ was a man with a divine mind or intellect (*nous*).[12] Against this, the catechesis focuses strongly on the humanity of Christ. While the creed mentioned only the birth from Mary and the crucifixion under

---

[6] On the application of the label "Arian" in ancient and modern treatments of non-Nicene theologians, see R. Williams 1987:1–22; and Lyman 1993.

[7] Vaggione 2000.

[8] Gregory of Nyssa *Against Eunomius* 1.176.

[9] WS 5.55.

[10] WS 5.63–64.

[11] WS 5.29–30.

[12] *Against Apollinaris*, PG 66:995.

Pontius Pilate, Theodore spoke to the candidates at length about the child-hood, life, teaching, and miracles of Christ.[13] For Theodore, if Christ was not fully human, then there was no point in the incarnation. If redemption could be accomplished by the divine mind (*nous*), then there was no need for God to join himself to human nature at all.[14] Theodore taught the candidates in no uncertain terms that Christology was a matter of soteriology. The baptism, obedience, death, and resurrection of Christ's humanity made humanity redeemable.[15] If Christ was not fully human, then the incarnation was for naught.[16]

Theodore reserved less time in his catechetical curriculum for the discussion of the Holy Spirit and the Church. The theological issues raised at the Council of Nicaea had focused on the relationship between the Father and the Son. However, the subsequent disagreements over the wording and theology of the creed also took up the issue of the status of the Holy Spirit. Theodore's arguments here are rather weak. He states plainly that the participants in the council simply added the name of the Holy Spirit because the real disagreement was about Christ. Theodore argued that by mentioning the Holy Spirit along with the Father and the Son, the intent was clearly to apply all the discussion of the Son's divinity to the Holy Spirit as well.[17] Theodore strengthened this assertion by connecting this piece of theology to Christian baptism. Citing Matthew 28.19, he appealed to the Trinitarian nature of baptism in the name of the Father, Son, and Holy Spirit as securing the full divinity of the Spirit.[18] Furthermore, if the Spirit were not fully divine, he would not be able to play his role as the one who secures the benefits of baptism.[19]

This baptismal focus ties in directly with Theodore's rather brief teaching on the church. Following the creed, Theodore linked the church and baptism, essentially defining the church for the candidates as a baptizing community.[20] He stressed in this context that the members of that community should be as closely knit together into one body as the two natures of Christ were in his one person.[21] This body, united in right worship of God, constituted the church of the creed as Theodore presented it to his baptismal students.[22]

---

[13] *WS* 5.62–63.
[14] *WS* 5.56. On the soteriological motivation of Theodore's Christology, see Greer 1961:66–85.
[15] *WS* 5.76–77.
[16] *WS* 5.51.
[17] *WS* 5.92.
[18] *WS* 5.94–95.
[19] *WS* 5.108. Of course, the non-Nicenes, employing a different notion of divinity, interpreted the mention of three names as distinguishing between three different essences and three different activities; see 2000:137.
[20] *WS* 5.111–112.
[21] *WS* 5.113–114.
[22] *WS* 5.112.

This summary outlines the basic theological material Theodore presented from the creed. A number of studies have used these homilies for the purpose of addressing questions related specifically to the subsequent Christological debates with which Theodore and his legacy became entangled during the course of the fifth and sixth centuries.[23] With the canonically questionable nature of the Fifth Council as a backdrop, several scholars have attempted to address the question of whether or not Theodore actually held the views he was accused of holding.[24] Not only is such an inquiry of questionable historical value for an inquiry into Theodore's catechesis, it also suggests a misleading approach to Theodore's catechetical curriculum.

This does not mean that a study of the fifth- and sixth-century Christological debates is unwarranted. Indeed, much work remains to be done on these developments and particularly on how they played out within and between the various religious communities and confessions involved. Rather, I refer here to the fact that most inquiries of this sort address theological rather than historical concerns. At the root is a concern over whether Theodore was rightly condemned at the Fifth Council. His condemnation, coming as it did well after his death and therefore based on charges he could not answer, was certainly not canonical. Thus the aim here is not to analyze Theodore's theology in order to determine whether or not he held erroneous views. This theological question has been addressed by other scholars and does not concern us directly here. Instead, this study sets out to analyze Theodore as a catechist. How Theodore structured his catechesis and the rhetorical devices he used to explain the Christian religion to those entering the community will command the focus in what follows.

Theodore's Pedagogy

An interest in the pedagogy of these homilies does not come from some alien source but rather from the sermons themselves. Throughout the catechesis, Theodore demonstrates a deep concern for the role he assumed as teacher of converts to Christianity. He repeatedly discusses the nature of his instruction and how he has structured his catechesis for maximal impact. He took his charge as catechist seriously; he cared about the effect of his teaching and the lessons that his students would hear and, he hoped, internalize through catechesis.[25]

---

[23] For a more detailed treatment of Theodore's teaching on the creed, which focuses on the question of whether or not Theodore was rightly condemned at Constantinople 553, see Gerber 2000.

[24] Among the many works from varying perspectives, see Jugie 1935; Richard 1943; Devreesse 1948; and Sullivan 1951.

[25] On the related notion of divine *paideia* in Theodore, see Becker 2006:112–125.

Theodore labored to explain in simple language theological concepts that were often quite abstruse and he did so in a context where the stakes could be very high. Well-educated and deeply learned theologians had wrestled with the concepts and terminology surrounding the relationship between the Father and the Son for most of the fourth century. The catechist found himself in the position of needing to present these same ideas to a lay audience, many of whom would not have had the philosophical background or knowledge of Christian scriptures available to the more highly educated among the clerical elites. In a context where the consequences of error were great, a priest like Theodore assumed a tremendous burden as he catechized these converts. The fourth-century debates had consistently been heated. As opinions shifted, imperial and popular support likewise vacillated. Bishops taking a number of different positions found themselves alternately exiled from their sees and reinstated. Furthermore, this was not a simple intellectual exchange. Accusations of false belief and heresy hung over these debates. People genuinely believed that their party rightly understood the issues and that those opposed to their approach were anathema, fit only to be condemned as heretics and purged from the Christian community along with their errors. The stakes were high, and clergy worked diligently to produce Christians loyal to them and to their notions of proper theology.

Recent work on Arianism makes this point very well. A careful look at the debates of the fourth century clearly shows a wide range of opinion on the proper understanding of the relationship between the Father and the Son.[26] However, Athanasius and a handful of likeminded theologians launched an active campaign to link together those who failed to accept the Nicene term *homoousios*. Anything less than acceptance of this notion of an identity between the Father and the Son was equated with the teaching of Arius. In this way, Athanasius and others constructed an Arian theology where one did not actually exist. In reality, however, theologians struggled with the implications of *homoousios* for myriad reasons, not necessarily because they accepted the theology of Arius.

This work has been invaluable for our understanding of many of the theological and political developments that took place between the first and second ecumenical councils. It would be misleading, however, to see in this only the fluidity of theological positions and categories that existed on the ground in the fourth century. We must also duly note the tremendous power of theological branding. A relatively small group was able to corral disparate positions together, effectively label them as heresy, and ultimately anathematize their

---

[26] Hanson 1988; Gwynn 2007; R. Williams 1987; and Vaggione 2000.

adherents. Theology mattered in this context. Even if we were to set a greater interpretative stress on power politics than on a detached pursuit of theological understanding, we must still recognize that the consequences of theological belief remained profound. The personal, communal, and political ramifications of one's beliefs could be considerable. Theodore's understanding of the weight of these matters pervades his catechesis. He tailored his instruction so that his pupils would come into the church with the proper understanding of the contentious matters of the creed. How he approached this task will occupy the remainder of this chapter.

Theodore's language of education

Given the acerbic atmosphere that could surround theological allegiances, it should hardly surprise that concerns about sound pedagogy would occupy the mind of a catechist. His sermons, in conjunction with the rest of the initiatory process, would constitute the foundation for the converts' understanding of the beliefs central to the community they were joining. Not only do Theodore's sermons bear the marks of someone who thought carefully about these matters, they also contain a surprising number of references to teaching and pedagogical strategy. A favorite biblical text of Theodore was Matthew 28.19–20, the command of Jesus to the disciples, "Go therefore and make disciples of all the nations, baptizing them in the name of the Father and of the Son and of the Holy Spirit, teaching them to observe all things that I have commanded you; and lo I am with you always, even to the end of the age." Theodore's understanding of catechesis as a period of instruction culminating in baptism fits very well with the themes of this text. He quotes it directly over a half dozen times throughout his sermons on the creed.

The Syriac text of Theodore's catechesis contains a range of terms dealing with teaching and the passing on of information.[27] Prominent among these are words deriving from the roots *ylp* (ܝܠܦ), *lmd* (ܠܡܕ), *šlm* (ܫܠܡ), *yd* (ܝܕ), and *ydʿ* (ܝܕܥ). The root *ylp* means "to know; to perceive, to be able." The form employed most often in the catechesis means "to teach, inform, or train" and likely translates Greek *didaskō* (διδάκσω).[28] Nominal forms derived from *ylp*, *yulpānā* (ܝܘܠܦܢܐ) and *malpānuṭā* (ܡܠܦܢܘܬܐ), recur as well. They share a similar semantic range including teaching and doctrine. They regularly translate related Greek terms *didakē* (διδακή) and *didaskalia* (διδασκάλια). These terms denote the basic material conveyed in the course of the catechetical lectures or some other source, such as a particular biblical text. They can also refer to "doctrine" in a more

27   Becker 2006:115.
28   Payne Smith 1879, 1:1599–1600; see the Peshitta of Matthew 28.20.

100

technical theological sense. In this case, they refer to a systematic statement on a particular theological point, such as the oneness of God or the divinity of the Holy Spirit. Alongside the various forms of *ylp*, the root *ydᶜ* also occurs. In the form employed, this verb bears the meaning "to make known, show, point out, tell, inform, instruct."[29] The root often translates Greek *gignōskō* (γιγνώσκω), "to know," with the form occurring in the catechesis generally representing *gnōrizō* (γνωρίζω) and expressing the idea of producing knowledge or causing it to come about in the subject of instruction.

The translator of Theodore's catechesis often employed forms of the root *lmd*, meaning "to put together, compile." However, the verbal form most often employed bears the meaning "to make a disciple, teach the Christian faith, convert" and represents Greek *mathēteuō* (μαθητεύω).[30] Two nouns deriving from this form also appear often in Theodore's catechesis. The text regularly employs *talmidā* (ܬܠܡܝܕܐ), the normal Syriac term for a disciple of Jesus, *mathētēs* (μαθητής). These were the students of Jesus but also his followers in a more intimate sense than the teacher-student relationship might suggest. The catechesis uses this term for both the original twelve disciples and the catechumens who are in the process of converting. Another noun frequently in use also comes from this same root. *Talmiduṯā* (ܬܠܡܝܕܘܬܐ) bears a range of meanings, all of which are relevant to the theme of education and teaching in these sermons. Mingana alternately translates it as "initiation," "teaching," or "discipleship." He prefers these terms, while also noting that it sometimes has the sense of "the 'catechumenate' or the state of being a 'catechumen.'"[31] The semantic range of this term makes it difficult to pinpoint the Greek equivalent. *Mathēma* (μάθημα) would offer a cognate of *mathētēs*, but *didakē* provides an alternative that is just as likely. Regardless, the repeated use of the root *lmd* nicely highlights the emphasis placed on the educational aspect of catechesis.

The frequent use of two additional terms further develops our understanding of Theodore's conscious concern for education. The root *šlm* appears in two forms. The basic meaning of the verb is "to come to an end, be finished, concluded." The verb appears regularly in a form that has the connotation of committing a lesson or idea to the hearer.[32] Greek *paradidōmi* (παραδίδωμι) probably lies behind the Syriac here, and the term is best translated with "to commit" or "to hand over."[33] Another form in which the root *šlm* occurs is the nominal form *mšlmānuṯā* (ܡܫܠܡܢܘܬܐ). Often rendered by Mingana as "teaching," *mšlmānuṯā* has

---

[29] Payne Smith 1879, 1:1554–1558. The verb used in the catechesis takes the causative Aphel form.
[30] Payne Smith 1879, 2:1954; see the Peshitta of Matthew 28.19.
[31] WS 5.104n2.
[32] Payne Smith 1879, 2:4183–4188. Again the Aphel recurs in the catechesis.
[33] Mingana prefers "to hand down," but often uses "to teach" as well.

a connotation of tradition. It likely translates *paradosis* (παράδοσις) and refers to something handed down from Christian forbearers or even from Christ himself.[34] The final critical term to appear in this context is *tawdiṭā* (ܬܘܕܝܬܐ). Given the creedal context of these sermons, this should be expected. The basic meaning of the term is "confession" or "profession," and it could translate either *homologia* (ὁμολογία) or *eucharistia* (εὐχαριστία). *Tawdiṭā* occasionally means confession or profession in the catechesis, but it also refers by extension to the substance of that profession, the doctrine that makes up the confession.[35]

The text heightens its effect by the proliferation of this pedagogical terminology, often within a single paragraph. Allow one example to suffice where many could be offered:

> After the words concerning God, they proceeded to the teaching [*malpānuṭā*] of the persons, which is the true teaching [*tawdiṭā*] of the Christian faith and the true knowledge [*idaʿṭā*] for those who become disciples [*meṭṭalmədin*] of Christ. Because the sentence denotes Divine nature, it refers to the three persons, but as the teaching [*malpānuṭā*] concerning the persons could not be considered as referring to one of them only, they rightly spoke to us of what is due to each person separately. At the beginning of their sentence they placed the Father from whom are the Son and the Holy Spirit. The Father is truly the one who is a Father alone, but we hold each one of the three persons to be God, because Christ included this true doctrine [*yulpānā*] in His teaching [*tawdiṭā*] concerning these three persons.[36]

This layered application of pedagogical language recurs throughout Theodore's sermons on the creed and testifies to his emphasis on catechesis as an educational system.

Theodore did not limit his discussion of pedagogy to the act of catechesis. Rather, he applied the language of education to many different subjects. He

---

[34] Payne Smith 1879, 2:4193.

[35] Payne Smith 1879, 2:1552.

[36] WS 5.29; *Homélies Catéchétiques* 2.10r: ܡܢ ܒܬܪ ܡܠܐ ܕܥܠ ܐܠܗܐ ܝܨܦܘ ܠܗܘܢ ܡܠܦܢܘܬܐ ܕܩܢܘܡܐ

presents Christ,[37] the disciples,[38] scripture,[39] and natural law[40] as teachers at various points in the catechesis. For example, in the previous quotation, "The words concerning God" mentioned at the beginning, refer back to the first line of the creed, "I believe in one God." The subject "they" mentioned throughout the passage refers to the bishops who composed the creed, in Theodore's language, "the blessed Fathers."[41] Thus the creed preserves and disseminates the teachings of this group whose esteem Theodore appeals to in the course of his own teaching.

Memory and repetition

As the organizing principle of the first ten catechetical sermons, the creed and its authors have a firm presence in Theodore's catechesis. Theodore, in the course of teaching the candidates the Christian faith, enters into a sort of dialog with the Fathers who wrote it. Keen to present them as teachers of the Christian faith, Theodore emphasizes the tight phrasing and summary nature of their creed. They did this intentionally so that the creed could be easily understood and committed to memory. In his fifth sermon he asserts:

> Our Fathers, however, took trouble to say all these things in short terms so that the hearers might learn them with ease, and so that we might also learn thoroughly every one of them from the Sacred Books. They wrote and arranged the Creed in short terms, and this is the reason why they said: *Who was born of the Virgin Mary and was crucified in the days of Pontius Pilate.* They only said the beginning and the end of the Economy that took place on our behalf, as the beginning of all grace is His birth of Mary, and its end is crucifixion.[42]

Theodore thus exhorted his audience to learn from the creed by committing it to memory. However, he also used the sparse wording of the creed as an opportunity to fill in much of the life of Jesus, demonstrating his particular interest in historical context and the historicity of the incarnation. He mentions

---

[37] *WS* 5.27.
[38] *WS* 5.94.
[39] *WS* 5.28.
[40] *WS* 5.44.
[41] *WS* 5.29.
[42] *WS* 5.63; *Homélies Catéchétiques* 6.34r: ܠܐ ܣܟܠܘܗܝ ܗܘܘ ܠܐܕܬܝ ܕܠܚܕܠܟ ܘܠܚܕܠܟ ܕܚܩܦܝܚܐ ܢܘܚܕܗ

the infancy of Jesus, as well as his baptism.[43] Throughout this presentation of Jesus' life, Theodore adds numerous references to his divinity and sinless life, drawing heavily on the Pauline corpus in doing so.[44] In this way, Theodore used the teaching of the Fathers as a mnemonic device. He preached a fuller version of Jesus' life and a theological interpretation of it based on a simple phrase in the creed.

Theodore's use of the creed as another mnemonic device is only one of the pedagogical strategies he used. In the course of presenting his lessons, Theodore employed a number of techniques to help his students retain the information he presented. He intentionally repeated things for the benefit of the catechumens. In particular, he often began a homily with a summary of the preceding one. Homily 2 begins, "Yesterday we spoke to your love sufficiently, and in the measure granted to us by the grace of God, of faith which is the foundation of the principle of religion. We approached the words of our profession of faith and showed how through faith in one God all the error of the polytheism of the Gentiles vanishes completely."[45] The first homily had explicated the beginning of the creed, "I believe in one God the Father." Theodore's lesson focused on the oneness of God as a refutation of pagan polytheism. This single point summarized that sermon. Theodore began the fourth homily in a similar fashion, saying, "Yesterday we endeavored to interpret to your love, according to our ability and in a succinct manner, the things said by our blessed Fathers concerning the Divinity of the Only Begotten, while we kept the remainder of them for another day."[46] In this instance as well, Theodore called to mind the subject of his teaching from the prior day while also emphasizing the main point he wanted his listeners to take to heart. This constant repetition of main themes appears throughout Theodore's catechesis as a mnemonic device.

Theodore often repeated his main points and themes within a single sermon. He sought to simplify the often very intricate implications theologians drew from the creed by fostering this mode of presentation. This habit has not always endeared Theodore to his readers, however. Mingana agrees with Harnack in his introduction to the catechesis that Theodore is "too prosaic and

43 *WS* 5.62, 67.

44 *WS* 5.68–71.

45 *WS* 5.27; *Homélies Catéchétiques* 2.8v: ܥܠ ܗܝܡܢܘܬܐ ܕܐܝܬܝܗ̇ ܫܬܐܣܬܐ ܕܪܫܐ ܕܬܘܕܝܬܐ ܕܕܚܠܬ ܐܠܗܐ ܠܘܬ ܚܘܒܟܘܢ ܐܝܟ ܕܡܨܝܐ ܠܢ ܒܛܝܒܘܬܐ ܘܕܐܠܗܐ ܐܬܡܠܝ ܡܠܠܢ. ܘܐܬܩܪܒܢ ܠܘܬ ܡ̈ܠܐ ܕܡܘܕܝܢܘܬܐ ܕܗܝܡܢܘܬܢ ܘܚܘܝܢ. ܕܐܝܟܢܐ ܒܗܝܡܢܘܬܐ ܕܚܕ ܐܠܗܐ ܟܠܗ̇ ܛܘܥܝܐ ܕܣܓܝܐܘܬ ܐܠܗ̈ܐ ܕܥܡ̈ܡܐ ܠܚܣܪܢܐ ܡܬܒܛܠܐ.

46 *WS* 5.43; *Homélies Catéchétiques* 4.20r: ܠܘܬ ܐܠܝܢ ܕܐܡܝܪ̈ܢ ܠܐܒܗ̈ܬܢ ܛܘܒܢ̈ܐ ܥܠ ܐܠܗܘܬܗ ܕܝܚܝܕܝܐ. ܐܬܡܠܝ ܐܝܟ ܚܝܠܢ ܐܬܦܢܝܢ. ܘܦܫܩܢ ܐܢܝܢ ܠܚܘܒܟܘܢ ܐܝܟ ܕܡܫܟܚܐ ܒܦܣܝܩܘܬܐ. ܟܕ ܢܛܪܢ ܠܫܪܟܗܘܢ ܐܚܪܢܐ ܒܝܘܡܐ.

monotonous."[47] This opinion concurs with that of Photius, whose ninth-century *Bibliotheka* includes a discussion of several theological works by Theodore. Photius did not know the catechesis, but he criticized the style of several other works by Theodore for their lack of a certain graceful artistry. He writes of Theodore, "There is much use of the oblique cases and participles, with frequent and ill-arranged repetition of the same idea; on returning to a concept one finds it more fully and circumstantially expounded than in the main account, which is utterly unmethodical."[48]

However one assesses the stylistic merits of Theodore's language, due effort ought to be expended upon understanding Theodore's own conception of what he is doing in his homilies. As he addressed his audience, Theodore reflected on the structure of his presentation and included a discussion of his aims. He carefully crafted his use of repetition as an aid for his students' comprehension.[49] This stated pedagogical aim speaks directly to Theodore's understanding of the catechesis and the deep pastoral concern he had to instruct the catechumens in their new faith. Throughout his presentation of the creed, Theodore combines repetition with an emphasis on a simplicity that is itself essential to his pedagogical method.

The Rhetoric of Simplicity

Theodore's rhetoric of simplicity demonstrates a genuine empathy for his students as they wrestled with the finer points of the theology he taught them. Several times during these homilies, the Syriac translates Theodore with *qlil qlil* (ܩܠܝܠ ܩܠܝܠ), "little by little."[50] Theodore used this phrase to emphasize that he packaged his teaching into small, hopefully digestible portions. In beginning his seventh sermon, he asserted, "This is the third day I am discoursing on this subject to your love, as I am anxious that you should learn it little by little [*qlil qlil*] and keep my words in your memory."[51] Homily 7 contains the third of five sermons on the topic of the Son. This material presents some of Theodore's most technically demanding of the whole catechesis. Here he reminded the catechumens, some of whom may indeed have struggled to follow along, that

[47] *WS* 5.17.

[48] Photius *Bibliotheca* 177.123a.

[49] Mingana makes a fleeting remark about student comprehension in his introduction, *WS* 5.17.

[50] One of two Greek phrases likely lies behind the Syriac *qlil qlil*: διὰ βραχέων and κατὰ μικρόν, both express a similar idea of something given out in small, manageable portions.

[51] *WS* 5.72; *Homélies Catéchétiques* 7.40v–41r: ܗܐ ܓܝܪ ܬܠܬܐ ܝܘܡܝܢ ܕܡܠܠ ܗܘܐ ܥܒܕܐ ܠܟܘܢ ܚܘܒܟܘܢ، ܡܡܠܠ ܐܢܐ ܡܛܠ ܕܚܦܝܛܘܬܐ ܐܝܬ ܠܝ ܕܒܡܠܠܐ ܩܠܝܠ ܬܐܠܦܘܢ، ܕܬܬܕܟܪܘܢ، ܠܡܕܥܢ ܗ̈ܘܝ ܕܡܠܟܘܢ، ܡܬܡܠܠܢ.

he had put considerable effort into breaking down the phrases of the creed and presenting them in manageable portions. He hoped that these smaller portions, repeated often, would stick in the memories of his students.

The most common way for Theodore to employ this *qlil qlil* was at the end of a sermon. He regularly begged the indulgence of his audience for the difficulty of the subject matter as he brought the homily to a close.[52] In concluding Homily 3, he said:

> We should be in need of many words if we intended to comment fully upon all things said by our blessed Fathers concerning the Divinity of the Only Begotten. In order, however, to lighten to you the burden of the many things that are said to you we shall utter them little by little [*qlil qlil*] so that you may better be able to hear and to learn them. With your permission, therefore, we shall put an end here to the things that were said to-day, and keep the things that follow (in the *credo*) to another day, and for all of them let us praise the Father, the Only Begotten Son and the Holy Spirit, now, always, and for ever and ever. Amen.[53]

Recognizing the potential burden presented by these difficult topics, Theodore reminded the catechumens of his efforts to compartmentalize his presentation and to give them manageable amounts to internalize during the course of a single sermon. In doing so, he also articulated his expectation that they would indeed learn and retain what he taught them.

Theodore often emphasized the mnemonic motivation behind his simplification. At the conclusion of his first homily, he said, "It is necessary that we should offer you an oral teaching about everything, little by little [*qlil qlil*], in order that you may be able to remember the things that are spoken to you, as these are indispensable to those who adhere to what has preceded."[54] Theodore expected his sermons to reach the catechumens and to have a lasting impact.

52 See the end of Homilies 1, 3, 5, 7, and 8.

53 *WS* 5.42–43; *Homélies Catéchétiques* 3.19v–20r: ܐܠܐ ܥܠ ܡ̈ܠܐ ܣ̈ܓܝܐܬܐ ܡܣܬܢܩܝܢ ܗܘܝܢ ܐܢ ܒܥܝܢ ܗ̄ܘܝܢ ܕܥܠ ܐܠܗܘܬܗ ܕܝܚܝܕܝܐ ܠܟܠܗܝܢ ܕܡܢ ܐܒܗ̈ܬܢ ܛܘܒܢ̈ܐ ܐܡܝܪ̈ܢ ܕܢܦܫܩ ܠܡܫܬܥܝܘ ܢܚܬܐ. ܕܠܐ ܕܝܢ ܢܗܠܝܢ ܕܡܬܐܡ̈ܪܢ ܕܣ̈ܓܝܐܬܐ ܢܝܩܪ̈ܢ ܥܠܝܟܘܢ ܩܠܝܠ ܩܠܝܠ ܡܫܡܥܝܢ ܠܟܘܢ: ܕܬܫܟܚܘܢ ܬܫܡܥܘܢ ܘܬܠܦܘܢ ܐܢܝܢ. ܘܗܫܐ ܒܥܒܕ ܗܢܐ ܒܦܘܣܩܢܐ ܕܝܠܟܘܢ ܐܘܣܦ ܒܗܘܢ ܠܗܠܝܢ ܕܝܘܡܢܐ ܐܬܡ̈ܠܠ. ܘܐܝܠܝܢ ܕܢܩܦܢ ܠܗܠܝܢ ܕܢܬܐܡ̈ܪܢ ܢܛܪ ܐܢܝܢ. ܠܝܘܡܐ ܐܚܪܢܐ. ܥܠ ܟܠܗܘܢ ܕܝܢ ܫܘܒܚܐ ܢܣܩ ܠܐܠܗܐ ܐܒܐ: ܘܠܒܪܐ ܝܚܝܕܝܐ: ܘܠܪܘܚܐ ܕܩܘܕܫܐ: ܗܫܐ ܘܒܟܠܙܒܢ ܘܠܥܠܡ ܥܠܡܝܢ ܐܡܝܢ܀

54 *WS* 5.26; *Homélies Catéchétiques* 1.8r: ܐܠܐ ܡܛܠ ܕܘܠܐ ܕܒܡܠܠܐ ܡܠܦܢܘܬܐ ܕܥܠ ܟܠܡܕܡ ܠܡܩܪܒܘ ܠܟܘܢ: ܕܬܫܟܚܘܢ ܐܦ ܠܡܬܕܟܪܘ ܐܢܝܢ ܠܗܠܝܢ ܕܡܬܐܡ̈ܪܢ ܡܬܡܠܠܢ: ܗܠܝܢ ܓܝܪ ܐܦ ܡܬܒ̈ܥܝܢ ܠܗܠܝܢ ܐܝܠܝܢ ܕܠܡܬܚܫܚܘ ܗܢܘܢ ܡܩܪܒܝܢ: ܐܝܟ ܕܢܩܦܢ ܠܗܠܝܢ ܕܩܕܡ.

The rhetoric of simplicity helped package his message into manageable lessons but also reinforced his expectations regarding their retention. At times, he voiced these expectations in the form of an admonition: "In the last days we coherently and sufficiently articulated to your love lessons on the doctrine concerning Christ according to the teaching of our blessed Fathers. Now it is up to you to remember the things spoken to you with such great diligence."[55] Theodore expected results from the efforts he put into his sermons and did not hesitate to communicate this to the catechumens.

Theodore was particularly sensitive to the idea that he might appear to overstep the bounds of what his hearers could bear. At times he almost apologizes, as in Homily 6, where he says, "I believe, however, that my speech has exceeded the limits as the words (which express) the Economy of the grace of Christ have only been delivered to us (in short terms) as given above."[56] He feared that he had needlessly complicated things by using so many more words than did the authors of the creed. Then he continued, "In order, therefore, that you may not receive a teaching which is not perfect and that we may not trouble you with many words, let us, by the permission of God, leave off here the things which will follow what has been said, and be satisfied with what has already been spoken to-day ..."[57] Theodore developed this theme of simplicity as an aid to the catechumens' learning.

This pedagogical aspect of simplicity in Theodore also finds a complement in a different rhetoric of simplicity with a long pedigree in Christian thought. This notion of simplicity, which appears in several of the epistles of the Pauline corpus, suggests a distrust of overly sophisticated thought, especially when that sophistication leaned in the direction of philosophical speculation. In Romans 1, Paul acknowledges his debt to Greek wisdom but also argues that the same Greek learning has essentially missed the forest for the trees: "So they are without excuse; for though they knew God, they did not honor him as God or give thanks to him, but they became futile in their thinking, and their senseless minds were darkened. Claiming to be wise, they became fools; and they exchanged the glory of the immortal God for images resembling a mortal human being or birds or

55 *WS* 5.82, translation mine; *Homélies Catéchétiques* 8.47v: ܡܠܦܢܘܬܐ ܕܥܠ ܡܫܝܚܐ ܗܕܐ، ܒܫܘܠܡܐ ܐܡܪ ܡܬܠܡܕܢܘܬܐ ܕܐܒܗ̈ܝܢ ܛܘ̈ܒܢܐ: ܗ̇ܫܐ ܕܝܠܟܘܢ ܗܝ ܕܬܥܗܕܘܢ ܠܗܝܢ ܚܘܒܟܘܢ، ܡ̈ܠܠܝܢ: ܕܐܡܠܠܢ، ܗ̣ܝ ܡܫܟܚ ܕܬܥܗܕܘܢ، ܠܗܝܢ ܗܠܝܢ ܕܠܘܬܟܘܢ، ܒܚܦܝܛܘܬܐ ܣܓܝܐܬܐ ܐܬܡܠܠ.

56 *WS* 5.72; *Homélies Catéchétiques* 6.40v: ܐܠܐ ܡܣܒܪܢܐ ܕܥܒܪܬ، ܠܡܫܘܚܬܐ ܕܡ̈ܠܬܐ ܗܠܝܢ ܕܐܬܡܠܠ ܥܠ ܗܝ ܡ̈ܠܐ ܕܡܕܒܪܢܘܬܐ ܕܛܝܒܘܬܗ ܕܡܫܝܚܐ ܗܠܝܢ ܠܢ ܐܫܬܠܡ.

57 *WS* 5.72; *Homélies Catéchétiques* 6.40v: ܡܛܠ ܕܠܐ ܢܗܘܐ، ܗܟܝܠ، ܡܠܦܢܘܬܐ ܕܠܐ ܓܡܝܪܐ: ܘܠܐ ܢܗܘܐ ܢܠܐܐ ܠܟܘܢ، ܒܣܘܓܐܐ ܕܡ̈ܠܐ: ܠܗܘܢ ܐܝܟܢܐ ܠܝ، ܡܦܣ ܐܠܗܐ ܢܫܒܘܩ ܗ̈ܢܝܢ ܕܢܩܦܢ ܠܗܠܝܢ ܕܐܬܐܡܪ. ܘܢܣܦܩ ܗܪܟܐ ܠܗܠܝܢ ܕܝܘܡܢܐ ܐܬܡܠܠ. ܘܢܗܒ ܬܫܒܘܚܬܐ ܠܐܒܐ ܘܠܒܪܐ ܘܠܪܘܚܐ ܕܩܘܕܫܐ: ܗܫܐ ܘܒܟܠܙܒܢ ܘܠܥܠܡ ܥܠܡܝܢ ܐܡܝܢ܀

four-footed animals or reptiles."[58] Thus the wisdom of the Greeks was not effective; it did not bear fruit where it should have. In other words, sophisticated wisdom could not be valued unequivocally.

Paul gives this theme fuller treatment in his first letter to the church in Corinth. He wrote 1 Corinthians when he heard that the church there was plagued with factions. In seeking to remedy this situation, he encouraged the church to simplicity and humility by offering a sustained discussion of the foolishness of the cross of Christ. He insisted that "God's foolishness is wiser than human wisdom, and God's weakness is stronger than human strength."[59] But Paul's notion of foolishness did not only apply to the cross. He insisted that the form and content of the message were alike foolish:

> When I came to you, brothers and sisters, I did not come proclaiming the mystery of God to you in lofty words or wisdom. For I decided to know nothing among you except Jesus Christ and him crucified. And I came to you in weakness and in fear and in much trembling. My speech and my proclamation were not with plausible words of wisdom, but with a demonstration of the Spirit and of power, so that your faith might rest not on human wisdom but on the power of God.[60]

Behind Paul's declaration of his own simplicity lies the idea that it would have been potentially deceptive if he had used clever speech or sought to woo his audience with sophistication. Humility and simplicity were preferable. Indeed they offered a proof of the truth of Paul's message.

Later Christians picked up on these themes and developed them within a variety of different contexts. Similar ideas appear repeatedly within the writings of the so-called Apostolic Fathers, written toward the end of the first century and the beginning of the second. These texts often denounce the arrogance and speculation of doubting or deceptive Christians. A favorite term for critiquing such ideas is *dipsychia* (διψυχία), double-mindedness. The term occurs several times in 1 and 2 Clement as well as the *Didache*. In the *Shepherd*

---

[58]   Romans 1.20–23: εἰς τὸ εἶναι αὐτοὺς ἀναπολογήτους·διότι γνόντες τὸν θεὸν οὐχ ὡς θεὸν ἐδόξασαν ἢ ηὐχαρίστησαν, ἀλλ᾽ ἐματαιώθησαν ἐν τοῖς διαλογισμοῖς αὐτῶν καὶ ἐσκοτίσθη ἡ ἀσύνετος αὐτῶν καρδία. φάσκοντες εἶναι σοφοὶ ἐμωράνθησαν, καὶ ἤλλαξαν τὴν δόξαν τοῦ ἀφθάρτου θεοῦ ἐν ὁμοιώματι εἰκόνος φθαρτοῦ ἀνθρώπου καὶ πετεινῶν καὶ τετραπόδων καὶ ἑρπετῶν.

[59]   1 Corinthians 1.25: ὅτι τὸ μωρὸν τοῦ θεοῦ σοφώτερον τῶν ἀνθρώπων ἐστίν, καὶ τὸ ἀσθενὲς τοῦ θεοῦ ἰσχυρότερον τῶν ἀνθρώπων.

[60]   1 Corinthians 2.1–5: Κἀγὼ ἐλθὼν πρὸς ὑμᾶς, ἀδελφοί, ἦλθον οὐ καθ᾽ ὑπεροχὴν λόγου ἢ σοφίας καταγγέλλων ὑμῖν τὸ μυστήριον τοῦ θεοῦ. οὐ γὰρ ἔκρινά τι εἰδέναι ἐν ὑμῖν εἰ μὴ Ἰησοῦν Χριστὸν καὶ τοῦτον ἐσταυρωμένον. κἀγὼ ἐν ἀσθενείᾳ καὶ ἐν φόβῳ καὶ ἐν τρόμῳ πολλῷ ἐγενόμην πρὸς ὑμᾶς, καὶ ὁ λόγος μου καὶ τὸ κήρυγμά μου οὐκ ἐν πειθοῖ[ς] σοφίας [λόγοις] ἀλλ᾽ ἐν ἀποδείξει πνεύματος καὶ δυνάμεως, ἵνα ἡ πίστις ὑμῶν μὴ ᾖ ἐν σοφίᾳ ἀνθρώπων ἀλλ᾽ ἐν δυνάμει θεοῦ.

of Hermas it appears over fifty times and constitutes one of the most important themes in the work: "Trust in the Lord, you who are double-minded, because he can do all things; he both turns away from you his wrath, and sends out plagues upon you who are double-minded. Woe to those who hear these words and disobey them; it would have been better for them not to have been born."[61] *Dipsychia* can simply refer to one's lack of faith or a weakness of mind producing a failure to adhere to Christian moral principles. Alongside this, however, the author refers to a double-mindedness that manifests itself in an arrogant sense that one's will and ideas are superior to God's. Relying on their own wisdom, the double-minded falter: "Thinking that they can find a better way, they go astray and wander about in misery, trudging through the wastelands."[62] The *Epistle of Barnabas* elaborates on this idea even more explicitly in urging that people not "be intimately associated with the lofty, but live with the humble and righteous. Accept as good the things that happen to you, knowing that nothing transpires apart from God. Do not be double-minded or double-tongued."[63] Simplicity emerges in these texts as a prominent Christian virtue. Properly maintained it should preserve the believer from numerous errors.

These first- and second-century pleas for Christian simplicity resonated with later generations as well. However intellectually rigorous Christian theology became or however well educated the practitioners of the art were, many Christians retained a robust suspicion of the excessively intellectual, especially when it could be characterized as prying into things that had not been revealed.[64] Denunciation of heresy was a prominent theme in Theodore's catechesis, and he often spoke to the candidates about the deceitful and erroneous theologizing of various heretics.[65] Heretics were often attacked for having overstepped the bounds of divinely ordained thought or worship. The fourth-century attacks on non-Nicene theology that culminated in the Council of Constantinople did just that.

An excellent example of the critique of insistence on theological precision can be found in the case of Eunomius. A fierce opponent of the term *homoousios* and its theological implications, Eunomius turned his considerable intellectual

---

[61] *Shepherd of Hermas* 23.6: Πιστεύσατε τῷ κυρίῳ, οἱ δίψυχοι, ὅτι πάντα δύναται καὶ ἀποστρέφει τὴν ὀργὴν αὐτοῦ ἀφ' ὑμῶν καὶ ἐξαποστέλλει μάστιγας ὑμῖν τοῖς διψύχοις. οὐαὶ τοῖς ἀκούσασιν τὰ ῥήματα ταῦτα καὶ παρακούσασιν· αἱρετώτερον ἦν αὐτοῖς τὸ μὴ γεννηθῆναι.

[62] *Shepherd of Hermas* 15.1: δοκοῦντες οὖν βελτίονα ὁδὸν δύνασθαι εὑρεῖν, πλανῶνται καὶ ταλαιπωροῦσιν περιπατοῦντες ἐν ταῖς ἀνοδίαις.

[63] *Shepherd of Hermas* 19.6–7: οὐδὲ κολληθήσῃ ἐκ ψυχῆς σου μετὰ ὑψηλῶν, ἀλλὰ μετὰ δικαίων καὶ ταπεινῶν ἀναστραφήσῃ. Τὰ συμβαίνοντά σοι ἐνεργήματα ὡς ἀγαθὰ προσδέξῃ, εἰδὼς ὅτι ἄνευ θεοῦ οὐδὲν γίνεται. Οὐκ ἔσῃ διγνώμων οὐδὲ δίγλωσσος·παγὶς γὰρ θανάτου ἐστὶν ἡ διγλωσσία.

[64] For the range of approaches to simplicity in the lives of saints, see Rubenson 2000.

[65] See, for example, *WS* 5.60, 62.

skills to the refutation of the Nicene doctrine. At times he saw considerable success, but ultimately his theology failed to satisfy even sympathetic non-Nicenes.[66] Eunomius insisted on precision of theological language above all else.[67] His confidence in the ability of humans to know God and in the ability of human language to describe God drove his approach to theological questions.[68] His insistence upon precision (*akribeia*) would ultimately be the source of his failure. To his opponents, his *akribeia* suggested an arrogant self-confidence. They found this approach all the more troubling since they believed that Eunomius' theology diminished Christ's divinity.[69] Thus Eunomius' theological method arguably diminished the Son while appearing to elevate Eunomius himself. This gave his critics considerable ammunition to use against him. But even his allies, who were in the process of trying to find an alternative to the formula of Nicaea, found that his relentless drive for *akribeia* lacked the flexibility necessary for the task.[70] The Cappadocians would ultimately respond to this type of theological argument with a strong insistence that the ontological distance between God and human beings meant that God was essentially unknowable outside his self-revelation. Gregory of Nyssa offers a statement representative of this conviction:

> The simplicity of the True Faith assumes God to be that which he is, viz., incapable of being grasped by any term, or any idea, or any other device of our apprehension, remaining beyond the reach not only of the human but of the angelic and of all supramundane intelligence, unthinkable, unutterable, above all expression in words ...[71]

In short, for the Cappadocians, God was not susceptible to human attempts at *akribeia*.[72] Ephrem the Syrian would take a different approach to the "Arian" theology he confronted. He derided Arian speculation as a grave theological concern.[73] In its place he offered a relentless stream of biblical imagery carefully

---

[66] Vaggione 2000:147.

[67] Eunomius *Liber apologeticus* 7.15; *Apologia apologiae* 2.284–285.

[68] Gregory of Nyssa *Against Eunomius* 1.162.

[69] Gregory of Nyssa *Against Eunomius* 1.186.

[70] Vaggione 2000:91.

[71] Gregory of Nyssa *Against Eunomius* 1.638: ἡ γὰρ ἁπλότης τῶν τῆς ἀληθείας δογμά τῶν τὸν θεὸν ὅπερ ἐστὶν ὑποτίθεται, οὔτε ὀνόματι οὔτε διανοήματι οὔτε τινὶ ἄλλῃ καταληπτικῇ ἐπινοίᾳ περιληφθῆναι δυνάμενον, οὐ μόνον ἀνθρωπίνης, ἀλλὰ καὶ ἀγγελικῆς καὶ πάσης ὑπερκοσμίου καταλήψεως ὑψηλότερον μένοντα, ἄφραστόν τε καὶ ἀνεκφώνητον καὶ πάσης τῆς διὰ λόγων σημασίας ἀνώτερον ...

[72] Vaggione 2000:265.

[73] *Hymns on Faith* 15.7: "Whoever makes 'inquiry' is a wounded member; may he be healed and not harm the whole body! And because he is poisoned, may the Healer of our pains cut him off and cast him out from the pasture!" Translation from Murray 1975:89.

directed toward upholding Nicene theology.[74] He took the route of poetical image over logical argument and, in doing so, left his unique stamp on the Syriac literary tradition. In the theological battle for hearts and minds, the ostensibly arrogant self-confidence and tireless pursuit of precision that characterized Eunomius' theology would ultimately fail to capture people's imagination. This kind of theologian could effectively be labeled a technician (*technologos*), one with a deft ability for argument but lacking the true Christian spirit necessary for theological understanding.[75]

In the Nicene examples discussed here, the authors engaged their audiences with the idea of simplicity and human shortcoming as one means of offering their preferred position as the correct position. None of these authors could be described as a simpleton, however. Indeed, the polemic against non-Nicenes was anything but anti-intellectual. The theological debates of the fourth century contained sophisticated and erudite argumentation on all sides of the issues. While the ideas and arguments were not at all simple, the rhetoric of simplicity tapped into a common expectation that the truth was straightforward. A complicated position, on the other hand, could bear the taint of deception or outright hubris. Speculative thought and prying into mysteries suggested tricks designed to lead astray the pure of heart, who would otherwise naturally find the simple truth satisfactory.

This description of the rhetoric of simplicity, however, raises questions. Is the idea merely rhetorical, actually hiding a reality that remains rather different? In other words, is simplicity really the deceptive position that masks its lie behind a false humility and a veneer of self-evident truth? On the one hand, these questions must receive an answer in the affirmative. This "simplicity" is not at all simple. On the other hand, in a certain qualified sense, those employing the rhetoric of simplicity were espousing self-evident truths. At least they were able to articulate an effective rhetoric of common sense, simplicity being a key component of this rhetorical presentation. In the case of Theodore's catechetical sermons, the rhetoric of simplicity joined other themes to construct what he presented as self-evident truth.

Sharing the Mind of the Community

We have seen Theodore's appeals to scripture and church tradition as means of legitimating his message. It remains to discuss another way in which Theodore argued for the self-evident nature of his teaching. In conjunction

---

[74] Though nearly forty years old, Murray 1975 remains the classic treatment of the theological symbolism in Aphrahat and Ephrem.

[75] Vaggione 2000:93.

with his appeals to texts, individuals, and traditions that had authority within his Christian community, Theodore consistently asserted that the content of his sermons was true as a matter of necessity. Scores of times throughout his teaching on the creed, terms suggesting the necessary or essential nature of the point Theodore asserts recur. The majority of these terms derive from the roots *wlā* (ܘܠܐ), *zdq* (ܙܕܩ), and *špr* (ܫܦܪ).[76]

The root *wlā* pertains to what is right or what ought to be the case.[77] The most common form of the term used in the catechesis is the abstract noun *wālitā* (ܘܠܝܬܐ).[78] It usually introduces a phrase whose meaning is assumed or which is presented as being necessarily true. The root *zdq* is used similarly. This root means "it is right, it ought, it is due."[79] The form appearing in the catechesis means "to justify" or "to declare righteous." This verb generally occurs in this forensic sense for the purpose of describing one aspect of Christian salvation.[80] The catechesis uses the root in this forensic sense only on occasion. It appears most often to present an assertion as simply right or correct, true as a matter of necessity. Forms of *špr* also appear. The basic root meaning, "to be beautiful, pleasing," is rarely the intended one.[81] Rather, the sense it often conveys is that something is right or appropriate. While we do not have the original Greek text of Theodore's sermons, we can compare similar constructions in extant Greek texts by Theodore. Theodore's commentaries on the Psalms and Minor Prophets regularly use the Greek terms *anagkaiōs* (ἀναγκαίως), *anagkē* (ἀνάγκη), *dei* (δεῖ), *kalos* (καλός), *dikaios* (δίκαιος), *dikaiōs* (δικαίως), *prepon* (πρέπον), and *eikotōs* (εἰκότως) in a similar fashion. We can safely assume that similar constructions lie behind the Syriac we have.

In the context of discussing baptism in the name of the Father, Son, and Holy Spirit, Theodore asserts that, "It was necessary [*zadeq*] for those who had rejected false gods and learned that Divine nature was one, eternal and the cause of everything, which is Father, Son and Holy Spirit, to receive through these names the gift of baptism which is bestowed for the sake of a wonderful

---

[76] Other terms with similar meanings also occur, though with much less frequency in the commentary on the creed. See, for example, ܐܡܠܟ, WS 5.185; ܦܠܐ, WS 5.137; ܬܚܫܚܬܐ, WS 5.228; ܚܫܚ, WS 5.196; ܠܠ, WS 5.152; and ܙܕܩܝܬ, WS 5.226.

[77] Payne Smith 1879, 1:1083–1084.

[78] This usually appears in an adverbial sense with a prefixed ܒ. Several times the translator also employed the adverbial form from the same root, ܘܠܝܬ.

[79] Payne Smith 1879, 1:1062–1063.

[80] For example, see the Peshitta of Romans 4.

[81] Payne Smith 1879, 2:4272–4273. Mingana translates it alternatively as "it is right," "is it fitting," or "it is with justice."

happiness and is the earnest of the future and ineffable benefits."[82] Theodore cannot actually provide a proof here. Rather, the necessity is something he simply asserts, expecting his students to adopt the position he puts forward. Similarly, he declares that "He is rightly [*bwāliṭā*] called the first-born of all the creatures, because He was first renewed, and then He renewed the creatures, while He is higher in honor than all of them."[83]

As we saw with his pedagogical language, the expressions concerning things that Theodore wants to present as obviously true also pile up upon one another. He declares:

> Since they took pains to teach us concerning His humanity, it is with justice [*bwāliṭā*] that before everything they set forth the reason for which Divine nature humbled itself to the extent of taking upon itself the form of a servant for us and of its caring for our salvation. It is with justice [*bwāliṭā*], therefore, that our Fathers, in beginning their teaching concerning the Economy of His humanity, formed the starting-point of their discourse from this purpose: For us children of men and for our salvation. It was also fitting [*špir*] on their part to place the words "for our salvation" after the words "for us children of men," in order that they might show the aim of His coming.[84]

With this kind of repetition, Theodore sought to leave the impression that the doctrine of the creed simply flowed naturally from one point to the next.

Theodore presented the teaching in his catechetical sermons as having many sources of authority. He repeatedly emphasized that scripture, tradition, and creedal statements coalesced to substantiate his preaching. He also made sure to present his lessons with the clarity and simplicity required of true wisdom. In case these more nuanced approaches failed to convince, Theodore

---

[82] WS 5.111–112; *Homélies Catéchétiques* 10.67v: ܐܠܬܗ̈ ܡܢ ܡܣܬܟܠܐܗ̈ܘ ܗܘܐ ܕܗܘ ܠܗܢ ܗܘܐ ܩܕܡ
[83] WS5.39; *HoméliesCatéchétiques* 3.17r: ܗ̈ܘܐ ܕܥ ܐܗܠ̈ ܐܠ ܐܗ̈ܒܙܐ: ܕܐܠܐ ܕܚܟܡ ܚܗ̈ܐ ܗܘ̈ܚܕ ܗܗ̈ ܕܐܠܟ̈ܗ ܗܘܟܠ
[84] WS 5.52; *Homélies Catéchétiques* 5.26v: ܗܘܡܝ. ܗܘܗ̈ ܐܢܚܗ̈ ܠܟܠ ܠܟܠܟܘܗ̈ ܕܐܗܣܟܟܗ ܒܝ ܐܗܠܝ.

resorted to attacking anyone who held a position at odds with his teaching. He attacked the adherents of contrary positions by insisting that they had depraved minds. In the context of explaining why the creed uses some language not found in scripture, Theodore declares:

> To those who have goodwill in religion the words written in the sacred Books would have been sufficient; these have been written also in the teaching of our blessed Fathers, who, however, because there are no adequate words easily to convince an evil mind, added of necessity to their teaching a statement which they chose in order to warn the children of the faith and refute the error of the heretics.[85]

This statement is designed to remove the charge of tampering with biblical teaching. Nevertheless, the implication for the hearers was clear. If they failed to agree, theirs were the evil minds. The simplicity of scripture's teaching and the careful guidance of the creed should be enough to satisfy the catechumens. Elsewhere, Theodore explicitly connected this theme with his emphasis on Christian teaching being simple when he said,

> but the measure of what we said was considered by us to be sufficient to all those who possess goodwill in religion, because to those who have an unwilling mind, even a long discourse will be of no avail, while to those who possess a good will a short discourse will suffice for the demonstration of the truth, when (this discourse) is drawn from the testimony of holy scripture.[86]

Theodore often urged his catechumens to be of good will in religion.[87] He emphasized that simplicity sufficed for the true and willing believer, while the double-minded person, the one who insisted on speculation and prying into

85 *WS* 5.104; *Homélies Catéchétiques* 10.62r–62v: ܠܐܝܠܝܢ ܗܘܐ ܕܪܓܝܓܝܢ ܛܒܐ ܒܕܚܠܬܐ ܕܐܠܗܐ ܣܦܩ ܠܗܘܢ. ܦܬܓܡܐ ܗܠܝܢ ܕܟܬܝܒܢ ܒܟܬܒܐ ܩܕܝܫܐ. ܐܬܟܬܒ ܕܝܢ ܐܦ ܒܡܠܦܢܘܬܐ ܕܐܒܗܝܢ ܛܘܒܢܐ. ܡܛܠ ܕܝܢ ܕܠܝܬ ܡܠܐ ܕܡܨܝܢ ܠܡܦܝܣܘ ܠܡܕܥܬܐ ܒܝܫܬܐ ܐܠܨܝܬ ܐܘܣܦܘ ܡܕܡ ܕܓܒܘܗܝ ܗܘܘ ܠܡܠܦܢܘܬܗܘܢ: ܠܙܘܗܪܐ ܕܒܢܝ ܗܝܡܢܘܬܐ ܘܡܟܣܢܘܬܐ ܕܛܘܥܝܝܐ ܕܗܪܣܝܘܛܐ:

86 *WS* 5.62; *Homélies Catéchétiques* 5.33v: ܐܠܐ ܡܫܘܚܬܐ ܠܢ ܡܬܚܫܒܐ ܕܗܘܝܢ ܕܐܡܪܢ ܠܐܝܠܝܢ ܕܪܓܝܓܝܢ ܛܒܐ ܒܕܚܠܬܐ ܕܐܠܗܐ ܐܝܬ ܠܗܘܢ. ܠܡܕܥܬܐ ܓܝܪ ܕܠܐ ܨܒܝܐ. ܐܦܠܐ ܡܫܠܡܘܬܐ ܕܡܠܐ ܕܡܬܐܡܪܢ ܡܘܬܪܐ ܡܕܡ. ܠܪܓܝܓܐ ܕܝܢ ܛܒܐ ܗܟܘܢ ܐܢܫ ܠܗ ܐܦ ܩܠܝܠ ܘܡܦܪܫܬܐ ܠܚܘܝܬܐ ܕܫܪܪܐ. ܐܡܬܝ ܕܡܢ ܣܗܕܘܬܐ ܕܟܬܒܐ ܩܕܝܫܐ ܢܬܐܡܪܢ.

87 This translates the Syriac ܪܓܝܓܐ ܛܒܐ ܒܕܚܠܬܐ ܕܐܠܗܐ. Often translated as "religion," ܕܚܠܬܐ ܕܐܠܗܐ literally means "fear of God"; see Payne Smith 1879, 1:864. This Syriac phrase often translates Greek *theosebeia* or *eusebeia*, meaning "piety or reverence." Theodore uses the term in a parallel passage extant in Greek (*Commentary on the Psalms* 45.16): "At any rate, for the one willing there is no difficulty in grasping the respect shown to the leaders of the churches, not only by their

mysteries, would never be satisfied. Of course, this was a common tactic in fourth-century theological polemic. In this situation where theological opponents shared a biblical text, they often spoke past one another in interpreting that text. They simply failed to grasp the theological vision that drove the interpretive method of their opponents. Such cases left a palpable sense that those on the other side of the theological divide were under a sinister, demonic influence. Their problem was an evil mind (*kakonoia*, κακονοία) as opposed to a good mind or will (*eunoia*, εὐνοία).[88] Eunomius used language very similar to Theodore's when he responded to the allegations of Basil of Caesarea, exclaiming "But these people really ought to give up! They have neither perceived the difference in the beings with wholesome eyes nor have they shown themselves right-minded judges of the actual objects—Judgment has hidden the truth from them on account of their ill-will."[89] Theodore introduces this commonplace of theological polemic into his catechetical classroom in order to preempt any abhorrent views from gaining traction among the candidates. This rhetoric was designed to leave the strong perception that those outside the community into which these candidates were about to be baptized were wholly other, not simply Christians of differing opinions but brazen heretics whose minds had been adversely affected by evil.

Theodore's entire approach to teaching the creed can be understood as an attempt to teach the baptismal candidates how to have this good kind of mind. We have seen how Theodore gave great attention to pedagogical method and placed considerable emphasis on teaching in these sermons, not only his own teaching but also the teaching of Christ, the Fathers, and their creed. He tried to parse the teaching of the creed in a way his students would find manageable. For many his instruction would have been very intellectually abstract material. Even his approach of teaching it "little by little" may well have rendered those not given to abstract reasoning a difficult time, and this in spite of Theodore's frequent repetition of key themes and language. Nevertheless, these sermons bear every mark of being delivered to a broad cross-section of society, not simply to an educated elite. Theodore does not engage in the heady intellectual discussion that forms the basis of Gregory of Nyssa's so-called *Great Catechism*.[90] These sermons were very carefully constructed to avoid extraneous philosophical

---

    own, but also by those opposed to the teaching of the true religion [*eusebeias*], who think them worthy of well-nigh complete reverence."

[88] Vaggione 2000:90.

[89] *Liber apologeticus* 23.1–4: Ἀλλ' οὗτοι μὲν μηθ' ὑγιαίνουσιν ὀφθαλμοῖς τὴν τῶν ὄντων κατανενοηκότες διαφοράν, μήτε δίκαιοι κριταὶ γενόμενοι τῶν πραγμάτων ἀφιέσθωσαν, διὰ κακόνοιαν ἐπικρυπτούσης αὐτοῖς τὴν ἀλήθειαν τῆς δίκης.

[90] Although this treatise bears the name "catechism," it has little resemblance to the lessons intended to introduce Christianity to those in the process of converting and pursuing baptism.

discussion and tedious use of technical terminology, which would have meant little to the majority of his audience.[91] Instead, we see an attempt to reach the full range of students Augustine had in mind when he wrote to the deacon Deogratias.[92] Theodore sought to produce likeminded members of a Christian community properly orientated toward God. This aim could not be served by the application of rigorous philosophical categories. Rather it called for a simple creed carefully explained.

As we saw in the introduction to the arrangement of Theodore's teaching on the creed, he concluded his teaching with a communal and liturgical focus.[93] The teaching of the creed led directly to the recitation of the creed preceding baptism. These combined acts would initiate the candidates into full membership in the Christian community. The context of Theodore's teaching was communal, with baptismal sponsors joining the candidates for these sermons. Theodore sometimes directed his preaching toward the sponsors, whom he hoped would join him in teaching the candidates by helping them to understand and memorize the creed.[94] Theodore thus employed the social ties involved in the process of catechesis to further engage the candidates and draw them more fully into the Christian community. These sponsors would continue to play a role in the process of initiation as the candidates approached baptism and the eucharist. The next chapter will take up Theodore's teaching on these rites and consider the role they played in making heavenly citizens out of baptismal candidates.

Rather this treatise is a philosophical discourse intended for monks studying theology. Lim (1995:164–171) takes this as paradigmatic of catechesis, which is highly misleading.

[91] There has been considerable debate on the subject of preaching and the composition of the late antique audience for preaching. For the view that late antique preaching was predominately, if not exclusively, directed towards elites, see MacMullen 1989. For a vigorous and compelling position to the contrary, see Maxwell 2006.

[92] See discussion in chapter two.

[93] *WS* 5.111–116.

[94] *WS* 5.21.

5

Teaching Liturgy and Performing Theology

HAVING CONSIDERED THE COMMUNAL and creedal aspects of Christian initiation, we turn here to the theme of cult and consider the role played by Theodore's discussion of the liturgy within his catechetical curriculum. The final five sermons in Theodore's educational program for baptismal candidates comment on the sacramental liturgies, three on baptism and two on the eucharist. The first sermon on each liturgy introduces in somewhat general terms the theological significance of the rite. The sermons then proceed to recount and interpret each statement and act involved in the performance of the liturgies. In particular, Theodore sought throughout these sermons to draw the catechumen's attention to some of the physical components of the liturgies' celebration. He focused on the actions, gestures, and dress of those celebrating the eucharist in order to highlight the liturgy as a participation in the life and doctrine of the church.

It has been the practice of liturgical scholars to approach a text such as Theodore's in the hope of reconstructing early liturgical forms. Some have used material from late fourth-century texts in conjunction with other liturgical texts from this period and earlier for the purpose of reconstructing some sort of a liturgical Ur-text. Other scholarly approaches have more highly valued the manifestation of particular liturgies and have sought to analyze the elements of a particular liturgy, noting its similarities and differences to other liturgies of similar or divergent periods and places.[1]

These approaches each have their merits and drawbacks. However, this study seeks to address a different set of questions and problems. While Theodore's catechesis does indeed provide considerable detail regarding the form and content of the liturgy in Antioch at the end of the fourth century, this was by no means his purpose in preaching. To be sure, the catechist did want to communicate these things to his students, but his aim in doing so was

---

[1] For the former view, see Dix 1954; also Saxer 1988. For the latter view, see Yarnold 1999; and Riley 1974. For a critique of a number of the methodological and theological assumptions of much of this literature, see Bradshaw 2002.

always to guide them in their experience of liturgy. His extended descriptions of each liturgical moment and consistent application of vivid language to these rites aimed to create the appropriate emotional response among his audience. Chapter four detailed the ways in which Theodore devoted the early sermons of his catechesis to a detailed explanation of the theological content of the creed. It is as if his words on the subject still hung in the air when he took up the teaching of the liturgy in the latter half of his catechetical curriculum. In initiating the catechumens into the mysteries of the Christian church, Theodore repeatedly emphasized the way in which each physical component of the liturgy was pregnant with theological meaning and how its performance brought one into contact with a heavenly reality.

Our main concern once again remains Theodore's pedagogy, more so than the details of what the liturgy actually entailed. Related to his presentation of this liturgical material is his understanding of what ritual is and how it functions. We will see rather quickly that Theodore worked with a correspondence theory of ritual in which the actions and dress of all the various actors corresponded to spiritual realities. Theodore taught that ritual actions enacted important theological concepts, such as the Trinity, while others brought the worshipper into God's presence and held out hope of future eschatological fulfillment.[2]

This dichotomy between ritual acts and ideas has dominated much of the discussion of ritual, both by practitioners and social scientists. Recently, however, this dichotomy has come in for a rather compelling critique. Catherine Bell, making extensive use of Bourdieu and other social theorists, challenges scholars of ritual who have assumed a distinction between ritual acts and the ideas to which those ritual acts point.[3] Bell argues that ritual does not do what it does by pointing to a set of ideas, but rather it works as a set of embodied practices. Ritual does not communicate ideas of power and hegemony, rather it embodies those power structures. Bell focuses on the role that ritual plays in reinforcing social structures, particularly power relations within a society. In doing so, she opens a fruitful discussion regarding strategies of ritualization, which includes such questions as how a ritual comes to be, who engages with it, and how hegemony and autonomy play out through its performance.[4]

Bell's approach to ritual has been very influential among ritual theorists, since it provides a way to understand ritual on its own terms rather than as a practice that points to a set of ideas that often vary markedly between different practitioners of the same rites. Our concern with Theodore's pedagogy, however,

---

118

presents some difficulties for the application of Bell's ideas. Theodore clearly did not think in Bell's terms. Indeed Bell argues that ritualized actors generally do not understand how ritual does what it does. Furthermore, Theodore taught the liturgy in order to insure that the catechumens understood what the rites meant, that they would think rightly about their ritual actions. Just as Theodore never separated theological profession from the believing community, he also never separated ritual action from ritual thought. In other words, Theodore's theory of ritual and the liturgical pedagogy that flows from it assumes the very dichotomy Bell aims to dismantle. Nevertheless, Bell's discussion of ritual contributes to our understanding of the role of ritual in these sermons and in the process of Christianization and conversion. The ritualized actions of baptism and the eucharist, as well as Theodore's teaching on these subjects, fit into the matrix of community and creedal theology we have been considering. Performing the rituals of the confessing community established the community, reinforced its hierarchy, and played a critical role in expressing what it meant to be an initiated Christian. Theodore's teaching of the liturgy from his position within the hierarchy of the church reinforced the community and the clergy as authoritative experts in the prevailing outlook of the community.

Communicating Awe-Inspiring Rites

Theodore's strategy for laying out the substance and significance of the baptismal and eucharistic liturgies relies heavily on vivid description of the correspondence between ritual act and the spiritual reality to which it points. We first encountered this emphasis on the awe-inspiring nature of Christian worship as a catechetical theme in chapter two. In expressing this awe, Theodore drew on his rhetorical education and produced elaborately detailed sermons on the liturgy, which strongly bear the marks of the rhetorical genre of *ekphrasis* (ἔκφρασις). The aim of an *ekphrasis*, or descriptive speech, was to engage the audience with a particularly striking account of an event, location, or piece of art.[5] Towards the end of the first century AD, Theon defined *ekphrasis* as "a descriptive speech which brings the subject matter vividly before the eyes."[6] Vividness, Greek *enargeia* (ἐνάργεια), was a hallmark of this descriptive technique. This vivid language aimed to captivate the audience and make them feel as though they were eyewitnesses. Quintilian and Longinus also talk in terms of speech that could bring distant things before the eyes of the audience to great rhetorical effect.[7] In

---

[5] See Webb 2001 and 2000 for general discussion of *ekphrasis*.

[6] Theon *Progymnasmata* 118.7: Ἔκφρασις ἐστὶ λόγος περιηγηματικὸς ἐναργῶς ὑπ' ὄψιν ἄγων τὸ δηλούμενον; trans. Webb 2000:221.

[7] Quintilian *Institutes* 6.2.31 and 8.3.62; Longinus *On the Sublime* 15.1–2.

producing an *ekphrasis,* the rhetor sought to describe an event or piece of art in so animated a fashion as to draw the audience members in and make them feel a part of it. Since the subject of an *ekphrasis* could be significantly removed from the audience both in time and space, the rhetor sought to describe the topic in such a way as to elicit a powerful emotional response.[8] The rhetorical handbooks regularly use the term *phantasia* (φαντασία) to describe this effect. They wanted to create an overwhelming mental image in their audience, one that would abolish any sense of disbelief. Though no easy task, confidence remained high that this lofty goal could be obtained.[9] In one particularly strong account of the abilities of such speech, Longinus claims that these "oratorical fantasies" have the power to enslave the hearer.[10]

Theodore's sermons apply many of these techniques in order to engage the catechumens with a vivid interpretation of what he wanted them to see as a totally new Christian life. Theodore structured these sermons to introduce the catechumens to the full range of the experience they were about to have but also took great pains to instruct them in the appropriate way to engage with these experiences intellectually and emotionally. The candidate was about to take part in a divine drama. Whether in baptism or the eucharist, he or she would witness firsthand and for the first time the priestly services. These liturgical services were supposed to express profound realities, and Theodore wanted to ensure that his pupils missed nothing. The candidates needed to know the stages of the rituals and their place in them. He instructed them about each component of the ritual experience: the registrar of baptism, the deacons, the priest, the font, the table, and the elements of the ritual meal, unpacking the significance of each of these, its appearance or dress, its physical nature, and the spiritual reality to which it corresponded. He also taught the catechumens their place in this liturgical drama. One cannot miss Theodore's profound conviction that catechumens needed instruction in worship. He taught them about their own posture, dress, and actions. He even treated the mental, emotional, and ethical states appropriate for the catechumens.

Theodore used these five sermons to guide his pupils through the many aspects of the liturgies they were about to experience. This chapter seeks to capture his concern for such a holistic introduction to liturgy. When the catechumens took part in the liturgies, he wanted them to know that they performed theological truths and experienced these truths as physically manifest in their bodies. Theodore did not leave the recognition of this process to chance; he never assumed that a spontaneous response to Christian teaching and liturgy

[8]   On the issue of *ekphrasis* as an emotional appeal, see Webb 1997.
[9]   For some examples of where it fell short, see Webb 1997:125.
[10] Longinus *On the Sublime* 15.9.

would be a proper response. He took pains to insure that ritual performance had its proper impact on the catechumen. Where the sermons on the Nicene Creed had taught the catechumens how they should believe in God, these five sermons present Theodore's attempt to teach them how to experience God.

Clerical Roles and Heavenly Reality

One aspect of the liturgical experience that deserves special attention pertains to the roles of the various clerics involved in the administration of the sacraments. The consecrated water, bread, and wine did not exhaust the symbols of the two liturgies. The officiating churchmen also fulfilled important symbolic functions in the course of the liturgies. Theodore invested their physical presence and appearance with great meaning. Their actions at the baptismal font or before the eucharist portrayed to all witnesses a heavenly reality that he urged the catechumens to recognize.

Theodore explained the role of the clergy most clearly in his teaching on the eucharistic liturgy, where the bread and wine are the most obvious symbols in the sacrament. They are the true body and blood of Christ and point to his death and resurrection as a memorial. They provide spiritual nourishment, sustenance for those who had entered the kingdom through baptism and who sought to persevere in the faith. However, throughout Theodore's discussion of the eucharist, the catechist sought to show complete correspondence between the physical manifestation of the liturgical act and the spiritual reality to which it corresponded. He seems to have in mind something like a defense against the very charge he leveled at the services of the heretics in his teaching on exorcism. Theodore clearly saw such heretical worship as a threat and took to mocking the services of the heretics by comparing them to theatrical performances:[11]

> As when in a theatrical performance and in a play you see kings and you do not consider them kings because of the imitation of their dresses, but all of them as a ludicrous representation and a burlesque worthy to be laughed at—they only show before the eyes things taken from the ordinary life of the world—so also the things performed by the heretics under the name of doctrine, whether it be their baptism or their

---

[11] Another example of this appears in John Chrysostom's anti-Jewish sermons. These sermons betray a deep concern regarding participation in anything other than "orthodox" Christian worship. For a fuller discussion, see Wilken 1983.

eucharist, deserve laughter; and we ought to turn away from them as from the service of Satan because all of them tend to strengthen impiety.[12]

Heretics had liturgical symbols, perhaps even ones that appeared to be the same as those taught by Theodore, but he insisted that they were empty, offering only a hollow imitation of the true Christian worship. Bolstered by this conviction, Theodore ridiculed the sacraments of the heretics by comparing them to a farcical play or base pantomime.[13]

The cosmological assumptions at work here come from a nearly ubiquitous, if not always technically detailed, Platonism not uncommon in Late Antiquity. In a nice turn of phrase, Polymnia Athanassiadi refers to this pervasive Platonic backdrop to religious discourse as "the late antique spiritual Commonwealth."[14] That which is truly real exists in heaven, while the things of this earth partake of reality only insofar as they reflect or participate in heavenly things. Theodore's "heretics" would have likely shared this cosmology and undoubtedly made similar claims regarding their own services. In fact, this problem was as widespread as the Platonism that stood behind the original claims. Iamblichus and Proclus both advocated highly ritualized interpretations of the *Chaldean Oracles* and did so based in part on a similar theory of correspondence between human worship and a divine reality.[15] In defending theurgy against the charges of Porphyry, Iamblichus admitted that there were cultic abuses, usually carried out by the uneducated and certainly not enjoying divine participation.[16] Nevertheless, he insisted on the validity of proper divination, arguing for the

---

[12] WS 6.42; *Homélies Catéchétiques* 13.97v: [Syriac text]

[13] For a recent treatment of classical views on the theater and theatrical performers, see Duncan 2006. For early Christian perceptions of theater, see Dox 2004; and Leyerle 2001.

[14] Athanassiadi 1999:180. The literature on late antique Platonism is truly colossal. Among the many available titles, see Bowersock 1990; and A. Smith 2004. While the intricacies of this phenomenon are interesting in their own right, they need not concern us here. The Platonism implicit in Theodore's teaching need not be any particular type or system. It need not even be thoroughly conscious on the part of Theodore or his audience. The important thing is that it exists for his audience, or at least Theodore believes it does, on the level of an assumed worldview.

[15] Athanassiadi 1999:164.

[16] *On the Mysteries* 3.13: Ταῦτα δὴ οὖν τὰ γένη μέσα συμπληροῦνται τὸν κοινὸν σύνδεσμον θεῶν τε καὶ ψυχῶν, καὶ ἀδιάλυτον αὐτῶν τὴν συμπλοκὴν ἀπεργάζεται, μίαν τε συνέχειαν ἄνωθεν μέχρι τοῦ τέλους συνδεῖ, καὶ ποιεῖ τῶν ὅλων τὴν κοινωνίαν εἶναι ἀδιαίρετον.

way in which *daimones*, or contingent divinities, ensured interaction with true divinity: "These classes of beings, then, bring to completion as intermediaries the common bond that connects gods with souls, and causes their linkage to be indissoluble. They bind together a single continuity from top to bottom, and render the communion of all things indivisible."[17] The Emperor Julian, who looked to the writings of Iamblichus as a model for his "pagan church," also noted the importance of divine intermediaries in securing right worship of the gods.[18] He also stressed another concern shared by his Christian opponents, the purity of the priest, who was also an intermediary. Julian articulated an elaborate program to ensure the ritual purity, moral rectitude, and philosophical acumen of his pagan priests as a further means of making sure that sacrifices were performed properly and temple worship did not fall into disrepute.[19] He did not want the human link between the one sacrificing and the divine to disrupt the requisite continuity between worshiper and divinity.

Theodore voices a similar set of concerns when he says that "Service of Satan is also that service which is found among the heretics under the name of religion, because although it has some resemblance to an ecclesiastical service, yet it is devoid of the gift of the grace of the Holy Spirit, and is performed in impiety."[20] Rather than a spiritual connection between sacramental elements and a heavenly reality, heretical sacraments corresponded with the evil work of Satan himself. Having raised the issue of theatrical performances, Theodore seems to have recognized that even as he critiqued the worship of those outside his church community as satanic farce, he also needed to ensure that the worship he taught rightly participated in the profound reality of God and the saints in heaven. The repeated insistence on the spiritual reality of the orthodox sacraments, along with their immutability, eternal permanence, and ineffability, suggest that he understood that his critique could be turned against him. Though apparently aware of this potential problem, he was nevertheless willing to use this charge against the heretics. Behind the claim of possessing the Holy Spirit and the charge of heretical impiety clearly stood the authority of the bishop and priest. As we saw in chapter three, the bishop held a position of great authority in the hierarchy of the Christian clergy. Occupying the place just below God invested the bishop with an ability to stand in the place of God and in this role to confirm the validity of Christian worship. However,

[17] *On the Mysteries* 1.5.
[18] *Letter to a Priest* 293.
[19] *Letter to a Priest* 298.
[20] WS 6.42; *Homélies Catéchétiques* 13.97r: ܗܡܚܬܐܐ ܕܡܟܢܐ ܙܠ ܐܡܚܬܐܐ ܐܗ ܦܠܗܗ ܗܐܗܗܟܐ ܟܚܣܠ ܟܚܡܐ
123

Theodore's method of refuting the opposition would really only appeal to those who already agreed with him. Insofar as his audience was generally sympathetic to, and even enthusiastic about, his teaching, it seems a mistake to look for a more sophisticated argument in this context. Theodore relied on his audience sharing the "good mind" he taught them to have as he preached the creed to them. Regardless of how convincing the argument might appear to an outsider, Theodore's position was clear enough. Only his liturgical drama possessed the kind of correspondence with reality that rendered it efficacious.

In the context of discussing earthly practice and heavenly reality, Theodore gave considerable attention to Christ as a priest according to the order of Melkizedek, a recurring theme in the biblical book of Hebrews.[21] Two main points in the catechist's exegesis of the relevant passages from Hebrews must be stressed in this context. Firstly, the sacrifice offered by Christ in his capacity as priest was a single sacrifice, a perfect unity. One could neither divide it nor repeat it nor duplicate it. Secondly, Christ offered this sacrifice in heaven and not on earth. The earth was not the proper realm for the manifestation of such ineffable and immutable perfection. Christ resided in heaven and perpetually offered his perfect sacrifice there.

This provides the context in which Theodore turned to the roles played by the clergy in the administration of the eucharist. The priest and deacons who attended at the service were types of a spiritual reality, just as were the bread and wine. The body and blood of Jesus resided in heaven with the risen Christ who performed the sacrifice there, while the bread and wine rested visibly on the altar. Likewise, the priest physically represented to the congregation a type of this sacrificing Christ:

> And because our Lord Christ, he offered himself as a sacrifice, and thus on account of this he became for us a high priest. But now we must know that the priest, this one who now draws near to the altar, this one who does not offer himself as a sacrifice, who is not even a true high priest, depicts him [Christ]. Nevertheless, just like an image [yuqnā] he performs the administration of this ineffable sacrifice through which he molds [ršam] for you, just like a fantasy [šragrāgyātā],

[21] WS 6.79–83; *Homélies Catéchétiques* 15. For the priesthood according to the order of Melkizedek, see Hebrews 5–7. The extant fragments of Theodore's commentary on the book of Hebrews include his discussion of Hebrews 7.3, in which he also discusses Christ as a high priest according to the order of Melkizedek.

a representation [*ṣalmā*] of heavenly ineffable things and supernatural and incorporeal hosts.[22]

In the drama of the liturgy, the priest portrayed Christ and acted out his service in heaven. Theodore drew such a tight connection between the sign and the thing signified that he felt the need in this case to point out to his audience that the priest did not offer up himself as a sacrifice; the analogy between Christ and the priest did not extend that far.

The particular language in this passage rewards a closer look. The priest stands as an image of Christ, who remains in heaven. The Syriac term *yuqnā* meaning "icon" is a transliteration of Greek *eikōn* (εἰκών). Though we would do well to avoid importing later notions of Christian icons into this context, the term is certainly employed here to draw a strong link between the priest and Christ. We ought to think in terms of a statue of the emperor that represented his imperial dignity and authority.[23] In the year 387, when the citizens of Antioch dared violate the statues of the Emperor Theodosius I, they rightly feared harsh retribution for this act of insolence. Theodore's language reinforces the strength of this image. The term *ṣalmā* has a range of meaning similar to *yuqnā* and also translates Greek *eikōn*.[24] *Ršam*, to mold, is often used of the plastic arts and pertains to the act of giving something shape. It can also be used of writing, particularly inscribing.[25] The Syriac term *šragrāgyātā* is a bit difficult in this context. It deals with images held in the mind but normally has a rather negative connotation. It most often deals with false images, occasionally even false images that torment a person. The translator of Theodore uses it in a significantly different sense here. In this context, emphasis is laid on the power of the mental image. It is best understood as capturing the meaning of the Greek term *phantasia,* which we encountered earlier in conjunction with the definition of *ekphrasis.*[26] Theodore wanted the catechumens to be captivated by the liturgy.

[22] WS 6.83 (translation modified); *Homélies Catéchétiques* 15.125r: ܡܚܣܢܐ ܕܗܕ ܕܡܚܠܟ [Syriac text]

[Syriac text lines]

[23] Lampe 1961:410.

[24] Payne Smith 1879, 2:3408–3409.

[25] Payne Smith 1879, 2:3985–3986.

[26] For the connection between Syriac *šragrāgyātā* and Greek *phantasmata*, see Payne Smith 1879, 2:3805. The negative uses of the term do predominate. In Genesis 19.11, 2 Kings 6.18, and Bar Hebraeus *Carmina de amore divine* 1.72, it is associated with blindness. In Wisdom of Solomon 17.3 it is used for a strange and troubling vision. Nevertheless, a similar range of meaning pertains to Greek *phantasia* and *phantasma*; see Lampe 1961:1471. Furthermore, in the Syriac text of Eusebius

He wanted the actions of the priest during the eucharist to bring heaven before the eyes of the catechumens, and the vivid prose of his lessons was structured to help them do that.

The deacons also had their own role to play in representing the heavenly reality of the sacrifice. Theodore developed various aspects of the way in which the deacons offered the image of the angelic hosts of heaven.[27] New Testament precedent had established angelic service to the incarnate Christ as a relatively common occurrence. For example, angels had declared the birth of Christ among the shepherds[28] and ministered to Christ following his temptation in the desert.[29] Likewise, Theodore set apart those holding the office of deacon because they served Christ through their ministry at the altar: "This name, however, is especially applied to those who perform this ministry, and are called by all 'deacons,' as they are alone appointed to perform this ministry, and represent a likeness of the service of the spiritual messengers and ministers."[30] The English "deacon" translates both the Greek *diakonos* (διάκονος) and Syriac *mšamšānā* (ܡܫܡܫܢܐ), both literally meaning "servant" or "minister."[31] We have already seen that the creation of deacons in the church originally came about because the apostles were being distracted from their ministry of preaching by spending too much time serving the communal meal.[32] Thus deacons initially gave assistance to the apostles and rendered service to the congregation. Theodore, maintaining the original meaning of *diakonos* (servant), redirected the focus of the activity carried out by the deacons. Their service, just like that of the angels in the New Testament, was rendered unto Christ. Theodore further expanded this image of angelic service to Christ by introducing Isaiah 6 and the awe-inspiring scene of a host of Seraphim declaring God holy while one of their number flew toward Isaiah to cleanse his lips with a fiery coal.[33] The catechist urged his pupils to consider this heavenly reality that the host of deacons reflected during the celebration of the liturgy. The clothing of the deacons also reflected their vocation of service to Christ. The catechist emphasized how the outer garment and stole of the deacons suggested service to Christ, who was present on the altar during

---

of Caesarea *Theophania* 4.6.31, *šragrāgyātā* is used in the context of images capable of overcoming a person.

27 *WS* 6.84–87; *Homélies Catéchétiques* 15.

28 Luke 2.14

29 Matthew 4.11

30 *WS* 6.84; *Homélies Catéchétiques* 15.125v: ܐܠܐ ܗܢܐ ܫܡܐ ܕܝܠܗ ܗܘ ܒܠܚܘܕܝܗ ܗܘ܆ ܕܗܠܝܢ ܕܥܒܕܝܢ ܬܫܡܫܬܐ ܡܫܡܫܝܢ ܘܡܬܩܪܝܢ ܡܢ ܟܠܢܫ ܗܠܝܢ ܗܘ ܡܫܡܫܢܐ܆ ܕܗܢܘܢ ܒܠܚܘܕܝܗܘܢ ܣܝܡܝܢ ܕܢܫܡܫܘܢ ܗܕܐ ܬܫܡܫܬܐ ܘܕܡܘܬܐ ܡܨܝܪܝܢ ܕܗܝ ܬܫܡܫܬܐ ܕܡܠܐܟܐ ܪܘܚܢܝܐ ܘܡܫܡܫܢܐ ܪܘܚܢܐ.

31 Lampe 1961:352A; and Payne Smith 1879 2:4227.

32 Acts 6.1–7; see discussion in chapter three.

33 *WS* 6.100–102; *Homélies Catéchétiques* 16.

the eucharistic meal. Theodore stated that the outer garments of the deacons befitted the elevated nature of the one they served. The sublimity of their clothing testified to the glory of Christ, before whom the deacons served.[34] The stole also suggested divine service as the deacons arranged it just as a household servant would have.[35]

Theodore did not discuss the vestments of the priest in the context of the eucharist. However, he did mention the clothing of the priest during the performance of the baptismal liturgy. When the priest approached the catechumens to anoint them following the exorcism, he wore a radiant white robe of linen, which was unique to this moment: "When you have, therefore, made your promises and engagements, the priest draws near to you, wearing not his ordinary garments or the covering with which he was covered before but clad in a robe of clean and radiant linen."[36] The new white linen symbolized the joy of the future heavenly existence that the catechumens would experience. Its luminous quality pointed to the radiant life to come. Likewise, the cleanliness of the robe indicated the repose and happiness of the world to come. The priest's appearance was clearly intended to be striking, particularly in contrast to that of the catechumens, who at this point wore nothing more than their undergarments.[37]

---

[34] The text contains a difficult turn of phrase here (*Homélies Catéchétiques* 15.126r): ܚܒ ܝ ܗܘܕ̈ ܠܗ ܕܒ ܗܘܕ. Mingana translates the sentence, "They have also an apparel which is consonant with their office, since their outer garment is taller than they are, as wearing such an apparel in such a way is suitable to those who serve" (*WS* 6.84). What it means for the garment of the deacon to be "taller than they are" is unclear. Tonneau and Devreesse (*Homélies Catéchétiques*, p501) translate this phrase as "parce que plus sublime qu'eux." This comes much closer to the meaning of the text. The garment is more sublime than or superior to the deacon himself. Theodore refers to the common practice of wealthy families dressing their household slaves in fine clothing. The clothing denoted a service to a superior master.

[35] Again the wording is difficult (*Homélies Catéchétiques* 15.126r): ܠܬܐ ܗܘܕ̈ ܡܢ ܕ ܡܕ̈ ܗܘܕ̈ܠܟ. Mingana renders this as, "They do not place the stole on their neck in a way that it floats on either side but not in front, because there is no one serving in a house who wears such an apparel" (*WS* 6.84-85). A better translation is, "They do not hang the stole upon their neck from both sides without it being in front of them." The point, however, is clear enough. They wear their stole in the same way as domestic servants.

[36] *WS* 6.45; *Homélies Catéchétiques* 13.99v: ܠܗ ܚܕ. ܕܘܡ̈ ܚܕܬ̈ ܐ ܡܩܬ̈ ܥܠܟ ܕܟܕܒ ܠܕ ܩܬ. The consistent position taken by many Christian sources in

[37] *WS* 6.36; *Homélies Catéchétiques* 13. The consistent position taken by many Christian sources in Late Antiquity is that baptism ought to take place with the candidate naked, Greek γυμνός. Γυμνός has a range of meaning from completely naked to simply plain or unadorned; see Lampe 1961:324B–325A. A recent article (Guy 2003) notes this range of meaning and suggests that something closer to the latter definition ought to be understood as the normal method of Christian baptism, as it is unlikely that a woman would be naked in the presence of a male deacon. The

Indeed, the priest depicted the promised state that awaited the candidates and that they had entered the catechumenate to attain.

The liturgies of baptism and the eucharist presented the catechumens with a vivid image of the heavenly reality into which they sought initiation. Their registration incorporated them into the physical earthly community. They came before the church officially and submitted their names along with those of their sponsors in the new faith. This process continued as the catechumens encountered exorcists, deacons, and priests. They interacted with these people in carefully constructed ways that were designed to point them to a supernatural reality. The activities of the clerics always centered on consecrated items: oil, water, bread, and wine. However, the contexts bore meaning every bit as much as the sacramental items. The baptismal font was often described as the womb of rebirth.[38] The altar cloths were the burial clothes of Jesus. The entire scene portrayed a heavenly reality. Indeed the clerics officiating at these rites each played a role that corresponded directly to a divine reality in heaven. The costumes of the clergy and all the surrounding props pointed to this truth.

Although Theodore had criticized the services of the heretics as false theatrical performances, one clearly sees how he presented to his catechumens a liturgical experience that entailed an engaging drama of its own. The sights and sounds that the catechumens encountered were designed for maximal dramatic impact.[39] The liturgical script communicated profound truths of the faith as the clerics acted them out through anointings, immersion of the catechumens in the water, and making the sign of the cross, to name just a few. Most importantly, however, the catechist sought to set his drama apart from that of the heretics by reiterating the idea that only the orthodox drama corresponded to a reality taking place in heaven. The orthodox alone acted on the cosmic stage

---

Apostolic Constitutions suggest that deaconesses actually entered the font with the women being baptized and so presumably would have anointed the naked women as well: Διακόνισσα οὐκ εὐλογεῖ, ἀλλ᾽ οὐδέ τι ὧν ποιοῦσιν οἱ πρεσβύτεροι ἢ οἱ διάκονοι ἐπιτελεῖ, ἀλλ᾽ ἢ τοῦ φυλάττειν τὰς θύρας καὶ ἐξυπηρετεῖσθαι τοῖς πρεσβυτέροις ἐν τῷ βαπτίζεσθαι τὰς γυναῖκας διὰ τὸ εὐπρεπές (*Apostolic Constitutions*, 8.28.6). Riley (1974:145n4) insists that whatever measures may have been taken to preserve propriety, the symbolism of nudity had to be somehow preserved. Theodore does not give much hint about whether he used γυμνός in a literal or figurative sense. It seems he simply relied on the rhetorical force of the term in speaking to an audience that would not have known one way or the other.

[38] Bedard 1951:17–36.

[39] Yarnold (1994:66) suggests that this emphasis on the "awe-inspiring" nature of the rites stems from a desire to capture some of the language and appeal of the pagan mysteries. He argues that late fourth-century catechists found this a desirable approach on account of the mass conversions following the conversion of Constantine. Whether the conversion of Constantine brought about such a mass of conversions or whether the mysteries played any role in shaping catechesis in the late fourth century does not affect my position here. One must note Theodore's use of very emotionally charged language.

under divine direction. Therefore, even if heretical services looked exactly the same as orthodox, they were actually empty rituals, performed by charlatans who neither knew nor reflected heavenly realities.

Physical Participation in the Liturgy

Thus far we have focused primarily on the passive experience of the catechumens. To press the metaphor of drama a bit further, we have seen the catechumens as the audience of a liturgical drama in which clerical actors with sacramental props put on an elaborate production choreographed by Christ for the purpose of reflecting a heavenly reality. However, the catechumens were not properly an audience to this cosmic drama. Rather, insofar as it was designed to incorporate them into the church and initiate them into its mysteries, it required the catechumens to participate. As actors alongside the clergy, they had their own roles to play. This section focuses more precisely on the catechumens as participants in these liturgies. We will turn here to the variety of ways in which catechumens participated physically in these rites.

Gesture

At various points in his discussion of the elements of the baptismal and eucharistic liturgies, Theodore described to the catechumens various gestures that they would perform during the services. In each case, these added to the meaning of what was taking place. He gave detailed attention to the physical position of the catechumens throughout the exorcism and signing. He described the exorcism by means of a courtroom scene with God as judge, Satan as the accuser, and the exorcist as the catechumens' advocate. Interestingly, Theodore told the catechumens little about what would happen to them during this court scene, such as what the exorcist might say or do to rid them of demonic influence. Rather, he focused on the courtroom setting and interpreted the actions of the catechumens in light of this vivid metaphor: "In this same way when the words called the words of exorcism are pronounced you stand perfectly quiet, as if you had no voice and as if you were still in fear and dread of the Tyrant."[40] Thus the catechumens, accused by Satan, remained silent while the exorcist pled their case. This state of fear and dread also found expression in the gestures assumed by the catechumens. They were to stand barefoot with heads bowed and arms outstretched. In this way, their posture would reflect the harsh servitude that had characterized their relationship with the Devil: "In all

[40] *WS*6.31; *HoméliesCatéchétiques*12.90v–91v: ܒܗ ܕܝܢ ܐܦ ܗܟܢܐ ܒܗܘܠܝܢ ܕܡܬܐܡܪܢ̈ ܡܘܡܬܢܘܬܐ: ܟܕ ܫܬܩܐ ܐܝܬ ܘܟܠܗܘܢ ܐܝܟ ܕܠܐ ܩܠܐ ܩܐܡ ܐܢܬ ܐܝܟ ܗܘ ܕܒܕܚܠܬܐ ܘܐܦ ܐܢܬ ܘܕܚܝܠ ܐܢܬ ܡܢ ܛܪܘܢܐ.

this you are in the likeness of the posture that fits the words of exorcism, as in it you have shown your old captivity and the servitude which through a dire punishment you have rendered to the Tyrant."[41] The catechumens also held this position as an appeal for mercy from God the judge. Gestures reminiscent of suppliants demonstrated the humility of the candidates who had served Satan but who had come to recognize their need for salvation through Christ and a realignment of their loyalties towards his Father.

However, such gestures accomplished more than supplication before God. They also stood as a reminder to the catechumens of their sinful past and the dominion that Satan had held over them. Theodore elaborated on the significance of the catechumens' bare feet in this context: "You stand also on garments of sackcloth so that from the fact that your feet are pricked and stung by the roughness of the cloth you may remember your old sins and show penitence and repentance of the sins of your fathers."[42] Such an experience probably would not have been painful but merely a bit uncomfortable. Nevertheless, the catechist sought to direct the minds of his students toward a spiritual reality through this feeling. If the catechumens held this image before their mind's eye, the discomfort caused by bare feet on sackcloth would reinforce the meaning of their gestures and they would be mindful of the humble and needy position in which they came for baptism.

The supplicating gestures of the catechumens continued as they fell to their knees to receive the words of the exorcism. They did this while keeping their heads bowed and their arms extended as they had earlier.[43] If the soles of their feet had not been sufficiently affected by the sackcloth underneath them, surely the thinner and more sensitive skin of their knees would have been. Not only would the discomfort remind the catechumens of their sin, the actual descent to the floor was to draw their minds to the complicity of every person in the fall of Adam: "As we have all of us fallen into sin and been driven to the dust by the sentence of death, it behooves us to 'bow our knees in the name of Jesus Christ,' as the blessed Paul said,[44] and to 'confess that Jesus Christ is Lord, to the glory of God His Father.'"[45] Again the gestures and posture of the catechumens reflected

---

[41] WS 6.36; *Homélies Catéchétiques* 13.93v: ܘܚܠܝܡ ܕܘܐ ܠܗܘܣܐ ܕܡܘܡܢܬܐ ܡܕܡܠܝܗ ܘܗܘܕܠܟܐ ܗܘ ܠܗܘܕܠܟܐ ܩܢܚܗ ܠܗܣܐ: ܘܡܠܗܟܕܚܗ ܗܘ ܕܒܝܙ ܠܟܕܐܢܐ ܦܠܚܗܘ ܚܡܗܡܚܕܟܠܐ ܡܕܢܕܢ.

[42] WS 6.32; *Homélies Catéchétiques* 12.91r: ܗܩܥܗ ܕܐ ܠܟ ܚܠ ܩܢܢܐ ܕܗܩܕܐ. ܘܗܠܟܣܕ ܕܠܐ ܗܘܐ ܗܘܘܕܚܗ ܗܘܗܕܚܝ. ܕܠܠܟܚ ܘܡܘܩܗ. ܚܩܕܗܐ ܘܗܘ ܗܠܚ ܚܝܒܚܗ ܠܚܬܗܐ ܠܐ ܘܗܟܕܘ ܗܕܟܕܘܗܗܟܗܣܐ ܕܣܟܬܚ ܠܟܗ ܘܗܗܗܘܦܗ ܚܠܐ ܣܬܝܗ ܕܠܚܩܬܝ.

[43] WS 6.36; *Homélies Catéchétiques* 13.

[44] Philippians 2.10–11.

[45] WS 6.36; *Homélies Catéchétiques* 13.93v: ܩܣܠܝܚܗܐ ܠܟܚ ܢܗܠܟܣ ܚܠܟ ܘܚܝܕ ܠܘܕ ܓܝܢܐ ܕܗܕܗܐ ܠܗܡ ܠܕܚܠܐ ܗܘ ܠܗܗܣܟܣ. ܠܘܕܐ ܠܟ ܕܝ ܘܗܚܡܕܘ ܕܣܚܗܣ ܕܣܚܗܣܕ ܗܝܣܢܐ: ܢܚܘܩ ܚܘܬܚܣ ܠܒܝ ܗܠܟܗ ܠܗܚܕܐ ܩܘܠܟܘܗܐ ܚܠܟܣܬܐ: ܘܘܗܘܕܘ

the spiritual reality of sin and the need for redemption that Theodore sought to ingrain through his teaching. The catechumens maintained this position throughout the exorcism, abjurations, promises, and signing. Only after all of this, when the sponsors had spread a linen orarium on their heads, did they rise to their feet:

> By your rising from your genuflection you show that you have cast away your ancient fall, that you have no more communion with earth and earthly things, that your adoration and prayer to God have been accepted, that you have received the stamp which is the sign of your election to the ineffable military service, that you have been called to heaven, and that you ought henceforth to direct your course to its life and citizenship while spurning all earthly things.[46]

Thus the catechumens' rising signified the overthrowing and reversal of what the kneeling had signified. These gestures provided a liturgical enactment of redemptive history: fall, redemption, and association with Christ, all of which assumed the ethical imperative to live in a manner worthy of redemption.[47] Furthermore, the performance of these gestures not only echoed the abjurations and promises made by the catechumens during the exorcism, they worked in conjunction with the words. The gestures, every bit as much as the words, constituted the admission of guilt, confession, and acceptance of Christ's authority.

Theodore further highlighted the efficacy of this act, stating, "but it is right that after you have cast away that posture and those memories you should draw nigh unto the Sacrament which implies participation in the future benefits."[48] Thus immediately following the exorcism, the catechumens entered the baptismal font. All of the words spoken in the font came from the priest, not the catechumens, but their actions and gestures still bore significance. As the priest said, "So-and-so is baptized in the name of the Father, and of the Son, and

---

ܘܒܬܪܟܢ ܩܐܡ ܗܘ ܡܢ ܟܘܪܥܗ: ܡܚܘܐ ܕܡܢ ܕܘܒܪܗ ܩܕܡܝܐ.

[46] WS 6.47; *Homélies Catéchétiques* 13.100v–101r:

[47] Elm 2003.

[48] WS 6.36; *Homélies Catéchétiques* 13.93v:

of the Holy Spirit,"[49] he immersed the catechumens in conjunction with each of the divine names. However, Theodore suggested an interesting conjunction of actions in this rite: "The priest places his hand on your head and says 'of the Father,' and with these words he causes you to immerse yourself in water, while you obediently follow the sign of the hand of the priest and immediately, at his words and at the sign of his hand, immerse yourself in water."[50] Thus the priests immersed the catechumens but they also immersed themselves. One could read this simply in light of the logistics of performing the rite. It would indeed have been difficult for the priest to immerse the catechumens without their cooperation. However, Theodore used this reality to develop the meaning of the ritual more fully. He interpreted the cooperation of the catechumens as a declaration of assent to the words of the priest: "By the downward inclination of your head you show as by a hint your agreement and your belief that it is from the Father that you will receive the benefits of baptism, according to the words of the priest."[51] As in the exorcism, the gesture of the catechumens implied their agreement with the words spoken as a part of the rite. The treatment of the exorcism stressed the words of the catechumens and mentioned none of the words of the exorcist, although surely the posture of the catechumens in that context was meant to show agreement with the words spoken by both parties. In baptism, however, the catechumens spoke no words, and the gesture of a bowed head indicated complete agreement with the words of the priest. In fact, Theodore explicitly states that the inclination of the head took the place of speech on the part of the catechumen: "If you were allowed to speak at that time, you would have said: 'Amen,' a word which we believe to mean that we subscribe to the things said by the priest."[52]

The consideration of actions performed by the catechumens helps develop another point as well. Theodore possessed a deep concern for the unity and singularity of baptism. In discussing the precise actions of the catechumens, he stressed this theme. Reiterating the Trinitarian formula and three immersions of the rite, he adds, "Your immersions are done in an identical way in order that you may know that each one of those names is equally perfect and

49 *WS* 6.58; *Homélies Catéchétiques* 14.108v: ܠܡܥܕ ܦܠܓ ܒܫܡ ܐܒܐ ܘܒܪܐ ܘܪܘܚܐ ܕܩܘܕܫܐ.

50 *WS* 6.62; *Homélies Catéchétiques* 14.111r: ܒܗܠܝܢ ܕܝܢ ܒܗܢܐ ܣܐܡ ܐܝܕܗ ܥܠ ܪܝܫܟ. ܘܐܡܪ. ܒܫܡ ܐܒܐ ܘܡܥܡܕ ܕܡܠܬܗ ܕܡܬܥܒܕ ܒܡܝܐ ܠܟܘܢ. ܐܢܬ ܕܝܢ ܡܫܬܥܒܕܬ ܘܢܚܬ ܐܢܬ ܒܬܪ ܪܡܙܐ ܕܐܝܕܗ ܕܟܗܢܐ. ܘܒܡܠܬܗ ܘܒܪܡܙܐ ܕܐܝܕܗ ܐܣܝܪ ܠܡܥܡܕ ܐܢܬ ܒܡܝܐ܀

51 *WS* 6.62; *Homélies Catéchétiques* 14.111r: ܘܐܝܟ ܗܘ ܕܒܪܡܙ ܡܘܕܐ ܐܢܬ ܒܪܟܢ ܪܫܟ ܘܡܗܝܡܢ ܐܢܬ ܒܗ: ܕܡܢ ܐܒܐ ܐܢܬ ܘܡܘܕܐ ܐܢܬ: ܕܡܢ ܐܒܐ ܡܩܒܠ ܛܒܬܐ ܕܡܥܡܘܕܝܬܐ. ܐܝܟ ܗܕܐ ܡܠܬܗ ܕܟܗܢܐ.

52 *WS* 6.62; *Homélies Catéchétiques* 14.111r: ܐܠܘ ܓܝܪ ܡܫܠܛ ܗܘܐ ܠܟ ܠܡܡܠܠܘ: ܗܝܕܝܢ: ܐܡܪ ܗܘܝܬ ܐܦ ܐܢܬ ܐܡܝܢ. ܗܕܐ ܡܠܬܐ ܕܡܗܝܡܢܝܢ ܠܟܠܗ ܕܫܡܗ ܡܩܒܠܝܢ: ܕܡܫܪܪܝܢ ܠܗܠܝܢ ܕܐܬܐܡܪ̈ ܡܢ ܟܗܢܐ.

able to confer the benefits of baptism."[53] The absence of distinctions between the three immersions provided the catechumens with the opportunity to act out a baptism that was a unified rite, performed ultimately by a single triune Godhead. Further opportunity to do this came through the departure from the font. Baptismal immersion was triple, but the catechumen only departed from the font once: "You immerse yourself in water three times, according to the words of the priests, but you go out of the water once in order that you may know that baptism is one, and also the grace which is accomplished in it by the Father, the Son, and the Holy Spirit who are never separated from one another as they are one nature."[54] Theodore urged the catechumens to see an image of the Trinity itself in the triple immersion followed by single departure from the water.

Into these few simple gestures of the catechumens, Theodore imported the whole of baptismal symbolism and Trinitarian doctrine. The gestures performed in the baptismal font constituted the assent of the catechumens to these ideas as well as their initiation into the faith. The gestures associated with the eucharistic liturgy, the rite that sustained Christians in the faith, also functioned similarly. We have seen the elaborate symbols of the eucharist and how the catechist presented them to his students. The catechumens really only performed one simple act in this context: they ate the bread and drank the wine. Again, Theodore's lengthy description of this meal, its depth and varieties of meaning, and the heavenly reality to which it pointed all culminated in the act of consuming the elements. At this point, the catechumens were to enter into that heavenly reality and take their place alongside the priests and deacons at the heavenly meal attended by Christ the high priest and his angels. Unlike exorcism and baptism, the gesture performed by the candidates in the eucharist would not serve as a constitutive element of the rite, but rather the rite would even go on without any individual parishioner being in attendance. Nevertheless, Theodore's approach to liturgical action stressed the participation of the catechumens as actors on a stage of cosmic significance when they partook of the eucharistic elements.

---

[53] WS 6.63; *Homélies Catéchétiques* 14.111v: ܠܡ ܕܚܠܝܢ ܣܓܝ ܥܡ ܥܠܡ ܡܬܢܚܬܝܢ . ܚܡܠܡ ܡܬܚܡܝܢ ܠܡܓܕ ܐܘܟܝ ܕܠܡ ܘܡܩܘܡ ܠܚܝܢܐ ܠܩܬܡ܃ ܘܒܕ ܡܠܚܡܘܡܝܐ.

[54] WS 6.63; *Homélies Catéchétiques* 14.111v–112r: ܣܘܒܐ ܠܘܕܡܝܐ ܠܚܘܕ ܠܘܐ ܢܝܣܡܐܐ ܘܠܬܩܝܐ܃ ܐܠܗ ܕܡ ܠܘܩܘܡܝܢ. ܠܚܕ ܠܘܐ ܗܘܝܢ ܠܡ ܚܕܐ ܥܠܟ ܘܚܘܢܐ. ܘܣܘܒܐܠܘܕܡܝܐ ܚܕܘܕܥܠܟ ܫܠܟܬ ܠܘܐ. ܠܡ ܘܗܘܟ ܕܣܘܒܐܝܡ ܡܠܚܡܘܡܝܐ ܘܣܘܒܐ ܝܡ ܠܚܡܘܡܝܐ ܘܡܡ ܠܚܕ ܠܡ ܚܕܐ ܘܚܘܣܐ ܘܡܘܕܟܐ. ܐܢܘ، ܘܡܡ ܣܘܝܐ ܠܒܠܚܕ ܠܐ ܡܘܩܕܟܝ.

Dress

Dress was an important social signifier in classical Roman society. It communicated social standing with some precision, and the law even stipulated what items of clothing were restricted to members of certain classes.[55] By Late Antiquity many of the laws had been relaxed, but dress still communicated much about a person's social standing. As such, dress offered another means by which Christian doctrine could be enacted by the catechumens. Just as the catechumens had expressed spiritual realities and made vows to God through gesture and posture, their attire also served much the same function. This element of the liturgical experience became relevant in the course of the exorcism and baptism. As the catechumens progressed through the stages of these rites, their clothing expressed the position they held before God at each point.

The catechumens removed everything other than their undergarments when they presented themselves before the exorcist. As with their posture in this situation, the dress of the catechumens served as a physical expression of their spiritual state. This minimal amount of clothing showed the catechumens for what they were without Christ, slaves and subjects of Satan.[56] Such a lowly state at the hands of a harsh master constituted an appeal to God, the judge in this courtroom scene, and presented another way for the catechumens to throw themselves upon the mercy of the court. The catechumens wore only their undergarments while kneeling during the words of exorcism, their declaration of abjuration and promise, and their signing. Only after the signing did the sponsors place a linen orarium upon their heads and help them to their feet:

> You were before standing bareheaded, as this is the habit of the exiles and the slaves, but after you have been signed he throws on your head linen, which is the emblem of the freedom to which you have been called. Freemen are in the habit of spreading linen on their heads, and it serves them as an adornment both in the house and in the marketplace.[57]

55 For a variety of approaches to the social significance of Roman dress, see the essays collected in Sebesta and Bonfante 1994. See also Vout 1996; and George 2002.

56 *WS* 6.35–36; *Homélies Catéchétiques* 13. See n37 above for a discussion of the range of meaning in the term γυμνός, naked. Here we see more clearly that the metaphor of nudity is what matters to Theodore rather than the actual nudity.

57 *WS* 6.47; *Homélies Catéchétiques* 13.101r: ܠܩܘܕܡ ܓܠܐ ܒܪܫܠܝܠܘܬܐ ܩܐܡ ܗܘܝܬ. ܡܛܠ ܕܗܢܘ ܐܣܟܡܐ ܕܫ̈ܒܝܐ ܘܕܥ̈ܒܕܐ: ܗܫܐ ܕܝܢ ܕܐܬܪܫܡܬ ܪܡܐ ܠܗ ܥܠ ܪܫܟ ܟܬܢܐ ܕܐܬܘܗܝ ܐܬܐ ܕܚܐܪܘܬܐ ܕܠܗ̇ ܐܬܩܪܝܬ. ܠܚܐܪ̈ܐ ܗܟܢ ܓܝܪ ܐܝܬ ܠܗܘܢ ܥܝܕܐ ܕܟܬܢܐ ܢܦܪܣܘܢ ܥܠ ܪ̈ܫܝܗܘܢ، ܘܗܘܐ ܨܒܬܐ ܗܘܐ ܠܗܘܢ، ܐܦ ܒܒܝܬܐ ܐܦ ܒܫܘ̈ܩܐ.

The orarium thus represented the newfound freedom from Satan that the catechumens had secured through the exorcism. Again clothing reinforced the spiritual reality that had taken place through the rites.

The catechumens then removed all their clothing before entering the baptismal font. Their nudity served to remind them of their father Adam. In the garden, Adam and Eve had stood before God unashamed of their nakedness because they had not known sin.[58] After the fall, they became aware of their nudity and that it was a source of shame.[59] Thus the nudity of the catechumens at this point was intended to draw attention to the shame of sin and the divide between God and humans resulting from that sin.[60] Upon leaving the font the catechumens received a shining white linen robe. This robe covered their nakedness and pointed to the promise of the heavenly state that still remained as a future promise. They had been cleansed and would, in their future heavenly condition, have no need for clothing. However, at present, the persistent reality of sin required them to cover their bodies.

Thus the clothing of the catechumens served primarily to denote the spiritual reality reflected in their actions. It joined words and gestures in the exorcism to declare the great need they had to rid themselves of satanic dominion and associate themselves with Christ. The orarium denoted the freedom from Satan acquired through exorcism. The nudity of the baptismal font reinforced the catechumens' stated need for salvation, and their white robes held out the promise of heavenly fulfillment of divine promise. At each stage, the attire of the catechumens served as a reminder to themselves of these realities. As they removed and added clothing, they acted out the realities that lay behind the sacramental rite in which they engaged.

Signing and anointing

Priests and exorcists were the primary actors in the anointing and signing of the catechumens. However, through the physical effects of these rites, the catechumens were meant to receive a spiritual transformation.[61] One sees this most clearly with the signing administered after the exorcism. After the words of exorcism and the abjurations and promises of the catechumens' declarations, the priest signed the catechumens. Theodore explained this with reference to the branding of animals and the tattooing of soldiers: "The sign with which you are signed means that you have been stamped as a lamb of Christ and as

58 Genesis 2.25.
59 Genesis 3.7.
60 WS 6.54; *Homélies Catéchétiques* 14. Filoramo 1999:402.
61 Kalleres 2002.

a soldier of the heavenly King."[62] The imagery is clear; the signing serves as a declaration that the one about to be baptized is wholly under the authority of God. Lambs are to be docile and devoted to their master. Likewise, soldiers are to be faithful. Both bear the marks of this service, and Theodore extends the attendant symbolism of branding to catechumens: "In this same way you also, who have been chosen for the Kingdom of Heaven, and after examination been appointed a soldier to the heavenly King, are first stamped on your forehead."[63] However, this signing bore another essential component—that is, its apotropaic function. The sign of the cross appearing on the forehead provided sure protection against Satan. Theodore explained that,

> we are rightly stamped in a place that is higher than our face, so that from far we may frighten the demons, who will not then be able to come near us and injure us, and so that we may be able to possess so much confidence with God that we look at Him with an open face, and display before Him the stamp by which we are seen to be members of the household and soldiers of Christ our Lord.[64]

Theodore wanted the catechumens to understand that the sign of the cross struck fear in the hearts of the demons. Thus they need not worry about diabolical attack. The demons could see from afar that Christians bore the mark of God and would hesitate to attack them. One must also note the reason that the sign frightened the demons. It demonstrated the confidence of the Christian who had entered into the presence of God and who had looked him in the face as one of his own.

Experiencing Heaven

Theodore presented to his catechumens a liturgical experience designed to affect the entirety of who they were as persons. In the course of the liturgy, the catechumens would speak words, perform actions, and adopt gestures that would transform them physically, mentally, and spiritually into Christians.

---

[62] WS 6.46; *Homélies Catéchétiques* 13.100r: ܡܚܫܠ ܓܠܝܕ̈ܐ ܗܘ ܕܓܒܪ̈ܐ ܗܘ . ܘܡܚܬ ܘܡܝܕܬ ܡܢ ܡܢܐ ܘܒܡܐܘ̈ܝܒ ܘܩܕ̈ܡ ܡܢ ܩܕ̈ܡ ܕܡܣܬܐ. ܠܝ ܩܠܣܐ ܘܡܠܟܐ ܚܡܬܐ. On the tattooing of soldiers, see Jones 1987.

[63] WS 6.46; *Homélies Catéchétiques* 13.100r: ܐܠܡ ܘ̈ܝܒ ܗܘ ܡܢ ܗܘ ܐܠܐ ܐܠܝ ܒܠܡ ܠܚܝܐ ܠܡܠܟܘܬܗܐ ܚܡܬܢܐ. ܐܝܠ̈ܝܒܐ. ܘܗܡܘܪ̈ܐ ܩܠܡ ܠܡܠܚܐ ܚܡܬܐ. ܚܡܘܡܣܐ̈ܐ ܠܠܐ ܣܡ ܟܢܣܝ ܚܬܐܠ ܐܢܐ ܠܚܕܐ.

[64] WS 6.47; *Homélies Catéchétiques* 13.100v: ܐܠܝܗܠܡ ܚܡܬܢܐ܇ ܘܠܟܝܠܕ ܡܝ ܩܙܝ̈ܩܐܠ ܗܡܢ ܡܬܚܠܡ ܘܡܟܬܢ. ܠܝ ܘܡܢ ܘܘܣܡܠ ܘܘܡܝ ܕܝܣܝܠܝܡ ܠܠܠ ܕܬܡܐ. ܘܠܠ ܡܚܣܠ ܡܬܚܣܝܢ ܠܡܗܡܗܕܗ ܠܡܗܡܐ܇ ܘܠܣܬܚܬܘ ܠܝ. ܘܡܗܡܗܓܕ ܓܠܡ ܠܝ ܩܕ̈ܨܡܐ ܠܡܗ ܐܠܣ܇ ܘܬܠܩܐ ܐܝܠܬܗܡܐ ܫܝܡܝ ܡܚܣܠ ܠܡܗܡ ܗܡܗ. ܠܢܐ ܕܠܟ ܠܠܚܕ ܣܡܣܝܡ ܡܕܡܡܣܝܣ ܘܕܘ ܡܗܣܝܣܝ ܕܠܡܗܝ ܚܬܡܐ ܘܩܠܟܬܐ ܘܡܢܘ. ܡܚܣܣܐ ⁘

Theodore's teaching on the Creed had presented to the catechumens the cognitive content of the faith. However, in their experience of the baptismal and eucharistic liturgies, they were actually to realize those truths. There the catechumens would declare their sinful state along with their intention to associate themselves with Christ. Their gestures and the posture of their bodies would likewise assert these things as truths that they had appropriated. Furthermore, they would be initiated into a lifelong experience of nourishing themselves on the eucharistic meal. The drama of the eucharistic liturgy portrayed spiritual realities that the catechumens would perform. This participation served to keep their minds focused on the things of Christ and his perpetual work on behalf of his people. Thus, throughout their liturgical experience, the actions of the catechumens were supposed to recall and cement the ideas that they had been taught. Theodore's instruction showed a deep concern to link ideas with actions and concentration on theological truths with the performance of those truths.

The experience that the catechist put before the catechumens also possessed a strong emotional component. He structured his explanations so as to maximize this aspect of the experience. He described the registration at the commencement of the catechetical process as a tremendously significant break with Satan and association with the kingdom of God. However, this act left the catechumens vulnerable to even greater attacks from Satan, with the result that catechumens needed exorcism. Here the exorcist spoke words that cast out Satan, and the catechumens rejected Satan and promised to cling to Christ. These words, bolstered by the signing with oil, ensured freedom from Satan and association with Christ. However, the catechumens still needed to receive baptism to be fully initiated. Baptism itself held out a future expectation: "The power of the holy baptism consists in this: it implants in you the hope of the future benefits, enables you to participate in the things which we expect, and by means of the symbols and signs of the future good things, it invests you with the gift of the Holy Spirit, the first-fruits of whom you receive when you are baptized."[65] In this way, Theodore sought to grant to each stage of the process the maximal import while always maintaining a focus on future fulfillment.

Even after baptism, Theodore continued this approach. Since they had received the sign of baptism, the catechumens possessed full membership in the church and the ability to partake of the eucharist. This ritual meal would offer them sustenance throughout the Christian life and would preserve them

---

[65] WS 6.53–54; *Homélies Catéchétiques* 14.105r: ܗܢܘ ܣܘܟܠܐ ܕܡܥܡܘܕܝܬܐ ܩܕܝܫܬܐ. ܡܗܘ ܠܟ ܣܒܪܐ ܕܛܒܬܐ
ܕܥܬܝܕܢ. ܡܫܘܬܦ ܠܟ ܠܣܘܥܪܢܐ ܕܗܠܝܢ ܕܡܣܒܪܝܢ. ܘܒܛܘܦܣܐ ܘܒܐܬܘܬܐ ܕܗܠܝܢ ܛܒܬܐ ܕܥܬܝܕܢ. ܡܠܒܫ ܠܟ
ܠܡܘܗܒܬܐ ܕܪܘܚܐ ܕܩܘܕܫܐ ܕܪܫܝܬܗ ܡܩܒܠ ܐܢܬ ܡܐ ܕܥܡܕ ܐܢܬ.

in Christ until the end of their lives. However, even then, a future reality still awaited them:

> We walk here in faith and not by sight because we are not yet in the reality as we are not yet in the heavenly benefits. We wait here in faith until we ascend into heaven and set out on our journey to our Lord, where we shall not see through a glass [1 Corinthians 13.12] and in a riddle but shall look face to face. These things, however, we expect to receive in reality through the resurrection at the time decreed by God, and now it is only by faith that we draw nigh unto the first-fruits of these good things: to Christ our Lord and the high priest of things that belong to us.[66]

Theodore maintained a constant tension between the possession of the benefits of Christianity and the future fulfillment. The vision of the Christian life that he offered to the catechumens is therefore thoroughly eschatological.[67] The rites of initiation and sustenance consistently increase in their profundity, but the fulfillment comes only at the resurrection. His holistic approach thus incorporated every aspect of his students' being into the liturgical experience, and he attempted to present each stage as possessing its own crescendo while always directing them to place their hope in a future consummation.

In articulating this holistic explanation of the liturgy, Theodore offered a textbook *ekphrasis* on the Christian experience. His language throughout is highly emotional, consistently putting before his students things that they had never experienced directly. Theodore was teaching his students how to be Christians, how to experience God. Consider another statement of Theodore on the eucharist:

> As often, therefore, as the service of this awe-inspiring sacrifice is performed, which is clearly the likeness of heavenly things and of which, after it has been perfected, we become worthy to partake through food and drink, as a true participation in our future benefits—it is necessary for us to picture in our mind, as in a fantasy [*šragrāgyātā*], that we are in heaven, and through faith, inscribe a vision of heavenly things in our

[66] *WS* 6.82; *Homélies Catéchétiques* 15.124r: ܒܗܝܡܢܘܬܐ ܗ̇ܘ ܓܝܪ ܡܗܠܟܝܢܢ. ܘܠܐ ܒܚܙܘܐ ܕܠܐ ܥܕܟܝܠ ܗܘܝܢ ܒܗܘܢ ܒܨܒܘ̈ܬܐ. ܡܛܠ ܕܠܐ ܗܘܝܢ ܥܕܟܝܠ ܒܗܘܢ ܒܛܒ̈ܬܐ ܫܡܝܢܝ̈ܬܐ. ܟܕ ܒܗܝܡܢܘܬܐ ܗ̇ܘ ܕܝܢ ܗܪܟܐ ܡܣܟܝܢܢ: ܥܕܡܐ ܕܠܫܡܝܐ ܣܠܩܝܢܢ ܘܪܕܝܢܢ ܠܘܬ ܡܪܢ. ܘܠܐ ܡܟܝܠ ܒܡܚܙܝܬܐ ܐܘ ܒܦܠܐܬܐ ܚܙܝܢ: ܐܠܐ ܐܦ̈ܝܢ ܠܘܩܒܠ ܐܦ̈ܝܢ ܚܙܝܢ. ܐܠܐ ܡܛܠ ܕܗܠܝܢ ܒܗܘ̣ ܒܩܝܡܬܐ ܒܙܒܢܐ ܕܦܣܝܩ ܡܢ ܐܠܗܐ ܟܕ ܣܝܡܬܐ ܡܣܟܝܢܢ ܠܡܩܒܠ: ܗܫܐ ܕܝܢ ܒܗܝܡܢܘܬܐ ܠܪܫܝܬܐ ܕܛܒ̈ܬܐ ܗܠܝܢ: ܠܡܫܝܚܐ ܡܪܢ ܘܪܒ ܟܘܡܪܐ ܕܗܠܝܢ ܕܝܠܢ ܩܪܒܝܢܢ:

[67] Mazza 1991; and Bruns 1995:390–402.

mind, while recognizing that Christ who is in heaven and who died for us, rose and ascended into heaven and is now being immolated.[68]

Theodore's emphasis on the eucharist in this passage has a dual focus. First, he must emphasize the awe-inspiring nature of the eucharistic meal. Thus his sermon effectively presents an *ekphrasis* on the liturgy. He explains in lofty language the events that take place during that ritual, seeking to make them present to the catechumens who have never experienced them. He is teaching them how to engage in the ritual.

Ultimately, however, he wants to stress the current, but ontologically quite distinct, actions of Christ in heaven. This experience is separated from him as well as from the uninitiated catechumens. His instruction amounts to an exhortation to the catechumens to see the eucharist itself as an *ekphrasis* of what is going on in heaven. The language he uses here also appears in the rhetorical handbooks. As we saw earlier, the aim of getting an audience to picture things in the mind as if they were present was a standard component of *ekphrasis*. That this would be described as the production of a "fantasy" is also very common. Quintillian discusses the power associated with the production of this type of fantasy:

> We name *visiones* what the Greeks call *phantasiai* and it is through these that images of absent things are represented to the mind in such a way that we seem to see them with our eyes and to be in their presence. Whoever has mastery of them will have a powerful effect on the emotions. Some people say that this type of man who can imagine in himself things, words and deeds well and in accordance with truth is εὐφαντασίωτος [skilled in summoning up *phantasiai*].[69]

---

[68] WS 6.83 (translation modified); *Homélies Catéchétiques* 15.125r: ܟܠ ܗܠܝܢ ܘܗܝ ܕܚܠܬܐ ܕܥܡܗܘܢ:
[69] Quintilian *Institutes* 6.2.29–30 (trans. Webb 1997:118): "Quas φαντασίας Graeci vocant (nos sane visiones appellemus), per quas imagines rerum absentium ita representantur animo ut eas cernere oculis ac praesentes habere videamus, has quisquis bene ceperit is erit in adfectibus petentissimus. Quidam dicunt εὐφαντασίωτον qui sibi res, voces, actus secundum verum optime finget."

Theodore employs a similar notion of the power of fantasies (*šragrāgyātā*).[70] Fantasies engage the intellect and emotions to make imagined things real to the person good at using them. Particularly vivid description, the kind that Theodore hoped to provide, could produce the feeling of "meeting face-to-face the characters in the orator's story."[71] Thus the benefit of such engagement was a personal encounter with the subject of the liturgy's *ekphrasis*, Christ himself. Theodore hoped to produce Christians who were *euphantasiōtos*, who had powerful skills of imagination that were focused on seeing heaven in their regular worship.

Theodore repeatedly urged the catechumens in highly vivid language to ruminate on certain things as they spoke the words and performed the actions of the liturgies. Christian initiation led the catechumens to perform actions designed to affirm their place in a cosmological reality. Theodore taught them that the gravity of these spiritual truths should occupy their minds. The gestures and postures assumed in the exorcism depicted and proclaimed through the body the same beliefs as did the words of the catechumens. The nakedness, the gestures of supplication, and the pain of the sackcloth all expressed the need for freedom from Satan and for association with Christ. In discussing the various reasons for these things, Theodore added, "You recall in your memory old tribulations in order that you may all the better know the nature of the things which you cast away and that of the things to which you will be transferred."[72] In this context, Theodore taught that actions both declared theological realities and served to keep those realities vividly before the minds of the catechumens.

[70] See n26 above for a discussion of *šragrāgyātā* and *phantasia*.
[71] Dionysius of Halicarnassus *Lysias* 7.
[72] WS 6.36; *Homélies Catéchétiques* 13.93v: ܘܗܟܢܐ ܟܕ ܟܘܠܗܘܢ ܕܝܬܘܒ ܬܗܘܐ ܬܬܕܟܪ ܠܥܬܝܩܬܐ ܠܐܘܠܨܢܐ܆ ܒܕܓܘܢ. ܒܝܢܬ ܥܠܝܟ ܦܘܪܣܠܗܘܢ. ܘܗܘܐ ܥܠܝܟ ܠܐܝܠܝܢ ܕܐܬܝܗܒ.

Conclusion

THEODORE'S *CATECHETICAL HOMILIES* present his attempt to craft a distinctive Christian *paideia* and to create initiated Christian citizens. While Nock sees these converts as the norm, MacMullen can hardly imagine that such converts were produced by the early church. Of course, even after receiving this sort of instruction, people were still entering the church with differing notions of what that meant and with a broad range of motives. To conclude otherwise would be to miss completely the radically changed position of Christianity by the end of the fourth century. But Theodore and other catechists took up the challenge of initiating new Christians and sought to create the kinds of Christians they thought should populate the church in its newfound position of prominence. They believed the rites were efficacious and preached this message forcefully. Theodore insisted that:

> You have been born again and have become a completely different person. You no longer belong to Adam, who was subject to change, because he was afflicted and overwhelmed by sin; you belong to Christ, who was entirely free from sin through his resurrection, and in fact had committed no sin from the beginning of his life.[1]

It seems Nock could have borrowed much of his language for describing Christian conversion directly from Theodore. We see in this quotation Theodore's high confidence in the rites of Christian initiation. He believed that they produced nothing shy of complete transformation. However, we have also seen that Theodore did not simply leave this transformation to chance. He used the systems of education and initiation he had inherited to make a vigorous argument for personal transformation. In the course of doing this, he crafted an imaginative worldview into which he sought to draw his catechumens.

1 *WS* 6.67 (trans. Yarnold 1994:3.25); *Homélies Catéchétiques* 14.114v: ܘܐܚܪܢܐ ܚܠܦ ܐܚܪܢܐ ܐܬܝܠܕܬ ܗܘܝܬ. ܠܐ ܡܟܝܠ ܐܝܬܝܟ ܡܢܗ ܕܐܕܡ. ܗܘ ܕܡܫܬܚܠܦܢܐ ܗܘܐ ܕܒܚܛܝ̈ܬܐ ܐܬܟܒܫ ܘܕܘܝ. ܐܠܐ ܕܡܫܝܚܐ ܗܘ ܕܠܡܫܪܝܘܬܐ ܕܟܠ ܚܛܗ̈ܝܢ ܗܘܐ ܒܝܕ ܩܝܡܬܐ. ܟܕ ܐܦܠܐ ܡܢ ܩܕܝܡ ܠܟܝܢ ܥܒܕ ܚܛܝܬܐ.

However, in looking at these sermons, we are led back to the problems posed in the Introduction regarding discussions of conversion, catechesis, and incorporation into the church. It is obvious that in looking at the catechetical teachings of Theodore we are clearly getting the clerical perspective on Christian initiation. These sermons are not able to describe the thoughts, feelings, and intentions of those entering the church at the close of the fourth century. In other words, our "representative sampling" of Christian converts remains elusive due to the nature of our sources. This study, then, can clearly indicate one presbyter's strategy for addressing people engaged in the process of becoming fully initiated members of the church with what he thought was essential about Christianity. The aim here is not to suggest that this particular approach is representative of all catechetical homilies or even necessarily suggest that a majority of other priests and bishops followed a similar curriculum. Rather, this study highlights the range of tools available to catechists as they sought to teach those entering the church. In particular, this study shows that late antique catechetical homilies could give considerable attention to the subjectivity of their audience, even to the particular needs and desires of the baptismal candidates.[2]

Attention to the subjective experience of catechumens began even before they had become baptismal candidates. Prior to hearing the initial catechetical lesson, we have seen that the candidates had already begun integrating themselves into the Christian community. Indeed, this process would have started long before a person sought baptism. The increasing prominence of the church, particularly as an important civic institution in the late fourth century, was a conscious part of Christian proselytism. Even the casual observer could not have failed to notice the conspicuous position of the church, particularly the person of the bishop, as an important powerbroker in the late Roman city. The temporal and spiritual benefits to be derived from association with this institution would have been readily apparent and must have played a considerable role in the desire to pursue baptism. We should certainly see this backdrop as at least part of the reason for the maintenance of the *disciplina arcani*. Liturgical enactment of a distinction between insiders and outsiders made formal ties to the community and its channels of power that much more valuable.

But catechesis assumed more than a simple awareness of the Christian community and its role in society. More importantly, it took the catechumen's involvement with the social structures of the community well beyond the level of admiration for its influence and a desire to appropriate that influence for personal gain. Those seeking to become baptismal candidates needed

---

[2]   S. Schwartz 2005:152.

established ties to the community in order to engage in the process of initiation. Augustine's *On the Catechizing of the Uninstructed* indicates the Carthaginian practice of holding classes for people considering taking that step. Egeria, Chrysostom, and Theodore all discuss the importance of having a baptismal sponsor before being accepted as a candidate. This situation demanded more than simply having an acquaintance that was already baptized. The expectation was that this sponsor would be prepared to speak to rather intimate details of the catechumen's moral accomplishments and earnest efforts to avoid sin. Egeria's description of registration for baptism as a courtroom scene strongly suggests the gravity of the scenario and even the need for a sponsor who could act as an advocate for the catechumen.

However, the role of the sponsor did not end with the scrutiny of the catechumen and his or her acceptance into the ranks of the baptismal candidates. Occasionally during the *Catechetical Homilies*, Theodore speaks directly to the sponsors, suggesting that they are expected to attend the regular Lenten instruction along with the candidate. Their charge was to aid the candidates by supplementing the preachers teaching, but they were also necessary for passing on the unwritten creed, which the candidate was expected to memorize. But this was not a relationship based entirely on gaining an intellectual understanding of Christianity, of learning the creed and the finer points of theology. The sponsor assisted with the performance of ritual components of initiation as well, particularly exorcism and the renunciation of Satan. This kind of relationship was designed to begin the process of integrating the candidate into the social structures and liturgical life of the local community.

A firm emphasis on teaching emerges in our discussion of the process of becoming part of the Christian community. Baptismal sponsors would have committed a considerable portion of Lent to attending catechetical sermons along with the baptismal candidates. In addition to this, we have seen the extensive discussion of teaching within Theodore's presentation of the creed. Theodore clearly thought of catechesis as offering a significant pedagogical moment that gave him the opportunity to teach doctrine as well as to teach the candidates how to engage with the liturgy.

This commitment of time, effort, and resources focused on teaching calls into question an interpretation of the evidence that would remove an intellectual component from the process of Christianization. An emphasis on the social network as an explanatory model over and against the model of intellectual conformity is a welcome development in a discussion too often focused on doctrinal texts. However, the complete rejection of an intellectual component is not warranted. The social network of the church was heavily invested in inculcating its values within those joining it. As in the case of Chrysostom's catechesis, those values could be predominately, although not exclusively, moral. Conformity to technical theology was not necessarily what catechesis aimed to produce. Theodore worked diligently to compress his theological teaching into small units that would be comprehensible to his hearers. He also often repeated the main themes of his teaching in hopes of instilling at least the broad strokes of his message, even if the finer points might elude some. Furthermore, in conjunction with his explanatory lessons on the creed, the candidates needed to work with their sponsors to memorize the creed, further reinforcing the main outlines of Christianity's cognitive content.

In this context of catechetical instruction, comprehensive theological understanding would not have been a reasonable goal. The general tenor of the church's teaching was actually preferable when it came to reaching an audience drawn from all segments of late Roman society. As in the case of Eunomius, a strong emphasis on technical precision could result in a failure to convince even those who shared one's general outlook. In this context, Theodore's emphasis on the self-evident nature of his doctrine and repeated use of the terms *eunoia* and *kakonoia* provide considerable insight into his catechetical curriculum. By appealing to people of "good mind" and people of "evil mind," Theodore could further simplify his theological instruction. With this language he sought primarily to create and further reify community boundaries.

By the time they got to the point of receiving Theodore's instruction, the candidates were already significantly invested in the structures of the Christian community. Some of the emphases in Theodore's teaching suggest that it was more important that he reinforce this affiliation than that he successfully pass on all the details of his theology. He consistently used theological education to urge the cultivation of a good mind or will (*eunoia*), essentially a mind that came into conformity with that of the community. Thus while Theodore presented rather technical matters of theology to his audience, each candidate did not necessarily need to comprehend and internalize it in all of its detail. In this way, Theodore's instruction left plenty of room for the less theoretically or intellectually inclined. Thus we should imagine that some candidates were engaged by the theological ideas that Theodore and other catechists taught, while other candidates responded to his commentary on the creed by merely agreeing to participate in the good mind of the community. Even when they failed to comprehend his entire message, they could rest assured that they were entering a community that rightly understood the truth about God and was therefore able to relate itself rightly toward God in worship. In this qualified way, the cognitive content of Christianity played an important role in the process of initiating baptismal candidates.

Theodore concludes his *Catechetical Homilies* with a detailed discussion of the baptismal and eucharistic liturgies the candidates were about to experience. We see clearly how he uses these liturgical commentaries to give considerable attention to the subjective experience of his catechetical students. Theodore's strong sense of correspondence between liturgical acts and what was occurring in heaven lays great emphasis on the role of the worshipper and places him or her in very close relation to Christ through partaking of the liturgy. The aim throughout is to teach the candidates how to experience God in the liturgy.

In this context, the use of the genre of *ekphrasis* plays a very important role. Through his catechetical *ekphrasis*, Theodore employs highly emotive language specifically for the purpose of presenting the distant realities of heaven as palpably close to the candidates in their own experience. In thus addressing the subjective experience of his audience, we can see Theodore's most obvious attempt to create for them a distinctly Christian imagination. Drawing on the background of his creedal instruction regarding Father, Son, Holy Spirit, and church community, Theodore lays out a *phantasia*, a vision, of how an initiated member of the church meets the divine through corporate worship. This *ekphrasis* entails the argument that if the candidates were to dwell on this vision with a right mind (*eunoia*), then they would encounter God and presently realize a taste of eternal life in heaven. This exhortation to join the community in cultivating this mental image of orientation towards God forms the basis for a Christianized way of imagining the world and the place of the individual and the church community within it.

Theodore articulates his vision of a Christian *paideia* through these three broad themes of community, creed, and cult. His catechetical teaching expects involvement with the community, gives considerable attention to the teaching of the creed, and instructs the catechumens regarding how to experience the liturgy. While these are three different themes within Theodore's teaching, we must also keep in mind the ways in which any attempt to draw a strict distinction between them fails. Part of the immersion into the church community involved teaching and the passing on of the community's theological priorities. As sponsors attended catechetical classes and worked with candidates to memorize the creed, the communal structures associated with catechesis reinforced the doctrinal teaching. We have seen ways that this sponsor-candidate relationship was used to instill ethical values too through the process of baptismal registration. Likewise, the eucharist took place within the context of the community as clergy and laity came together to play their role in the ritual drama. Theodore pressed a highly theologized understanding of baptism and the eucharist. He insisted that these ritual acts expressed the theology of the community. Particularly in the case of baptism, the rite itself would constitute assent to the theology of the church on the part of the one being baptized. Thus community, creed, and cult were arranged to overlap and reinforce each other as tools of Christian initiation.

The study of these approaches to Theodore's presentation of his catechesis shows a considerable diversity of ways that Christianity could be made meaningful to people seeking initiation. Rather than seeing some of these ways as "Christian" and some of them as lacking in a distinctly Christian motivation (as in the case of Theodoret's Bedouin), it is more helpful simply to describe them in all of their diversity and imagine that people entered the church for reasons they found important. In the case of any individual candidate, mastery of theological content could be high or low, as could frequency of church attendance and engagement with the worship of the church. Likewise, the depth of a person's integration into the functions of the community could vary widely, both in regard to those functions that we would tend to describe as "religious," such as the liturgy or the pursuit of a clerical office, and those that we would tend to describe as "secular," such as benefitting from the bishop's court or ostensible largesse. The relative importance of these various forms of engagement with Christianity would certainly have varied considerably from individual to individual, as he or she strategized about how much involvement was desirable. To some the community may have been of central importance. Others may have found the liturgical life of the church very meaningful. Still others may have found the theological message of divine incarnation for the purpose of addressing the human condition a compelling narrative to integrate into their lives. For many others, a combination of these factors was surely at work. Each of these factors, however, should be seen as plausible tools used during the initiation process to make citizens of the church out of baptismal candidates. Each had an important role to play in cultivating a distinctly Christian imagination and in making Christianity believable to a considerable portion of the late Roman world. The Christian *paideia* crafted by late antique clergy ultimately presented a well-rounded culture of social ties, ideas, and participatory rituals. This matrix of factors allowed late Roman Christians to feel persuaded and ultimately to accept in large numbers a new religion that made sense to them and engaged them in meaningful ways.

Bibliography

Primary Literature

ʿAbdišōʿ. *Catalog.*

>Ed.: Assemmani, J. S. 1725. Ebediesu, *Enumeratio librorum omnium ecclesiasticorum. BO* 3.1:1–362. Rome.

Acts of the Council of Chalcedon.

>Ed.: Schwartz, E. 1932–1938. *Acta conciliorum oecumenicorum* 2.1-6. Berlin.
>Trans.: Price, R. and Gaddis, M. 2005. *The Acts of the Council of Chalcedon.* 3 vols. TTH 45. Liverpool.

Acts of the Council of Constantinople of 553.

>Ed.: Staub, J. 1971. *Acta conciliorum oecumenicorum* 4.1. Berlin.
>Trans.: Price, R. 2009. *The Acts of the Council of Constantinople of 553.* 2 vols. TTH 51. Liverpool.

Apostolic Constitutions.

>Ed.: Metzger, M. 1985. *Les constitutions apostoliques.* SCh 320. Paris.
>Trans.: ANF 7:385–508.

Apostolic Tradition.

>Ed.: Geerlings, W. 1991. *Traditio Apostolica. Apostolische Überlieferung. Lateinisch, griechisch, deutsch.* Fontes Christiani 1. Freigurg.
>Trans.: Dix, G. and Chadwick, H. 1992. *The Treatise of the Apostolic Tradition of St. Hippolytus of Rome, Bishop and Martyr.* London.

Apuleius. *Metamorphoses.*

>Ed. and Trans.: Hanson, J. A. 1989. *Metamorphoses.* LCL 44, 453. Cambridge, MA.

Athanasius of Alexandria. *Apology against the Arians.*

>Ed.: Opitz, H. G. 1940. *Athanasius Werke,* 2:87–168. Berlin.
>Trans.: NPNF[2] 4:97–148.

Augustine. *City of God.*

>Ed.: Dombart, B. and Kalb, A. 1955. *De civitate Dei.* CCL 47–48.
>Trans.: Bettenson, H. 2003. *City of God.* London.

———. *De catechizandis rudibus.*

  Ed.: PL 40.

  Trans.: Christopher, J. P. 1946. *The First Catechetical Instruction: De Catechizandis Rudibus.* Westminster, MD.

Codex Theodosianus

  Ed.: Mommsen, T. and Meyer. P. M. 1905. Theodosiani libri XVI cvm Constitutionibus Sirmondianis et Leges novellae ad Theodosianum pertinentes. Berlin.

  Trans.: Pharr, C. 1952. *The Theodosian Code and Novels, and the Sirmondian Constitutions.* Princeton.

Chronicle of Siirt.

  Ed. and Trans.: Scher, A., Dib, P., and Griveau, R. 1907–1919. *Histoire nestorienne (Chronique de Séert).* PO, 4:3; 5:2; 7:2; 13:4. Paris.

Cyprian of Carthage. *Letters.*

  Ed.: Hartel, W. 1871. CSEL 2.

  Trans.: Clarke, G. W. 1984. *The Letters of St. Cyprian of Carthage.* New York.

———. *On the Glory of Martyrdom.*

  Ed.: Hartel, W. 1871. *De laude martyrii.* CSEL 3.1:26–52.

  Trans.: ANF 5:579–587.

Cyril of Jerusalem. *Catechesis.*

  Ed.: Reischl, W. K. and Rupp, J. 1969. *Cyrilli Hierosolymarum archiepiscopi opera quae supersunt omnia.* Hildesheim.

  Trans.: McCauley, L. P. and Stephenson, A. A. 1969. *The Works of Saint Cyril of Jerusalem.* Washington, DC.

———. *Mystagogy 1–5*

  Ed.: Piédagnel, A. and Paris, P. 1988. *Catécheses mystagogiques.* SCh 126. Paris.

  Trans.: McCauley, L. P. and Stephenson, A. A. 1969. *The Works of Saint Cyril of Jerusalem.* Washington, DC.

———. *Procatechesis.*

  Ed.: Reischl, W. K. and Rupp, J. 1967. *Cyrilli Hierosolymarum archiepiscopi opera quae supersunt omnia. Hildesheim.*

  Trans.: McCauley, L. P. and Stephenson, A. A. 1969. *The Works of Saint Cyril of Jerusalem.* Washington, DC.

Dionysius of Halicarnassus. *Lysias.*

  Ed.: Jacoby, C., Usener, H., and Radermacher, L. 1995. *Dionysii Halicarnasei quae exstant.* Stuttgart.

  Trans.: Usher, S. 1974. *The Critical Essays.* LCL 465. Cambridge, MA.

Egeria. *Travels.*
>   Ed.: Maraval, P. 1997. *Journal de voyage.* SCh 296. Paris.
>   Trans.: Wilkinson, J. 1971. *Egeria's Travels.* London.

Ephraem. *Hymns on Faith.*
>   Ed.: Beck, E. 1955. *Des heiligen Ephraem des Syrers Hymnen de fide.* CSCO 154.
>   Louvain.

Eunomius. *Apologia apologiae* (outline and summary).
>   Ed.: Vaggione, R. P. 1987. *Eunomius: The Extant Works.* Oxford Early
>   Christian Texts. Oxford.

————. *Liber apologeticus.*
>   Ed. and Trans.: Vaggione, R. P. 1987. *Eunomius: The Extant Works.* Oxford
>   Early Christian Texts. Oxford.

Eusebius of Caesarea. *Church History.*
>   Ed.: Schwartz, E., Mommsen, T. and rev. Winkelmann, F. 1999. *Eusebius
>   Werke 2.1-3. Die Kirchengeschichte.* GCS. Berlin.
>   Trans: Lake, K. 1964–1965. *The Ecclesiastical History.* LCL 153, 265.
>   Cambridge, MA.

————. *On the Theophania.*
>   Ed.: Lee, S. 1842. *On the Theophania, or, Divine Manifestation of Our Lord and
>   Saviour Jesus Christ; a Syriac Version.* London.

————. *Life of Constantine.*
>   Ed.: Heikel, I. A. 1902. *Eusebius Werke 1.1.* GCS. Leipzig.
>   Trans.: Cameron, A. and Hall, S. G. 1999. *Eusebius, Life of Constantine.*
>   Oxford.

Facundus of Hermiane. *Defense of the Three Chapters.*
>   Ed. and Trans.: Clément, J. -M., Vander Plaetse, R., and Fraïsse-
>   Bétoulières, A. 2002–2006. *Défense des trois chapitres (à Justinien).* 4 vols.
>   SCh 471. Paris.

Gregory of Nazianzus. *Oration 4.*
>   Ed.: *PG* 35:532–664.
>   Trans.: King, C. W. 1888. *Julian the Emperor, Containing Gregory Nazianzen's
>   Two Invectives and Libanius' Monody with Julian's Extant Theosophical Works.*
>   London.

Gregory of Nyssa. *Contra Eunomium.*
>   Ed.: Jaeger, W. W. 1921. *Gregorii Nysseni Opera.* Berlin.
>   Trans.: NPNF[2] 5.

The Hymn to Demeter.
>   Ed.: Richardson, N. J. 1974. *The Homeric Hymn to Demeter.* Oxford.
>   Trans.: Rayor, D. 2004. *The Homeric Hymns.* Berkeley.

Iamblichus. *On the Mysteries.*
> Ed. and Trans.: Clarke, E. C., Dillon, J. M. and Hershbell, J. P. 2003.
> *Iamblichus: On the Mysteries.* Atlanta, GA.

John Chrysostom. *Baptismal Instructions.*
> Ed.: Wenger, A. 1970. *Jean Chrysostome. Huit catéchèses baptismales.* SCh 50.
> Paris.
> Ed.: *PG* 49:223–240.
> Trans.: Harkins, P. W. 1963. *Baptismal Instructions.* New York.

———. *Homilies on the Acts of the Apostles.*
> Ed.: *PG* 60:13–384.
> Trans.: NPNF[1] 11:1–330.

———. *Homilies on the Epistle to the Romans.*
> Ed.: *PG* 60:391–682.
> Trans.: NPNF[1] 11:335–566.

———. *Homilies on the First Epistle to the Corinthians.*
> Ed.: *PG* 61:9–382.
> Trans.: NPNF[1] 12:1–269.

———. *Homilies on Hebrews.*
> Ed.: *PG* 63:9–236.
> Trans.: NPNF[1] 14:335–524.

———. *Homilies on the Statues.*
> Ed.: *PG* 49:15–222.
> Trans.: NPNF[2] 9:312–489.

———. *Letter to Theodore.*
> Ed.: Dumortier, J. 1966. *À Théodore.* SCh 117. Paris.
> Trans.: NPNF[2] 9:111–116.

John of Antioch. *Chronicle.*
> Ed. and Trans: Mariev, S. 2008. *Historia chronica.* Corpus fontium historiae
> Byzantinae 47. Berlin.

Julian the Apostate. *Letter to a Priest.*
> Ed.: Bidez, J. 1960. *Œuvres complètes.* Paris.
> Trans.: Wright, W. C. 1913. *The Works of the Emperor Julian* 2:293–339. LCL
> 29. Cambridge, MA.

———. *Against the Galileans.*
> Ed.: Neumann, C. J. 1880. *Juliani imperatoris librorum contra Christianos quae
> supersunt.* Leipzig.
> Trans.: Hoffmann, R. J. 2004. *Julian's Against the Galileans.* New York.

Justin Martyr. *The First Apology.*
> Ed.: Goodspeed, E. J. 1914. *Die ältesten Apologeten: Texte mit kurtzen*

Einleitungen. Göttingen.

    Trans.: ANF 1:163–187.

Liturgy of Saint James.

    Ed.: Mercier, B. C. 1946. *La liturgie de saint Jacques.* PO 26. Paris.

    Trans.: ANF 7:537–550.

Longinus. *On the Sublime.*

    Ed.: Russell, D. A. 1964. *On the Sublime.* Oxford.

    Trans.: Arieti, J. A. and Crossett, J. M. 1985. *On the Sublime.* New York.

Narsai. *On the Three Doctors.*

    Ed.: Martin, F. 1899. "Homélie de Narsès sur les trois docteurs nestoriens." *Journal Asiatique* 9e Série 14:446–492.

    Trans.: Martin, F. 1900. "Homélie de Narsès sur les trois docteurs nestoriens." *Journal Asiatique* 9e Série 15:469–525.

Origen. *Commentary on Matthew.*

    Ed.: Girod, R. 1970. Commentaire sur l'Évangile selon Matthieu. SCh 162. Paris.

———. *Against Celsus.*

    Ed.: Borret, M. 1967. *Contre Celse.* SCh 132, 136, 147, 150, 227. Paris.

    Trans.: Chadwick, H. 1980. *Contra Celsum.* Cambridge.

Palladius. *Dialogue on the Life of St. John Chrysostom.*

    Ed.: Malingrey, A. M. and Leclercq, P. 1988. *Dialogue sur la vie de Jean Chrysostome.* SCh 341–342. Paris.

    Trans.: Meyer, R. T. 1985. *Dialogue on the Life of St. John Chrysostom.* Ancient Christian Writers 45. New York.

Photius. *Bibliotheca.*

    Ed.: Henry, R. 1959–1977. *Photius, Bibliothèque.* 8 vols. Paris.

    Trans.: Wilson, N. G. 1994. *The Bibliotheca: A Selection.* London.

Pliny the Younger. *Letters.*

    Ed.: Guillemin, A. -M. 1927–1947. *Epistulae.* 4 vols. Paris.

    Trans.: Walsh, P. G. 2006. *Complete Letters.* Oxford.

Prudentius. *Peristephanon.*

    Ed.: CSEL 61:291–431.

Quintilian. *Orations.*

    Ed.: Cousin, J. 1975. *Institution Oratoire.* Paris.

    Trans.: Russell, D. A. 2001. *The Orator's Education.* Cambridge, MA.

Rufinus. *Church History.*

    Ed.: Winkelmann, F. 1999. *Eusebius Werke* 2.2. Berlin.

    Trans.: Amidon, P. R. 1997. *The Church History of Rufinus of Aquileia, Books 10 and 11.* New York.

Socrates. *Church History*.

Ed.: Hansen, G. C. 1995. *Socrates, Kirchengeschichte*. GCS. Berlin.

Trans.: NPNF[2] 2:1–178.

Sozomen. *Church History*.

Ed.: Bidez, J. and Hansen, G. C. 1960. *Sozomenus, Kirchengeschichte*. GCS. Berlin.

Trans.: NPNF[2] 2:179–427.

Themistius. *Orations*.

Ed.: Downey, G. and Schenkl, H. 1965. *Themistii orationes quae supersunt*. Leipzig.

Trans.: Heather, P. J. and Moncur, D. 2001. *Politics, Philosophy, and Empire in the Fourth Century: Select Orations of Themistius*. TTH. Liverpool.

Theodore of Mopsuestia. *Against Apollinaris* (Greek fragments).

Ed.: *PG* 66:991–1002.

Ed.: Swete, H. B. 1882. *Theodori Episcopi Mopsuesteni in Epistolas B. Pauli commentarii: The Latin Version with Greek Fragments* 2:312–322. Cambridge.

Trans.: McLeod, F. G. 2009. *Theodore of Mopsuestia* 148–157. The Early Church Fathers. London.

———. *Against Eunomius* (Greek fragments).

Ed.: *PG* 66:1002–1004.

Ed.: Swete, H. B. 1882. *Theodori Episcopi Mopsuesteni in Epistolas B. Pauli commentarii: The Latin Version with Greek Fragments* 2:322–323. Cambridge.

———. *Against the Allegorists* (Syriac fragments).

Ed. and Trans.: Van Rompay, L. 1982. *Fragments syriaques du Commentaire des Psaumes: (Psaume 118 et Psaumes 138-148)*. CSCO 189–190. Louvain.

———. *Against the Defenders of Original Sin* (Greek fragments).

Ed.: *PG* 66:1005–1012.

Ed.: Swete, H. B. 1882. *Theodori Episcopi Mopsuesteni in Epistolas B. Pauli commentarii: The Latin Version with Greek Fragments* 2:332–337. Cambridge.

———. *Against the Macedonians*.

Ed. and Trans: Nau, F. 1913. *Théodore de Mopsueste: Controverse avec les Macédoniens*. PO 9:637–667. Paris.

———. *Catechetical Homilies*.

Ed. and Trans.: Tonneau, R. and Devreesse, R. 1949. *Les Homélies Catéchétiques. Reproduction phototypique du ms. Mingana Syr. 561 (Selly Oak Colleges' Library, Birmingham)*. Vatican City.

Ed. and Trans.: Mingana, A. 1932. *Commentary of Theodore of Mopsuestia on the Nicene Creed*. Edited by Alphonse Mingana. WS 5. Cambridge.

Ed. and Trans.: Mingana, A. 1933. *Commentary of Theodore of Mopsuestia on the Lord's Prayer and on the Sacraments of Baptism and the Eucharist.* WS 6. Cambridge.

———. *Commentary on Hebrews* (Greek fragments).

Ed.: Staab, K. 1933. *Pauluskommentar aus der griechischen Kirche, 200-212.* Neutestamentliche Abhandlungen 15. Münster.

———. *Commentary on the Epistle to the Romans* (Greek fragments).

Ed.: Staab, K. 1933. *Pauluskommentar aus der griechischen Kirche, 113-172.* Neutestamentliche Abhandlungen 15. Münster.

———. *Commentary on the Epistle to Titus.*

Ed.: Swete, H. B. 1882. *Theodori Episcopi Mopsuesteni in Epistolas B. Pauli commentarii: The Latin Version with Greek Fragments* 2:233–257. Cambridge.

———. *Commentary on the Gospel of John* (Greek fragments).

Ed.: Devreesse, R. 1948. *Essai sur Théodore de Mopsueste, 305–419.* Studi e Testi 141. Vatican City.

Trans.: Kalantzis. G. 2004. *Theodore of Mopsuestia: Commentary on the Gospel of John.* Strathfield, NSW.

———. *Commentary on the Gospel of John* (Syriac fragments).

Ed. and Trans.: Voste, J.-M. 1940. *Theodori Mopsuesteni Commentarius in Evangelium Iohannis Apostoli.* CSCO 115–116. Paris.

———. *Commentary on the First and Second Epistles to the Corinthians* (Greek fragments).

Ed.: Staab, K. 1933. *Pauluskommentar aus der griechischen Kirche, 172-200.* Neutestamentliche Abhandlungen 15. Münster.

———. *Commentary on the First Epistle to Timothy.*

Ed.: Swete, H. B. 1882. *Theodori Episcopi Mopsuesteni in Epistolas B. Pauli commentarii: The Latin Version with Greek Fragments* 2:67–188. Cambridge.

———. *Commentary on the Psalms.*

Ed.: Devreesse, R. 1939. *Le Commentaire de Théodore de Mopsueste sur les Psaumes, (I-LXXX).* Studi e Testi, 93. Vatican City.

Trans.: Hill, R. C. 2006. *Commentary on Psalms 1-81.* Atlanta, GA.

———. *Commentary on the Second Epistle to Timothy.*

Ed.: Swete, H. B. 1882. *Theodori Episcopi Mopsuesteni in Epistolas B. Pauli commentarii: The Latin Version with Greek Fragments* 2:189–232. Cambridge.

———. *Commentary on the Twelve Prophets.*

Ed.: Sprenger, H. N. 1977. *Theodori Mopsuesteni Commentarius in XII [i.e. Duodecim] Prophetas.* Göttinger Orientforschungen 1. Wiesbaden.

Trans.: Hill, R. C. 2004. *Commentary on the Twelve Prophets.* Washington DC.

―――. *On the Incarnation* (Greek fragments).

  Ed.: *PG* 66:969–994.

  Ed.: Swete, H. B. 1882. *Theodori Episcopi Mopsuesteni in Epistolas B. Pauli commentarii: The Latin Version with Greek Fragments* 2:290–312. Cambridge.

  Trans.: McLeod, F. G. 2009. *Theodore of Mopsuestia*, 126–147. London.

―――. *On the Perfection of Observances*, Syriac fragment.

  Ed. and Trans.: Draguet, R. 1972. *Commentaire de livre d'Abba Isaïe (logoi I–XV) par Dadišo (VIIe s.).* CSCO 327. Louvain.

―――. *On the Priesthood* (Syriac fragments).

  Ed. and Trans: Mingana, A. 1934. *Early Christian Mystics.* WS 7:95–98, 217–217.

―――. *Response to the Emperor Julian.*

  Ed. and Trans.: Guida, A. 1994. *Replica a Giuliano Imperatore: adversus criminationes in Christianos Iuliani Imperatoris.* Biblioteca patristica 24. Florence.

Theodoret. *Church History.*

  Ed.: Parmentier, L. 1911. *Theodoret, Kirchengeschichte.* GCS 19. Leipzig.

  Trans.: NPNF[2] 3:33–159.

―――. *A History of the Monks of Syria.*

  Ed.: Canivet, P. and Leroy-Molinghen, A. 1977. *Théodoret de Cyr, Histoire des moines de Syrie.* SCh 234, 257. Paris.

  Trans.: Price, R. M. 1985. *A History of the Monks of Syria.* Kalamazoo, MI.

Theon. *Progymnasmata.*

  Ed.: Patillon, M. and Bolognesi, G. 2002. *Progymnasmata.* 2nd ed. Paris.

Secondary Literature

Abramowski, L. 1991. "The Theology of Theodore of Mopsuestia." In *Formula and Context: Studies in Early Christian Thought*, 1–36. London.

―――. 1992. "Was hat das Nicaeno-Constantinopolitanum (C) mit dem Konzil von Konstantinopel 381 zu tun?" *Theologie und Philosophie* 67:481–513.

Alexander, P. S. 1994. "Jerusalem as the Omphalos of the World: On the History of a Geographical Concept." In *Jerusalem: Its Sanctity and Centrality to Judaism, Christianity, and Islam*, ed. L. I. Levine, 104–119. New York.

Allen, P. 1999. "Severus of Antioch and Pastoral Care." In *Prayer and Spirituality in the Early Church*, ed. P. Allen, W. Mayer, and L. Cross, 2:387–400. Brisbane.

Ando, C. 2008. "Decline, Fall, and Transformation." *Journal of Late Antiquity* 1.1:31–60.

Angus, S. 1925. *The Mystery-Religions and Christianity: A Study in the Religious Background of Early Christianity.* London.

Athanassiadi, P. 1999. "The Chaldean Oracles: Theology and Theurgy." In Athanassiadi and Frede 1999:149–184.

Athanassiadi, P., and M. Frede, eds. 1999. *Pagan Monotheism in Late Antiquity.* Oxford.

Bailey, L. K. 2010. *Christianity's Quiet Success: The Eusebius Gallicanus Sermon Collection and the Power of the Church in Late Antique Gaul.* South Bend.

Baldovin, J. F. 1987. *The Urban Character of Christian Worship: The Origins, Development, and Meaning of Stational Liturgy.* Rome.

———. 1993. "A Note on the Liturgical Processions in the Menologion of Basil II (MS. VAT. GR. 1613)." In *ΕΥΛΟΓΗΜΑ: Studies in Honor of Robert Taft, S.J.*, ed. E. Carr, S. Parenti, A. A. Theirmeyer, and E. Velkovska, 26–39. Rome.

Barnes, M. R., and D. H. Williams, eds. 1993. *Arianism after Arius: Essays on the Development of the Fourth Century Trinitarian Conflicts.* Edinburgh.

Barnes, T. D. 1978. "Emperors and Bishops, AD 324–344: Some Problems." *American Journal of Ancient History* 3:53–75.

———. 1981. *Constantine and Eusebius.* Cambridge, MA.

———. 1993. *Athanasius and Constantius: Theology and Politics in the Constantinian Empire.* Cambridge, MA.

———. 1995. "Statistics and the Conversion of the Roman Aristocracy." *Journal of Roman Studies* 85:135–147.

Beard, M., J. North, and S. Price. 1998. *Religions of Rome.* 2 vols. Cambridge.

Beck, R. 2006. *The Religion of the Mithras Cult in the Roman Empire: Mysteries of the Unconquered Sun.* Oxford.

Becker, A. 2004. "Bringing the Heavenly Academy down to Earth: Approaches to the Imagery of Divine Pedagogy in the East Syrian Tradition." In *Heavenly Realms and Earthly Realities in Late Antique Religions*, ed. R. S. Boustan and A. Y. Reed, 174–191. Cambridge.

———. 2006a. *Fear of God and the Beginning of Wisdom: The School of Nisibis and Christian Scholastic Culture in Late Antique Mesopotamia.* Philadelphia.

———. 2006b "The Dynamic Reception of Theodore of Mopsuestia in the Sixth Century: Greek, Syriac, and Latin." In *Greek Literature in Late Antiquity: Dynamism, Didacticism, Classicism*, ed. S. F. Johnson, 29–47. Aldershot.

Becker, A. H., and A. Y. Reed, eds. 2003. *The Ways That Never Parted: Jews and Christians in Late Antiquity and the Early Middle Ages.* Tübingen.

Bedard, W. M. 1951. *The Symbolism of the Baptismal Font in Early Christian Thought.* Washington, DC.

Behr, J. 2011. *The Case against Diodore and Theodore: Texts and Their Contexts.* Oxford.

Bell, C. 1992. *Ritual Theory, Ritual Practice.* Oxford.

Bourdieu, P. 1977. *Outline of a Theory and Practice.* Trans. R. Nice. Cambridge.

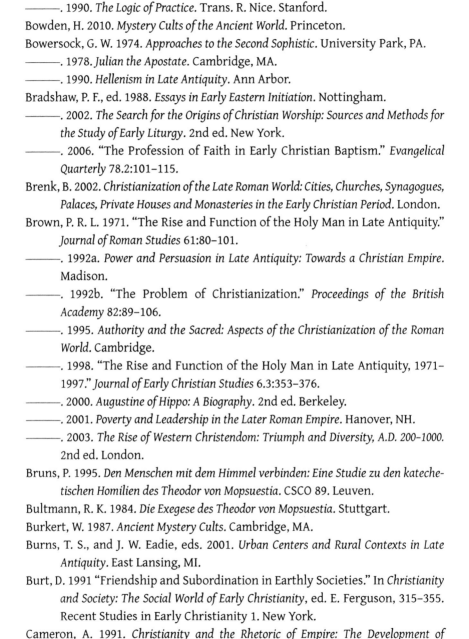

————. 1990. *The Logic of Practice.* Trans. R. Nice. Stanford.

Bowden, H. 2010. *Mystery Cults of the Ancient World.* Princeton.

Bowersock, G. W. 1974. *Approaches to the Second Sophistic.* University Park, PA.

————. 1978. *Julian the Apostate.* Cambridge, MA.

————. 1990. *Hellenism in Late Antiquity.* Ann Arbor.

Bradshaw, P. F., ed. 1988. *Essays in Early Eastern Initiation.* Nottingham.

————. 2002. *The Search for the Origins of Christian Worship: Sources and Methods for the Study of Early Liturgy.* 2nd ed. New York.

————. 2006. "The Profession of Faith in Early Christian Baptism." *Evangelical Quarterly* 78.2:101–115.

Brenk, B. 2002. *Christianization of the Late Roman World: Cities, Churches, Synagogues, Palaces, Private Houses and Monasteries in the Early Christian Period.* London.

Brown, P. R. L. 1971. "The Rise and Function of the Holy Man in Late Antiquity." *Journal of Roman Studies* 61:80–101.

————. 1992a. *Power and Persuasion in Late Antiquity: Towards a Christian Empire.* Madison.

————. 1992b. "The Problem of Christianization." *Proceedings of the British Academy* 82:89–106.

————. 1995. *Authority and the Sacred: Aspects of the Christianization of the Roman World.* Cambridge.

————. 1998. "The Rise and Function of the Holy Man in Late Antiquity, 1971–1997." *Journal of Early Christian Studies* 6.3:353–376.

————. 2000. *Augustine of Hippo: A Biography.* 2nd ed. Berkeley.

————. 2001. *Poverty and Leadership in the Later Roman Empire.* Hanover, NH.

————. 2003. *The Rise of Western Christendom: Triumph and Diversity, A.D. 200–1000.* 2nd ed. London.

Bruns, P. 1995. *Den Menschen mit dem Himmel verbinden: Eine Studie zu den katechetischen Homilien des Theodor von Mopsuestia.* CSCO 89. Leuven.

Bultmann, R. K. 1984. *Die Exegese des Theodor von Mopsuestia.* Stuttgart.

Burkert, W. 1987. *Ancient Mystery Cults.* Cambridge, MA.

Burns, T. S., and J. W. Eadie, eds. 2001. *Urban Centers and Rural Contexts in Late Antiquity.* East Lansing, MI.

Burt, D. 1991 "Friendship and Subordination in Earthly Societies." In *Christianity and Society: The Social World of Early Christianity,* ed. E. Ferguson, 315–355. Recent Studies in Early Christianity 1. New York.

Cameron, A. 1991. *Christianity and the Rhetoric of Empire: The Development of Christian Discourse.* Sather Classical Lectures 55. Berkeley.

————. 2002. "The 'Long' Late Antiquity: A Late Twentieth-century Model." In *Classics in Progress,* ed. T. P. Wiseman, 165–191. Oxford.

Carter, R. E. 1962. "Chrysostom's *Ad Theodorum Lapsum* and the Early Chronology of Theodore of Mopsuestia." *Vigiliae Christianae* 16.2:87–101.

Chadwick, H. 1948. "The Fall of Eustathius of Antioch," *Journal of Theological Studies* 49:27–35.

Chitty, D. J. 1966. *The Desert a City: An Introduction to the Study of Egyptian and Palestinian Monasticism under the Christian Empire.* Crestwood, NY.

Clayton, P. B. 2007. *The Christology of Theodoret of Cyrus: Antiochene Christology from the Council of Ephesus (431) to the Council of Chalcedon (451).* Oxford.

Cobb, P. B. 1992. "The Eucharist: The Liturgy of the Word in the Early Church." In Jones, Wainwright, Yarnold, and Bradshaw, 1992:219–230.

Cribiore, R. 1996. *Writing, Teachers, and Students in Graeco-Roman Egypt.* Atlanta.

———. 2001. *Gymnastics of the Mind: Greek Education in Hellenistic and Roman Egypt.* Princeton.

———. 2007. *The School of Libanius in Late Antique Antioch.* Princeton.

Crook, Z. A. 2004. *Reconceptualizing Conversion: Patronage, Loyalty, and Conversion in the Religions of the Ancient Mediterranean.* Berlin.

Daly, L. J. 1971. "Themistius' Plea for Religious Tolerance." *Greek, Roman and Byzantine Studies* 12:65–79.

Dawson, D. 1992. *Allegorical Readers and Cultural Revision in Ancient Alexandria.* Berkeley.

Day, J. 2001. "Adherence to the *Disciplina Arcani* in the Fourth Century." *Studia Patristica* 35:266–270.

———. 2007. *The Baptismal Liturgy of Jerusalem: Fourth- and Fifth-Century Evidence from Palestine, Syria and Egypt.* Aldershot.

Devreesse, R. 1930. "Par quelles voies nous sont parvenus les commentaires de Théodore de Mopsueste." *Revue Biblique* 39:362–377.

———. 1948. *Essai sur Théodore de Mopsueste.* Studi e Testi 141. Vatican City.

Dix, G. 1954. *The Shape of the Liturgy.* Westminster.

Doval, A. J. 2001. *Cyril of Jerusalem, Mystagogue: The Authorship of the Mystagogic Catecheses.* Washington, DC.

Downey, G. 1955. "Education and Public Problems as Seen by Themistius." *Transactions and Proceedings of the American Philological Association* 86:291–307.

———. 1957. "Themistius and the Defense of Hellenism in the Fourth Century." *The Harvard Theological Review* 50.4:259–274.

———. 1959. "Ekphrasis." *Reallexikon für Antike und Christentum* 4:921–944.

———. 1961. *A History of Antioch in Syria: From Seleucus to the Arab Conquest.* Princeton.

———. 1962a. "Allusions to Christianity in Themistius' Orations." *Studia Patristica* 5:480–488.

———. 1962b. *Antioch in the Age of Theodosius the Great*. The Centers of Civilization Series. Norman, OK.

Dox, D. 2004. *The Idea of the Theater in Latin Christian Thought: Augustine to the Fourteenth Century*. Ann Arbor.

Drake, H. A. 2000. *Constantine and the Bishops: The Politics of Intolerance*. Baltimore.

———. 2005. "Models of Christian Expansion." In Harris 2005:1–14.

Drijvers, J. W. 2004. *Cyril of Jerusalem: Bishop and City*. Supplements to Vigiliae Christianae. Leiden.

Dujarier, M. 1967. "Sponsorship." In *Adult Baptism and the Catechumenate*, ed. J. Wagner, 45–50. New York.

Dumortier, J., ed. 1966. *A Théodore*. SCh 117. Paris.

Duncan, A. 2006. *Performance and Identity in the Classical World*. New York.

Duthoy, R. 1969. *The Taurobolium: Its Evolution and Terminology*. Leiden.

Elliott, T. G. 1978. "The Tax Exemptions Granted to Clerics by Constantine and Constantius II." *Phoenix* 32.4:326–336.

Elm, S. 2003. "Inscriptions and Conversions: Gregory of Nazianzus on Baptism (*Or. 38–40*)." In *Conversion in Late Antiquity and the Early Middle Ages: Seeing and Believing*, ed. K. Mills and A. Grafton, 1–35. Rochester, NY.

Faivre, A. 1977. *Naissance d'une hiérarchie: les premières étapes du cursus clérical*. Paris.

Festugière, A. J. 1959. *Antioche païenne et chrétienne: Libanius, Chrysostom et les moines de Syrie*. Paris.

Filoramo, G. 1999. "Baptismal Nudity as a Means of Ritual Purification in Ancient Christianity." In *Transformations of the Inner Self in Ancient Religions*, ed. J. Assmann and G. A. G Stroumsa, 393–404. Leiden.

Finn, R. D. 2006. *Almsgiving in the Later Roman Empire: Christian Promotion and Practice (313-450)*. Oxford.

Foerster, R. 1900. "Andreas Dudith und die zwölfte Rede des Themistios." *Neue Jahrbucher für Pädagogik* 6:74–93.

Frank, G. 2000. *The Memory of the Eyes: Pilgrims to Living Saints in Christian Late Antiquity*. The Transformation of the Classical Heritage 30. Berkeley.

———. 2001. "'Taste and See': The Eucharist and the Eyes of Faith in the Fourth Century." *Church History* 70.4:619–643.

Frankfurter, D. 2003. "Syncretism and the Holy Man in Late Antique Egypt." *Journal of Early Christian Studies* 11.3:339–385.

Frede, M. 1999. "Monotheism and Pagan Philosophy in Later Antiquity." In Athanassiadi and Frede 1999:41–68.

Gaddis, M. 2005. *There Is No Crime for Those Who Have Christ: Religious Violence in the Christian Roman Empire*. The Transformation of the Classical Heritage 39. Berkeley.

George, M. 2002. "Slave Disguise in Ancient Rome." In *Representing the Body of the Slave*, ed. T. Wiedemann and J. Gardner, 41–54. London.

Gerber, S. 2000. *Theodor von Mopsuestia und das Nicänum: Studien zu den katechetischen Homilien*. Supplements to Vigiliae Christianae 51. Boston.

Grafton, A., and M. H. Williams. 2006. *Christianity and the Transformation of the Book: Origen, Eusebius, and the Library of Caesarea*. Cambridge, MA.

Greer, R. A. 1961. *Theodore of Mopsuestia, Exegete and Theologian*. London.

———. 2007. "Pastoral Care and Discipline." In *Cambridge History of Christianity*. Vol. 2, *Constantine to c. 600*, ed. A. Casiday and F. W. Norris, 567–584. Cambridge.

Gregory, T. E. 1979. *Vox Populi: Popular Opinion and Violence in the Religious Controversies of the Fifth Century A.D.* Columbus.

Guy, L. 2003. "'Naked' Baptism in the Early Church: The Rhetoric and the Reality." *Journal of Religious History* 27.2:133–142.

Gwynn, D. M. 2007. *The Eusebians: The Polemic of Athanasius of Alexandria and the Construction of the "Arian Controversy."* Oxford.

Hahn, J. 2004. *Gewalt und religiöser Konflikt: Studien zu den Auseinandersetzungen zwischen Christen, Heiden und Juden im Osten des römischen Reiches (von Konstantin bis Theodosius II)*. Berlin.

Hall, S. G. 1973. "Paschal Baptism." *Studia Evangelica* 6:239–251.

Hanson, R. P. C. 1988. *The Search for the Christian Doctrine of God: The Arian Controversy 318-381*. Edinburgh.

Harkins, P. W. 1963. *John Chrysostom: Baptismal Instructions*. New York.

Harl, K. W. 2001. "From Pagan to Christian in Cities of Roman Anatolia during the Fourth and Fifth Centuries." In Burns and Eadie 2001:302–322.

Harmless, W. 1995. *Augustine and the Catechumenate*. Collegeville, MN.

Harries, J., and I. Wood, eds. 1993. *The Theodosian Code: Studies in the Imperial Law of Late Antiquity*. London.

Harris, W. V. 1989. *Ancient Literacy*. Cambridge, MA.

———, ed. 2005. *The Spread of Christianity in the First Four Centuries: Essays in Explanation*. Leiden

Hayward, P. A., and J. Howard-Johnston, eds. 1999. *The Cult of Saints in Late Antiquity and the Middle Ages: Essays on the Contribution of Peter Brown*. Oxford.

Heather, P. J., and D. Moncur. 2001. *Politics, Philosophy, and Empire in the Fourth Century: Select Orations of Themistius*. TTH. Liverpool.

Hill, R. C. 1981a. "*Akribeia*: A Principle of Chrysostom's Exegesis." *Australian and New Zealand Theological Review* 14.1:32–36.

———. 1981b "On Looking Again at *Synkatabasis*." *Prudentia* 13:3–11.

———. 2001. "Theodore of Mopsuestia, Interpreter of the Prophets." *Sacris Erudiri* 40:107–129.

———. 2004. "His Master's Voice: Theodore of Mopsuestia on the Psalms." *Heythrop Journal* 45:40–53.

———. 2005. *Reading the Old Testament in Antioch*. Leiden.

Hoffman, R. J., ed. 2004. *Julian's Against the Galileans*. Amherst, NY.

Hopkins, K. 1998. "Christian Number and its Implication." *Journal of Early Christian Studies* 6:185–226.

Hübner, S. 2005. *Der Klerus in der Gesellschaft des spätantiken Kleinasiens*. Altertumswissenschaftliches Kolloquium 15. Stuttgart.

Hunt, E. D. 1993. "Christianizing the Roman Empire: The Evidence of the Code." In Harries and I. Wood 1993:143–158.

James, W. 1902. *The Varieties of Religious Experience*. New York.

Joannou, P.-P. 1972. *La législation impériale et la christianisation de l'Empire Romain (311–476)*. Rome.

Johnson, M. E. 1999. *The Rites of Christian Initiation: Their Evolution and Interpretation*. Collegeville, MN.

Jones, A. H. M. 1950. "The *Aerarium* and the *Fiscus*." *Journal of Roman Studies* 40:22–29.

———. 1959. "Were Ancient Heresies National or Social Movements in Disguise?" *Journal of Theological Studies* 10:280–297.

Jones, C. P. 1987. "Stigma: Tattooing and Branding in Graeco-Roman Antiquity." *Journal of Roman Studies* 77:139–155.

Jones, C., G. Wainwright, E. Yarnold, and P. F. Bradshaw, eds. 1992. *The Study of Liturgy*. London.

Jugie, M. 1935. "Le 'Liber ad baptizandos' de Théodore de Mopsueste." *Echoes d'Orient* 34:255–271.

Kalleres, D. 2002. "Exorcising the Devil to Silence Christ's Enemies: Ritualized Speech Practices in Late Antique Christianity." PhD Diss., Brown University.

Kaster, R. A. 1988. *Guardians of Language: The Grammarian and Society in Late Antiquity*. The Transformation of the Classical Heritage 11. Berkeley.

Kelly, J. N. D. 1995. *Golden Mouth: The Story of John Chrysostom—Ascetic, Preacher, Bishop*. Ithaca.

Kennedy, G. A. 1983. *Greek Rhetoric under Christian Emperors*. Princeton.

Kermode, F. 1979. *The Genesis of Secrecy: On the Interpretation of Narrative*. Cambridge, MA.

Kidner, F. L. 2001. "Christianizing the Syrian Countryside: An Archaeological and Architectural Approach." In Burns and Eadie 2001:349–379.

Kihn, H. 1880. *Theodor von Mopsuestia und Junilius Africanus als Exegeten: nebst einer kritischen Textausgabe von des letzteren Instituta regularia divinae legis*. Freiburg.

Kile, C. 2005. "Feeling Persuaded: Christianization as Social Formation." In *Rhetoric and Reality in Early Christianities*, ed. W. Braun, 219–248. Waterloo, Ontario.

Lamberton, R. 1986. *Homer the Theologian: Neoplatonist Allegorical Reading and the Growth of the Epic Tradition*. Berkeley.

Lamoreaux, J. 1995. "Episcopal Courts in Late Antiquity." *Journal of Early Christian Studies* 3.2:143–167.

Lampe, G. W. H. 1961. *A Patristic Greek Lexicon*. Oxford.

Lane Fox, R. 1987. *Pagans and Christians*. New York.

Lassus, J. 1938. "L'église cruciforme de Kaoussié." In Stillwell, Elderkin, Waagé, and Waagé 1934–1974, 2.5–44.

Laurie, T. 1853. *Dr. Grant and the Mountain Nestorians*. Boston.

Leyerle. B. 2001. *Theatrical Shows and Ascetic Lives: John Chrysostom's Attack on Spiritual Marriage*. Berkeley.

Liebeschuetz, J. H. W. G. 2001. *Decline and Fall of the Roman City*. Oxford.

Lim, R. 1995. *Public Disputation, Power, and Social Order in Late Antiquity*. The Transformation of the Classical Heritage 23. Berkeley.

Lyman, R. 1993. "A Topography of Heresy: Mapping the Rhetorical Creation of Arianism." In Barnes and Williams 1993:45–62.

Lynch, J. H. 1986. *Godparents and Kinship in Early Medieval Europe*. Princeton.

MacCormack, S. 1981. *Art and Ceremony in Late Antiquity*. The Transformation of the Classical Heritage 1. Berkeley.

MacMullen, R. 1984. *Christianizing the Roman Empire (A.D. 100–400)*. New Haven.

———. 1989. "The Preacher's Audience (AD 350–400)." *Journal of Theological Studies* 40.2:503–511.

———. 2006. *Voting about God in Early Church Councils*. New Haven.

Marcone, A. 2008. "A Long Late Antiquity?: Considerations on a Controversial Periodization." *Journal of Late Antiquity* 1.1:4–19.

Markus, R. A. 1990. *The End of Ancient Christianity*. Cambridge.

Marrou, H. I. 1982. *A History of Education in Antiquity*. Trans. G. Lamb. Madison.

Maxwell, J. L. 2006. *Christianization and Communication in Late Antiquity: John Chrysostom and his Congregation in Antioch*. Cambridge.

Mayer, W. 2001. "Patronage, Pastoral Care, and the Role of the Bishop at Antioch." *Vigiliae Christianae* 55:58–70.

Mayer, W., and P. Allen. 2000. "Through a Bishop's Eyes: Towards a Definition of Pastoral Care in Late Antiquity." *Augustinianum* 40:345–397.

Mazza, E. 1991. "Liturgie, vie chrétienne, eschatologie dans les Catéchèse Mystagogiques de Théodore de Mopsueste." In *Liturgie, éthique et peuple de Dieu*, ed. A. M. Triacca and A. Pistoia, 219–238. Rome.

McLeod, F. G. 1999. *The Image of God in the Antiochene Tradition*. Washington, DC.

———. 2005. *The Roles of Christ's Humanity in Salvation: Insights from Theodore of Mopsuestia*. Washington, DC.

———. 2007. "Narsai's Dependence on Theodore of Mopsuestia." *Journal of the Canadian Society for Syriac Studies* 7:18–38.

———. 2009. *Theodore of Mopsuestia*. London.

McLynn, N. 1996. "The Fourth Century Taurobolium." *Phoenix* 50:312–330.

Menze, V.-L. 2008. *Justinian and the Making of the Syrian Orthodox Church*. Oxford.

Metzger, M., ed. 1985. *Les Constitutions Apostoliques*. SCh 320. Paris.

———. 1989. "La conversion dans les 'Constitutions apostoliques.'" In *Liturgie, conversion et vie monastique*, ed. A. M. Triacca and A. Pistoia, 229–242. Rome.

Mills, K., and A. Grafton, eds. 2003. *Conversion in Late Antiquity and the Early Middle Ages: Seeing and Believing*. Rochester, NY.

Mingana, A. 1933–1985. *Catalogue of the Mingana Collection of Manuscripts: Now in the Possession of the Trustees of the Woodbrooke Settlement, Selly Oak, Birmingham*. 4 vols. Cambridge.

Murray, R. 1975. *Symbols of Church and Kingdom: A Study in Early Syriac Tradition*. Cambridge.

Mylonas, G. E. 1961. *Eleusis and the Eleusinian Mysteries*. Princeton.

Nassif, B. 1996. "'Spiritual Exegesis' in the School of Antioch." In *New Perspectives on Historical Theology: Essays in Memory of John Meyendorff*, ed. B. Nassif, 343–377. Grand Rapids.

Nicholson, O. 2009. "Constantinople: Christian City, Christian Landscape." In *Conversion to Christianity: From Late Antiquity to the Modern Age: Considering the Process in Europe, Asia, and the Americas*, ed. C. B. Kendall, O. Nicholson, W. D. Phillips, Jr., and M. Ragnow, 245–284. Minneapolis.

Noakes, K. W. 1992. "Initiation: From New Testament Times until St Cyprian." In Jones, Wainwright, Yarnold, and Bradshaw 1992:112–127.

Nock, A. D. 1933. *Conversion: the Old and the New in Religion from Alexander the Great to Augustine of Hippo*. Oxford.

Norris, R. A. 1963. *Manhood and Christ: A Study in the Christology of Theodore of Mopsuestia*. Oxford.

Payne Smith, R. 1879. *Thesaurus Syriacus*. 2 vols. Oxford.

Penn, M. P. 2005. *Kissing Christians: Ritual and Community in the Late Ancient Church*. Philadelphia.

Perler, O. 1969. *Les Voyages de saint Augustin*. Paris.

Perrin, M.-Y. 2008. "*Arcana mysteria* ou ce que cache la religion. De certaines pratiques de l'arcane dans le christianisme antique." In *Religionen: Die religiöse Erfahrung*, ed. M. Riedel and T. Schabert, 119–142. Würzburg.

Phillips, L. E. 1996. *The Ritual Kiss in Early Christian Worship*. Cambridge.

Rapp, C. 1999. "'For Next to God, You Are My Salvation': Reflections on the Rise of the Holy Man in Late Antiquity." In *The Cult of Saints in Late Antiquity and the Middle Ages: Essays on the Contribution of Peter Brown*, ed. P. A. Hayward and J. Howard-Johnston, 63–82. Oxford.

———. 2000. "The Elite Status of Bishops in Late Antiquity in Ecclesiastical, Spiritual, and Social Contexts." *Arethusa* 33.3:379–399.

———. 2005. *Holy Bishops in Late Antiquity: The Nature of Christian Leadership in an Age of Transition*. The Transformation of the Classical Heritage 37. Berkeley.

Reinink, G. J. 1995. "'Edessa Grew Dim and Nisibis Shone Forth': The School of Nisibis at the Transition of the Sixth-Seventh Century." In *Centres of Learning: Learning and Location in Pre-Modern Europe and the Near East*, ed. J. W. Drijvers and A. A. MacDonald, 77–89. Leiden.

Richard, M. 1943. "La tradition des fragments du traité Περί ἐνανθρωπήσεως de Théodore de Mopsueste." *Le muséon* 46:55–75.

Riley, H. M. 1974. *Christian Initiation: A Comparative Study of the Interpretation of the Baptismal Liturgy in the Mystagogical Writings of Cyril of Jerusalem, John Chrysostom, Theodore of Mopsuestia, and Ambrose of Milan*. Washington, DC.

Roberts, M. 1989. *The Jeweled Style: Poetry and Poetics in Late Antiquity*. Ithaca.

Rousseau, P. 1998. "'The Preacher's Audience': A More Optimistic View." In *Ancient History in a Modern University*, ed. T. Hillard and E. A. Judge, 391–400. Grand Rapids.

Rubenson, S. 2000. "Philosophy and Simplicity: The Problem of Classical Education in Early Christian Biography." In *Greek Biography and Panegyric in Late Antiquity*, ed. T. Hägg and P. Rousseau, 110–139. The Transformation of the Classical Heritage 31. Berkeley.

Rutter, J. B. 1968. "The Three Phases of the Taurobolium." *Phoenix* 22.3:226–249.

Salzman, M. R. 2002. *The Making of a Christian Aristocracy: Social and Religious Change in the Western Roman Empire*. Cambridge, MA.

Sandwell, I. 2005, "Outlawing 'Magic' or Outlawing 'Religion'?" In Harris 2005:87–124.

———. 2007. *Religious Identity in Late Antiquity: Greeks, Jews, and Christians in Antioch*. Cambridge.

———. 2010. "John Chrysostom's Audience and His Accusations of Religious Laxity." In *Religious Diversity in Late Antiquity*, ed. D. M. Gwynn, S. Bangert, and L. Lavan, 523–542. Leiden.

Saterlee, C. 2000. *Ambrose of Milan's Method of Mystagogical Preaching*. PhD diss., University of Notre Dame.

Saxer, V. 1988. *Les rites de l'initiation chrétienne du IIe au VIe siècle: esquisse historique et signification d'après leurs principaux témoins*. Spoleto.

Schöllgen, G. 1998. *Die Anfänge der Professionalisierung des Klerus und das kirchliche Amt in der syrischen Didaskalie.* Münster.

Schwartz, D. L. 2011. "Keeping Secrets and Making Christians: Catechesis and the Revelation of the Christian Mysteries." In *Revelation, Literature and Community in Late Antiquity*, ed. P. Townsend and M. Vidas, 131–151. Texts and Studies in Ancient Judaism 146. Tübingen.

Schwartz, S. 2005. "Roman Historians and the Rise of Christianity: The School of Edward Gibbon." In Harris 2005:145–160.

Sebesta, J. L., and L. Bonfante, eds. 1994. *The World of Roman Costume.* Madison.

Smith, A. 2004. *Philosophy in Late Antiquity.* London.

Smith, J. Z. 1990. *Drudgery Divine: On the Comparison of Early Christianities and the Religions of Late Antiquity.* Chicago.

Soler, E. 2006. *Le sacré et le salut à Antioche au IVe siècle ap. J.-C.: Pratiques festives et comportements religieux dans le processus de chistianisation de la cité.* Beirut.

Souter, A. 1964. *A Glossary of Later Latin.* Oxford.

Spoerl, K. M. 1993. "The Schism at Antioch Since Cavallera." In Barnes and Williams 1993:101–126.

Stark, R. 1996. *The Rise of Christianity: A Sociologist Reconsiders History.* Princeton.

Stewart, C., and R. Shaw, eds. 1994. "Introduction: Problematizing Syncretism." In *Syncretism/Anti-Syncretism: The Politics of Religious Synthesis*, ed. C. Stewart and R. Shaw, 1–26. London.

Stillwell, R., G. W. Elderkin, F. O. Waagé, and D. B. Waagé, eds. 1934-1972. *Antioch-on-the-Orontes.* 5 vols. Princeton.

Stroumsa, G. G. 1996. *Hidden Wisdom: Esoteric Traditions and the Roots of Christian Mysticism.* Leiden.

Sullivan, F. A. 1951. "Some Reactions to Devreesse's New Study of Theodore of Mopsuestia." *Theological Studies* 12.2:179–207.

———. 1956. *The Christology of Theodore of Mopsuestia.* Rome.

Swete, H. B., ed. 1880. *Theodori Episcopi Mopsuesteni in Epistolas B. Pauli commentarii: The Latin Version with the Greek Fragments.* 2 vols. Cambridge.

Taves, A. 2009. *Religious Experience Reconsidered: A Building Block Approach to the Study of Religion and Other Special Things.* Princeton.

Thome, F. 2004. *Historia Contra Mythos: die Schriftauslegung Diodors von Tarsus und Theodors von Mopsuestia im Widerstreit zu Kaiser Julians und Salustius' allegorischem Mythenverständnis.* Studien zur alten Kirchengeschichte 24. Bonn.

Tonneau, R., and R. Devreesse. 1949. *Les Homélies Catéchétiques. Reproduction phototypique du ms. Mingana Syr. 561 (Selly Oak Colleges' Library).* Studi e Testi 145. Vatican City.

Trombley, F. R. 1994. *Hellenic Religion and Christianization c. 370–529.* 2 vols. Leiden.

———. 2004. "Christian Demography in the *territorium* of Antioch (4th–5th c.)." In *Culture and Society in Later Roman Antioch*, ed. I. Sandwell and J. Huskinson, 59–85. Oxford.

Trout, D. 1996. "Town, Countryside, and Christianization at Paulinus' Nola." In *Shifting Frontiers in Late Antiquity*, ed. H. Mathisen and H. Sivan, 175–186. Aldershot.

Turner, V. 1995. *The Ritual Process: Structure and Anti-Structure*. New York.

Tyng, D. 1931. "Theodore of Mopsuestia as an Interpreter of the Old Testament." *Journal of Biblical Literature* 50:298–303.

Vaggione, R. P. 2000. *Eunomius of Cyzicus and the Nicene Revolution*. Oxford.

Van Dam, R. 2002. *Kingdom of Snow: Roman Rule and Greek Culture in Cappadocia*. Philadelphia.

———. 2003. *Becoming Christian: The Conversion of Roman Cappadocia*. Philadelphia.

Van Gennep, A. 1960. *The Rites of Passage*. Trans. M. B. Vizedom and G. L. Caffee. Chicago.

Vanderspoel, J. 1995. *Themistius and the Imperial Court: Oratory, Civic Duty, and Paideia from Constantius to Theodosius*. Ann Arbor.

Viciano, A. 1996. "Das formale Verfahren der antiochenischen Schriftauslegung: Ein Forschungsüberblick." In *Stimuli. Exegese und ihre Hermenutik in Antike und Christentum: Festschrift für Ernst Dassman*, ed. G. Schöllgen and C. Scholten, 370–405. Jahrbuch für Antike und Christentum 23. Münster.

Vosté, J.-M. 1925. "La chronologie de l'activité littéraire de Theodore de Mopsueste." *Revue Biblique* 34:54–81.

Vout, C. 1996. "The Myth of the Toga: Understanding the History of Roman Dress." *Greece & Rome* 43.2:204–220.

Wallace-Hadrill, D. S. 1982. *Christian Antioch: A Study of Early Christian Thought in the East*. Cambridge.

Ward-Perkins, B. 2005. *The Fall of Rome: And the End of Civilization*. Oxford.

Webb, R. 1997. "Imagination and the Arousal of the Emotions in Greco-Roman Rhetoric." In *The Passions in Roman Thought and Literature*, ed. S. M. Braund and C. Gill, 112–127. Cambridge.

———. 2000. "Picturing the Past: Uses of Ekphrasis in the Deipnosophistae and other Works of the Second Sophistic." In *Athenaeus and His World: Reading Greek Culture in the Roman Empire*, ed. D. Braund and J. Wilkins, 218–226. Exeter.

———. 2001. "The *Progymnasmata* as Practice." In *Education in Greek and Roman Antiquity*, ed. Y. L. Too, 291–316. Leiden.

Wessel, S. 2004. *Cyril of Alexandria and the Nestorian Controversy: The Making of a Saint and of a Heretic*. Oxford.

Wickham, C. 2005. *Framing the Early Middle Ages: Europe and the Mediterranean 400–800.* Oxford.

Wilken, R. L. 1983. *John Chrysostom and the Jews: Rhetoric and Reality in the Late 4th Century.* The Transformation of the Classical Heritage 4. Berkeley.

Williams, M. H. 2006. *The Monk and the Book: Jerome and the Making of Christian Scholarship.* Chicago.

Williams, R. 1987. *Arius: Hersey and Tradition.* London.

Wrede, W. 1901. *Das Messiasgeheimnis in den Evangelien.* Göttingen.

Yarnold, E. 1992. "Initiation: The Fourth and Fifth Centuries." In Jones, Wainwright, Yarnold, and Bradshaw 1992:129–144.

———. 1994. *The Awe-Inspiring Rites of Initiation: The Origins of the RCIA.* 2nd ed. Collegeville, MN.

———, ed. 2000. *Cyril of Jerusalem.* New York.

Young, F. M. 1989. "The Rhetorical Schools and Their Influence on Patristic Exegesis." In *The Making of Orthodoxy: Essays in Honour of Henry Chadwick,* ed. R. Williams, 182–199. Cambridge.

———. 2003. "Alexandrian and Antiochene Exegesis." In *A History of Biblical Interpretation,* ed. A. J. Hauser and D. F. Watson, 334–354. Grand Rapids.

Zaharopoulos, D. Z. 1989. *Theodore of Mopsuestia on the Bible: A Study of His Old Testament Exegesis.* New York.

Index

CPSIA information can be obtained at www.ICGtesting.com
Printed in the USA
BVOW08s1305140813

328349BV00008B/249/P